THE CAPITALS OF NATIONS

THE CAPITALS OF NATIONS

The Role of Human, Social, and
Institutional Capital in Economic Evolution

LALITA SOM

Oxford University Press is a department of the University of Oxford.
It furthers the University's objective of excellence in research, scholarship,
and education by publishing worldwide. Oxford is a registered trademark of
Oxford University Press in the UK and in certain other countries

Published in India by
Oxford University Press
YMCA Library Building, 1 Jai Singh Road, New Delhi 110 001, India

© Oxford University Press 2014

The moral rights of the author have been asserted

First Edition published in 2014

All rights reserved. No part of this publication may be reproduced, stored in
a retrieval system, or transmitted, in any form or by any means, without the
prior permission in writing of Oxford University Press, or as expressly permitted
by law, by licence, or under terms agreed with the appropriate reprographics
rights organization. Enquiries concerning reproduction outside the scope of the
above should be sent to the Rights Department, Oxford University Press, at the
address above

You must not circulate this work in any other form
and you must impose this same condition on any acquirer

ISBN-13: 978-0-19-945273-6
ISBN-10: 0-19-945273-3

Typeset in ITC Giovanni Std 9.5/13
by The Graphics Solution, New Delhi 110 092
Printed in India at Rakmo Press, New Delhi 110 020

To my grandparents

Contents

FOREWORD BY PERCY S. MISTRY	ix
PREFACE	xv
ACKNOWLEDGEMENTS	xvii
HUMAN, SOCIAL, AND INSTITUTIONAL CAPITAL	xix

I Theoretical Framework

1.	Analytical Framework	3
2.	Human Capital	8
3.	Social Capital	23
4.	Institutional Capital	45
5.	The Relationship between Human, Social, and Institutional capital	68

II Case Studies

6.	Industrial Revolution in Britain	83
7.	Early Industrial Revolution in America	102
8.	Japan's Growth Experience: Post–Second World War and Recent Times	115
9.	China: The Manufacturing Sector	131
10.	India: The Services Sector	163

III Micro Analysis

11. Theory of the Firm 191

IV Conclusion

12. Concluding Comments 217

APPENDIX A.1 222
APPENDIX A.2 233
BIBLIOGRAPHY 235
INDEX 267
ABOUT THE AUTHOR 274

Foreword

Development—economic, social, and human—is the story of humankind; an intricate tapestry that remains a work-in-progress. Its weave has preoccupied anthropologists, historians, economists, social scientists, governments, and laymen through the ages. The story of mankind has engaged historians for millennia. Yet, development attracted serious intellectual effort only after the Bretton Woods Agreement in 1946 when emergence from two World Wars, which were fought in relatively quick succession in the space of three decades, obliged former global powers to begin decolonizing large areas of the world they had dominated for three centuries.

In retrospect, that process was undertaken in ignorance of what really influenced economic and social development. Achieving independence and sovereignty were pressing imperatives for independence movement leaders in former colonies. That 'demand pull' was accompanied by 'supply-side' pressures, of increasing fiscal incapacity and growing public disaffection with retaining empires, on the part of colonizers. Both drove decolonization with undue haste during the 1950s and 1960s. Insufficient provisions (intellectual and material) were made for what proved to be difficult transitions and the unintended consequences that followed the decolonizing process.

Since the 1950s, thinking about 'development' has been dominated by the dismal science of economics, aided and abetted by the two Bretton Woods institutions—the World Bank (WB) and the International Monetary Fund (IMF). Unsurprisingly, it has been blinkered by a rigid academic-cum-bureaucratic approach to inquiry—an approach that became a vested interest in its own right. It excluded too long concepts from other disciplines that might have fostered better understanding sooner.

Earlier perspectives on what determined rapid, successful development were based almost entirely on notions of: efficient resource mobilization and allocation to offset innate capital scarcity; endowments of natural resources; adequacy of infrastructure and investment (given the extractive nature of colonization); macroeconomic policy; micro-efficiencies involving the productivity of labour, capital and multi-factor productivity; the macro-/micro-efficiency of capital use (input–output ratios); the role of markets and firms; private property ownership, entrepreneurship, and the like. The burning issue of the twentieth century, not yet laid to rest, was the choice of communism, socialism, or capitalism as the ideology of political governance over the economy. Yet despite a vast amount of research into these quintessentially economic issues, the outcomes of development proved to be different from what the dominant economic theories of the time seemed to suggest.

Far too many countries endowed with abundant natural resources (in Africa, Latin America, and some in Asia, such as India and Indonesia) did not develop as predicted. Instead, they experienced crisis after crisis through failure to manage their economies properly, thus crippling their societies. Those that chose communism or socialism over capitalism and markets failed (though China is an interesting case study about which ideology prevailed). By contrast, a few countries in Asia with no natural resources (and no colonies to provide them) developed rapidly on their wits. Their market models succeeded beyond expectations, outperforming countries that made another choice.

Such outcomes prompted rethinking about non-economic variables and influences in determining the trajectories and outcomes of development. Increasing attention was focused between the 1980s and the 1990s—an era of over-indebtedness in emerging markets followed by aggressive structural and sectoral adjustment policies, often misconceived by the WB and IMF—on the role and utility of technology, knowledge, skills, people, cultures, governments, governance, and institutions (public and private) in determining development outcomes. Were these dimensions as critical for successful development as the classically economic determinants?

That question reinforced growing intellectual interest in 'institutional economics' which attempted to pull together ideas and concepts previously confined to the disciplines of organizational and administrative behaviour. It gave rise to notions of 'capital' that embraced something more than money or financial capital; in particular embracing human, social, and institutional capital. Previously, economics treated human capital as 'labour'—one of the three classical, if simplified, factors of production—along with land and capital. Economics gave short shrift to other concepts about the attributes that enabled societies to cohere and prosper, invariably through a wide variety of complex, sophisticated institutions (private, public, voluntary, and mixed). These emerged not only as repositories and generators of wealth, but also of knowledge, cultures, practices, innovation, and competition.

It is in introducing and dealing with the recent evolution of knowledge about development outside classical economics that this book by Dr Lalita Som comes into its own. It makes a seminal contribution to a growing (if nascent and incomplete) body of knowledge about what is necessary, beyond good economics, to make countries and societies function and prosper. To be sure, it acknowledges that they cannot do so without the resources, factors and variables that classical economics acknowledges and understands, that is, without skills, capital, markets, productivity, competitiveness, technologies, entrepreneurship, etc. Where it stands out is in shedding light on what human, social, and institutional capital are, how they are nurtured and develop, and how they foster development. This book is a major contribution to the body of work that is in progress on understanding these concepts and the issues they raise.

In adding to its own value, the book acknowledges that while trying to be comprehensive, it is not the definitive 'Holy Grail' on this challenging subject. For example, it points to the extreme difficulties encountered in defining, quantifying, and measuring these three types of capital and providing formulaic interpretations of how they grow, accumulate, and influence outcomes.

To give but one example, although many people might grasp the concept of human capital instinctively, even the more sophisticated among them might have difficulty conceptualizing the measurement of it. Economics provides one approach to doing so by calculating the net present value (NPV) of the projected lifetime earnings of an individual at an appropriate discount rate and using that figure as a valuation of the 'capital' that an individual represents. The advantage of such an approach is that it enables human capital to be measured without taking into account all the qualitative differences that make up different forms of human capital. But what this measure does not do is indicate whether human capital in the form of a rock star, or a professional cricketer or footballer, though measured as being more valuable, is more critical to economic and social development than in the form of an engineer, scientist, entrepreneur, civil servant, software programmer, ballerina, author, or poet. So other ways of differentiating across different types of human capital and measuring it better need to be contrived and the book points to the direction of travel in that regard.

Similarly, it points to the difficulty of defining and measuring social capital; amorphous and abstruse as that concept is. The book questions whether social capital (or what Talcott Parsons evocatively called 'latency') is actually a form of 'capital' or not. Ways of measuring it are even more elusive. Yet we have an instinctive notion of what social capital might be. It is the invisible glue that binds society and determines our behaviour vis-à-vis one another; that is, social capital is a composite of our culture, traditions, values, beliefs (including in particular the cohesion caused by religious beliefs as well as the discord they generate when they conflict and collide), as well as such notions as trust, compliance, and a willingness to accept rules for the common good. We have a sense of social capital existing despite our inability to define or measure it. We know that societies, where implicit trust is high and compliance with rules is strong, are those societies in which the cost of almost every economic and social transaction is lower. Yet we find it difficult to imagine exactly which combinations or which proportions of notions like attitudes, cultures, trust, beliefs, and value systems, are optimal or how they are blended together in the mix that constitutes social capital. We recognize some of the ingredients but do not have a clear fix on the recipe.

When it comes to the notion of institutional capital, as the book makes clear, we have a sense of the vast array of different institutions that exist in our economies to make them work. These range from transnational corporations (whether domestic or foreign) to small and medium enterprises, microenterprises, sole proprietorships, partnerships, government agencies and ministries, judiciaries, legislatures, temples, churches, mosques, social and sporting clubs, and a plethora of non-governmental voluntary organizations. Developed societies are relatively rich in their endowments of institutions of every conceivable sort in every one of the above categories; developing societies are much less so. The quantum and quality of institutional capital (which is itself a derivative combination of human and social capital in different forms and mixes) is obviously much higher in the developed world.

Yet institutions are edifices and mechanisms that provide the framework within which human and societal endeavours are focused to particular purposes, shaped, and propagated. They provide the structures and repositories needed for learning, experimentation, innovation, and competition. These, in turn, produce outputs and drive markets for goods and services. In short, institutions drive and regulate economic and social activity and development. At the same time, we know that successful institutions, which survive over time, not only shape, but also continually adjust, adapt and evolve to their economic, social and political environments, do not just die. A vast array of knowledge of different forms of institutions has been built up outside the realms of classical economics which, in the main, acknowledges institutions only through the theory of the firm; a limp, inadequate acknowledgement of the importance of institutional capital.

Again, some forms of institutional capital can be measured loosely through, for example, the market capitalization of a publicly listed company. Other forms are almost impossible to put a price tag on; although try we must, using a methodology that is logical and reasonable. Yet, as the book points out we are still a considerable distance away from doing that and much remains to be done on the knowledge frontier.

Finally, the book makes an invaluable contribution in relating what it says about the importance of human, social, and institutional capital for actual development experience in different parts of the world—developing and developed. It does so by anecdotally and analytically providing many useful insights and observations that provoke thought and point to where future research needs to be done.

In writing this fascinating, illuminating book, albeit in academic style and idiom, Dr Som demonstrates, with laudable erudition, her mastery of a difficult subject; one that is of import to everyone interested in understanding the process of development. One can only hope that it will be the first of many of her books on the subject in coming years, if only because this one suggests that it may be the tip of a large iceberg of unexplored knowledge that needs to be plumbed more fully to its invisible depths.

Percy S. Mistry

Preface

There is a general consensus that there exists no unique or pure theoretical framework for economic development, and that it needs to be coordinated with others to provide the best possible explanation. Taking that thought forward, the book analyses three intangible forms of capital—human capital, social capital, and institutional capital—to identify the dynamic between them, as the crucial determinant of economic growth and development and to understand the process of economic evolution. The inspiration for combining these three intangible forms of capital stems from the assumption of a characteristic of human behaviour which is a response to both the limitations and the potential of human cognition and the fact that none of these forms of capital on their own are sufficient in, and of, themselves, in explaining economic growth and development. The presence of three intangible forms of capital as drivers introduces the possibility of complex forms of associations not only between the outcome and the drivers of the outcome, but amongst the drivers themselves. This is in addition to the potential feedback effects from the economic growth indicators to human capital, institutional, and social dimensions.

The book makes an earnest attempt to showcase and identify the dynamic and complex forms of associations between the three intangible forms of capital, that is, human capital, social capital, institutional capital as well as economic growth and evolution. The case studies in the book help the reader to understand the process of economic evolution across geography and time through the prism of these three intangible capitals. This book has significantly relied on historical facts and has drawn upon the studies of others but it is more than simply a survey of the literature. It weaves a broad argument, while the case studies (depicting historical examples across geography and time) help in testing the aspects of the argument. I am aware that any attempt at integration of different fields and evidence across time, geography, and studies is usually considered lacking in rigour to purists, partly because one can never do justice to the different features and their inherent predispositions. I am equally aware that the book does not present its hypotheses through detailed econometric analysis and instead depends on words to convey the flavour of the message to the general reader.

Over the course of writing this book, the most significant event that affected the global economic system was the financial crisis of 2007–8. Seven years later, the legacy of that crisis is still heavy on the world and the most enduring distresses of that crisis have been increase in inequalities, unemployment and destruction of trust. The interaction of the three intangible capitals places these demanding challenges in perspective and the attempt at rebuilding trust and creating better quality jobs to address the challenge of inequalities will require that policymakers concentrate their efforts towards these three capitals.

The theme running through this book is that social capital works more efficiently when interacting with both human capital and institutional capital. The essential interaction and the inter-linkage between human, social, and institutional capital is the novelty of this narrative and adds to the existing treatise explaining the differences in growth patterns across regions and time.

Through the dynamic relationship between human capital, social capital, and institutional capital in the book, the historical growth experiences of Britain and America during the Industrial Revolution are explained, Japan's high growth post-WWII and its recent lackadaisical growth experiences are explained, as well as the contemporary growth experiences of China and India. In addition, an analysis of the interaction between the three at the micro-level explains questions such as the existence of the firm and its boundaries.

Acknowledgements

This book has taken long years in the making and this has involved many people who saw me through the long but enjoyable course of writing it. This has been a voyage of discovery and I have learnt much along the way. I would like to extend my deep appreciation to all those who taught me directly or indirectly, talked things over, read, wrote, offered comments, allowed me to quote their remarks, and assisted in the editing and proofreading.

I would like to express my special gratitude to Percy Mistry, who planted the idea for this book in my mind a number of years ago and inspired me to follow it through. Over these years, he has offered me unwavering support, convincingly conveyed a spirit of enthusiasm and excitement with regard to research and scholarship, and continually shared ideas and challenged my thinking. Without his guidance and persistent encouragement, this book would not have been possible.

I thank my family for all the love and advice they have given me over the course of writing this book.

Human, Social, and Institutional Capital

After the Second World War and into the early 1960s, optimism marked much of the scholarly theory about the economic future of the developing world. The orthodoxy of the time was that the diffusion of capital and development assistance would start the process of economic evolution. This orthodoxy was systematized in the writings of neoclassical economists, notably Solow's seminal 1957 growth model. But the remarkable economic expansion of East Asia in contrast with the prevailing orthodoxy made it apparent that growth of real per capita income cannot be fully accounted for by increases in quantities of physical capital and labour inputs alone.[1]

Consequently, various departures from the orthodoxy that signalled a growing intellectual disillusionment came into existence to explain the puzzle of the 'residual'—the six-sevenths of output growth—that could not be attributed to growth in physical capital and labour in Solow's study. In order to explain the residual, theoretical developments focused on human capital, institutions, the nature and sequence of political and economic linkages, and lately on social capital came into being. While all these forms of capital and factors are essential for growth and evolution, none of them are sufficient in and of themselves. The theories of growth and their assumptions of substantive rationality of an under-socialized model of person, whose attributes are fixed independently of the relations into which (s)he enters, excluded any analysis of the contingent and dynamic process that, create and retain novelty and that, in real economic life, generates much of the observed economic dynamism. These theories' restrictive assumptions also ignored the complexity of the dynamic interaction between economic, social, and behavioural aspects in the process of economic growth. However, in the past two decades the concept of 'social embeddedness'[2] has become an influential one in the social sciences. The influence of social relations on economic activity has been the central theme of the literature on social capital. The concept of social capital introduced individuals, who are socially embedded, into disciplines such as economics.

If the goal is to grow the wealth of nations and societies, this will involve knowledge[3] and its growth. When knowledge grows, societies progress.[4] As new knowledge is discovered and used to solve problems, an economy evolves as an ever-changing structure of opportunities and constraints. The growth of knowledge depends on the diversity of individual initiative, but also on the relationships—formal and informal—between individuals. The growth of knowledge in any context needs a certain framework that provides the 'absorptive capacity' that makes the diffusion of knowledge possible. If human capital is embodied knowledge, institutions are structures which provide (relatively) stable frameworks for the creation of new knowledge. Formal and informal institutions are both consequences of the human dependence on patterns to guide understanding and action. Formal and informal institutions, their practice, and adoption (sometimes as an axiomatic truth) together form institutional capital, which allows firms and economies to create and sustain competitive advantage. Interpersonal exchange networks or connections are important in the creation and growth of knowledge because knowledge can be combined and shared through these connections. Collective norms and values significantly influence the success of human interaction. Social capital facilitates human interaction which enables knowledge to be created, shared, combined, and diffused and enables individuals and social groupings to achieve outcomes they could not otherwise achieve.

This book seeks to integrate the interplay between the three intangible forms of capital[5]—human capital, social capital, and institutional capital—in explaining economic growth and evolution. The inspiration for combining these intangible forms of capital stems from the assumption of a characteristic of human behaviour which is a response to both the limitations and the potential of human cognition and the fact that none of these forms of capital are sufficient on their own to explain economic growth and evolution.

Context

It is commonplace for all types of laypersons to complain that economists appear to know little about the reality of the world they inhabit. Instead they see economists as reducing the world in a way that fits the precepts that they can measure. That critique stems from: (a) the obsession with mathematical technical formalism that economics claims; (b) its peremptory dismissal of concepts from other social sciences on the grounds that they are diffuse, inadequately conceptualized, imprecisely defined, and inadequately measured; and (c) a lack of interest in the evolutionary path of its own discipline (from Adam Smith), which evolved from a much wider concept of 'political economy'—a concept embracing more of the real world rather than the distorted, fictional one which economists give the impression of preferring to inhabit. In the process economics, has lost its connection to other social sciences and disciplines, and its explanatory power.

Economics has been criticized for overlooking the broader thinking of sociologists, social psychologists, organizational behaviourists, anthropologists, and perhaps psychologists. As Talcott Parsons—among the most prominent sociologists of his era—observed, due to its spurious proclivities, the study of economics should be kept separate from the study of sociology and its derivative social sciences, because of its methodological differences and intellectual division of labour—one dealing with society and the other with the individual (Velthius 1999).[6]

Social sciences other than economics also seem more proficient (because economics limits its perspective to that which it can measure and manage conceptually/definitionally) at observing wider phenomena that make societies (and nations) tick. The inability of economics to incorporate elements from other social sciences—especially those related to human and social behaviour, the quality of institutions and the interaction between institutions,[7]—has meant that economics has never been able to explain any universal theory of 'evolutionary development' satisfactorily or holistically, except in its own very limited and terms.

Attempts have been made from the late 1960s and onwards to increase the explanatory power of economics—especially when it comes to understanding what constitutes economic evolution—by integrating the understanding of other social sciences with economics. Since the mid-1960s, the field of economics has become increasingly concerned with why individuals might not behave rationally, why markets might not work as they should, why/how non-market dimensions and relations can influence or determine the nature of transactions, and why an understanding of these is desirable. It has become increasingly apparent to the thinking economists that answers to these questions lie in disciplines outside traditional economics as it has been taught since the 1950s. The work on human capital can be considered as the starting point of taking economics to other social sciences. Similarly, what is now considered classical economics work on information asymmetries/imperfections has introduced sociological concepts to economics. These forays have allowed economics to consider the social as explaining the non-market. Institutional economics has also helped explain the social by using market imperfections. Introducing the concept of social capital into mainstream economic thinking represents yet another attempt to include elements from other social sciences to economics and to take the study of the social dimensions of evolution and development more seriously. All this has been part of the 'bringing social sciences to economics' wave.

At the same time, other social sciences have also strengthened their interest in the material world, for example, human capital has been deployed in a variety of ways across the social sciences. This book is a further attempt in addressing the social by integrating human capital, social capital, and institutional capital to explain the evolution of nations.

In economics, conventional notions of capital (natural, physical, financial, and technological) have failed to explain the reasons for chronic and continued under-development in many parts of the world—that is, sub-Saharan Africa, South Asia, and Latin America—despite substantial external infusions of physical and financial capital since 1950. That failure has led to re-examining assumptions about capital that have been used to explain how evolution occurs. Schultz (1961) and Becker (1962) introduced the notion of human capital, arguing that a society's endowment of educated, trained, and healthy workers determined how productively the orthodox factors could be utilized. The landmark articles of Romer (1986, 1987) and Lucas (1988) on the role of human capital triggered that re-assessment with more inclusive analysis of historical development processes being undertaken—using (as yet inadequately formed) constructs of human capital—to augment explanations relying on tangible capital accumulation. Since then human capital has been credited as the quintessential and inevitable factor in determining development.

In political science, Robert Putnam (1993) showed that the local civic associations laid the foundations for social trust, creating the conditions underpinning economic development. In sociology, Peter Evans (1995) demonstrated that a state was 'developmental' only when its public institutions and the state-society relations were efficient. The concept of social capital is majorly rooted in anthropology and social anthropology, which has focused on what makes societies function. The concept encompasses shared norms, values, and understandings that facilitate cooperation and collective action within groups. The central idea of the social capital theory is that the nature and quality of social relations have a definite and autonomous effect on economic evolution (Coleman 1988).

Institutional economists consider economic development as a function of the extent and complexity of economic transactions, which are determined by institutional capital. North (1990) argued that institutions, that is, the legal structures, and normative 'rules of the game' were crucial to understanding economic performance. In addressing the differences in institutional capital that exist throughout countries, political economists believe the differences are either deviations from best practice, which will converge as nations catch up to leading countries, or the distillation of more durable historical choices for a specific kind of society (Hall and Soskice 2000).

Development theorists and practitioners, by using notions of intangible capital, have analysed how development occurred in the West and in Japan over the last two centuries, as well in East Asia in the last four decades. Economists have so far examined these three variables individually and separately. They have not yet attempted to understand fully the relationships between them to develop a holistic, comprehensive view of how human, social, and institutional capital interact in contributing to the processes and structures of economic evolution. This book analyses these intangible forms of capital to identify the dynamics of the interactions between them as crucial determinants of economic development.

Objective of this Book

'The economic problem of society is not merely a problem of how to allocate given resources... It is a problem of the utilization of knowledge not given to anyone in its totality' (Hayek 1945). Since the 1990s, economists have been interested in the conditions under which new knowledge is produced. They have underlined that development of new knowledge is a localized, path-dependent and interactive process. The production of knowledge is cumulative[8] and integrative.[9] The accumulation of knowledge as an input allows recognition of competences (human capital). Competences express the ways through which knowledge is elicited, used, and applied to specific contexts and also the ways through which agents manage their interactions with each other (social capital). Interaction amongst agents is facilitated through a certain framework or a structure (institutional capital) which can guide action and thus help create new knowledge. Social capital is a key factor in understanding knowledge creation.

This book attempts to redefine social capital in the context of human and institutional capital. The social capital literature is clearly divided and unclear on questions of social capital's content, causes, and origins. By providing a clear relational context in which the concept of social capital can be legitimately applied and intellectually justified, this work delineates the causes, origins, and content of social capital as something distinct from, yet integrally and inextricably related to, the more commonly accepted notions of human and institutional capital.

All societies face a wide diversity of social dilemmas and collective-action problems. To overcome those dilemmas, agreements are needed. Agreements can be based on mutual learning about how to work better together; one person agreeing to follow someone else's commands; or they can be based on the evolution or construction of a set of norms or rules that define how a certain activity will be carried out repeatedly over time and how commitments will be monitored and sanctions imposed for non-performance. These arrangements are self-organizing governance systems that are created in local settings to cope with a variety of private and public problems. In addition, the laws established by formal legislative, executive, and judicial bodies are an important source of the rules used by groups of individuals. With such measures in place, human capital present in the form of groups of individuals can then be effectively channelled to solve problems they face as a group.

In a bid to understand the persistent differences in economic growth performance across countries and regions, this book goes beyond traditional economic variables to include a combination of human, institutional, and social capital, and the interaction among them. The book's theme is that social capital (itself an inadequately understood composite of norms, beliefs, values, and trust) is an indispensable adhesive that interacts with, and binds together, different types of human capital in a multitude of permutations and combinations, to form purpose-specific institutional capital. Institutional capital operates in ways that, in turn, through feedback loops that are not yet properly understood, continually strengthen the quality, quantity, and content of the human and social capital from which it is formed. The 'stock' of varied institutions that any particular society possesses is dynamic and continually evolving in nature as older institutions atrophy, decline, disappear, or transform to address the constantly changing needs and purposes, while newer institutions of different kinds continue to come up. The extent to which such institutions are efficient and effective, while being robust and durable, yet adaptable and flexible in responding to continual changes in their operating environments (through continuous or discontinuous processes of evolution and 'creative destruction'), reflects the quality, quantity, and strength of both the human and social capital that such institutions are made up of. It is instinctively obvious that these three distinct variables: human capital, social capital, and institutional capital, cannot, and do not, work in isolation. This book aims to show that the essential interaction and the linkage between human, institutional, and social capital could account for certain idiosyncratic determinants, and thus explain the differences in economic evolution across regions, assuming that international trade in goods and services can circumvent problems of physical capital to a certain extent.

Theoretical Developments

Developmental failures have featured in mainstream economics literature since the time of 'modernization theorists' (such as, Parsons, Levy, and Inkeles), which were at the heart of arguments justifying colonialism. These approaches held that adoption of Western (predominantly Judeo-Christian, Euro-American rationalist) values, practices, and resources would help overcome pervasive backwardness and establish necessary preconditions for material prosperity, while disregarding traditional (non–Euro American) societies. The weakness of such thinking was exposed by the rise of Japan.

The subsequent discrediting of modernization theory in both its sociological and economic forms led to its replacement in the 1970s by dependency and world-systems' theorists, who held social relations among corporate and political elites to be the primary mechanism of capitalist exploitation.

In the 1980s and 1990s, neo-classical and public choice theories assigned no distinctive properties to social relations. Here the units of analysis were either firms or 'rational' individuals. They focused on the strategic choices of rational individuals interacting under various constraints, holding that firms existed primarily to lower the transactions costs of exchange; given undistorted market signals, the optimal size and combination of groups would duly emerge. Although many schools of thought dominated the mainstream during this time, it was Austrian economics[10] that provided significant tenets absorbed by mainstream economic theory.

Different waves of developmental models since the 1950s, focusing on factors including capital accumulation, technological change, human capital, and institutions protecting property rights, have explained only a small proportion of the variation in the rate of growth. Most researchers responded to the puzzle of under-development by re-specifying the growth model and adding variables thought to capture missing factors not explained by the textbook models, such as the Solow model.[11] These models crowded out or ignored the contribution of social relations and other institutional arrangements mediating the space between states and markets and failed to make the connection between the different components determining growth and evolution. The wide range of variables that influence the economic evolution, the complexity of interactions/interrelationships among them, may invalidate the typical growth pattern as suggested by the Solow model.

What did all these theoretical developments and concomitant policy prescriptions mean for countries which had gained independence from their colonial masters around and after 1950s? The newly independent countries trying to develop in the latter half of the twentieth century had to accommodate in its growth process: (a) a series of eccentric choices and odd compromises along the continuum between *laissez-faire* capitalism and communism, determined by a bitter philosophical, political, and military conflict between two opposing models of socio-economic organization that has taken nearly seven decades to resolve; (b) an advanced international economic order that circumscribed sovereignty in economic decision making; (c) a variety of idiosyncratic country or regional determinants driven by geography, history, ethnicity, and religion; and (d) an array of multilaterally derived and imposed imperatives governing the global trading and financial systems that have been shaped since 1950 to serve principally the economic and security interests of a relatively few developed countries. In coping with these external influences, most emerging countries (and their international interlocutors) have realized only belatedly that what they had considered of paramount importance (that is, augmentation and accumulation of physical and financial capital) for economic evolution was actually less important than developing indigenous intangible capital, in the absence of which physical and financial capital were likely to be misused or wasted.

This realization has necessitated a more sophisticated appraisal of the 'social dimension'. The social capital literature, in its broadest sense, represents a first approximation to the answer to this challenge. It is a literature to which all the social science disciplines have contributed, and which has generated a remarkable consensus regarding the role and importance of institutions and communities. The idea of social capital has also allowed scholars, policymakers, and practitioners from different disciplines to appreciate that different disciplines have a vital, distinctive, and frequently complementary contribution to offer to inherently complex problems (Woolcock 2002). The concept has helped explain the links between political economy, social structure and human agency (Woolcock and Narayan 2000). Social capital has also contributed to help international institutions, such as the World Bank, in their earlier discussions on participation, which reflected on the links between governance, social structure, power, and identity. The World Bank adopted and promoted the idea of social capital as the 'missing link' in explaining development, or its absence, as 'the glue that holds society together' (Fine and Lapavitsas 2004).

Consequently, the post-1980 period has seen a resurgence of interest in the social and institutional dimensions of economic evolution, following pioneering work in this field by Hirschman (1958) and Adelman and Morris (1967), who detailed the critical role of formal and informal institutions in determining a range of developmental outcomes. After more than 30 years of neglecting the role of national and local institutions, a remarkable series of publications gave social scientists greater confidence in addressing long-neglected social and institutional themes. In economics, North (1990) argued that formal and informal institutions were crucial for understanding economic performance. The work of Joseph Stiglitz and Mancur Olson on incomplete and asymmetric information and institutional rigidities continued to be prominent. In political science, Putnam (1993) showed that the density and scope of local civic associations laid the foundations for the widespread dissemination of information and social trust, which creates essential conditions for economic development. In sociology, Evans (1992) demonstrated that whether a state was 'developmental' or 'predatory' was crucially dependent on both the capacity of its public institutions and the nature of state–society relations. By the late 1990s, the development literature on institutional capacity, social networks, and community participation began to be loosely focused on variants of the concept of 'social capital' (Woolcock 2002).

The Issue of 'Capital'

Indiscriminate application and use of the adjectives 'human', 'social', and 'institutional' to the noun 'capital' is part of what Baron and Hannan (1994) refer to as the emergence of 'a plethora of capitals'. 'Sociologists', they lament, 'have begun referring to virtually every feature of social life as a form of capital'. Economists reject the analogy to capital as defined by traditional economics, although there is an agreement on their importance. Regardless of whether one agrees or disagrees with the objections to the metaphor of capital, the terms are now firmly entrenched in the language used by social scientists.

Physical capital has three characteristics: 'extension in time, deliberate sacrifice for future benefit, and alienability' (Arrow 1999). Physical capital has a rate of return and can be readily measured by summing past investment net of depreciation (Solow 1999). Additionally, to qualify as 'capital' an entity must possess an opportunity cost (Baron and Hannan 1994). Capital in any form qualifies as capital only if it makes humans more productive when they use it in combination with other forms of capital[12] (Castle 1998). In addition, the other essential properties of physical capital goods are: transformation capacity, durability, flexibility, substitutability, decay, reliability, ability to create one capital form from another, opportunities for (dis)investment (Robinson et al. 2000).

Transformation capacity relates to the essential characteristics of capital goods, that is, goods to make goods by transforming inputs into outputs and is itself not necessarily transformed. All intangible capitals—human capital, social capital, and institutional capital—can be combined with other inputs to provide services that meet human needs.

Durability associated with physical capital refers to capital's ability to retain its identity after and during the process of providing services (Robinson et al. 2000). All the intangible capitals dealt with in this book are little affected by time or use (except social capital which possesses different degrees of durability).

Flexibility refers to the range and number of services available from a capital source. Like physical capital whose services can only be used to meet highly specialized needs (inflexible capital forms) and whose services can be used to provide a wide range of services (flexible capital forms), intangible capitals can be either flexible or inflexible.

The economic way of thinking asks about complements and substitutes and the three intangible capitals can be used both as complements and substitutes.

Decay (maintenance) refers to the manner in which the service capacity of durables is reduced (maintained). Physical capital's service potential decays after use, with the passage of time, and from the absence of maintenance. But unlike physical capital, all the three intangible capitals appreciate with use (Robinson et al. 2000).

Reliability concerns the predictability of capital's service delivery. Dependability has two dimensions—longevity and intensity. Unpredictability of intensity or duration usually reduces the value of all forms of capital (physical and intangible).

Ability to create other capital forms refers to capital's ability to be used to create the same or different kinds of capital. However, what is created is distinct from the original capital used in the creation process. Likewise, all the intangible capitals can be used to strengthen existing levels of intangible capitals or be used to create new forms of intangible capitals.

Investment (disinvestment) opportunities refer to one's ability to create new capital (or destroy existing capital). The intangible capitals are produced in a similar way that a machine is produced, by combining inputs (in a production function). The capital metaphor helps to conceptualize this production process. The investment (disinvestment) processes used to create (destroy) intangible capitals vary in intensity and durability.

Existing capital may be transferred from its creator to others by gift, inheritance, sale, or rental. In the strict sense of the word, alienability is not a characteristic of the intangible capitals (Robinson et al. 2000).

Although the intangible capitals seem to possess most of the characteristics of physical capital, there is still reluctance in accepting intangible capital as a form of 'capital'. This is partly because for example the work on social capital has focused on the consequences of the lack of it rather than on its content and creation. It is contended that the spread of its subject matter (rather than the depth of analysis) has been used to justify the usefulness of the concept. It is quite normal to witness emergent and nascent discourses facing problems of reception, definition, measurement, and operationalization until further theoretical and empirical research aids in entrenching such concepts in economic analysis and their ultimate translation into material practices of intervention.[13]

There is a widespread acceptance that the capital metaphor is not needed to show that institutions make a difference and human capital is now accepted as a real form of capital. But the capital metaphor seems to be necessary for social capital as it is the first attempt to forge an important conceptual space for taking the social dimension seriously and to convey it is an essential complement to natural, physical, and human capital.

This book takes the view derived from Ostrom that all forms of capital are essential for economic growth and evolution, and none of them are sufficient in and of themselves. To refer to social relations as 'capital', is not a sociological heresy or a sell-out to economics: it simply reflects the reality that social relationships are one of the ways in which people cope with uncertainty, extend their interests, realize their aspirations, and achieve outcomes they could not attain on their own. While capital is certainly a set of social relations (some are economic and some non-economic), not everything is capital. The economic content to capital, that is, a permanent motion in search of profit, is affected through social capital's role in the adoption of new technologies, as social relations are significant in the diffusion of information.

Structure of the Book

The book addresses the concept of social capital in the context of human and institutional capital. The book is divided into three parts. The first part of this book deals with chapters on theories related to human, social, and institutional capital as well as the analytical framework. Chapter 5 deals with how human capital, social capital, and institutional capital are interlinked and how that link explains economic growth and development. The second part of the book deals with macro case studies, explaining how the link between human, social, and institutional capital might have contributed to the growth of Britain and America in a historical context, that is, via the Industrial Revolution. It also looks at the growth experience of Japan in the post-WWII period. The book then explores the effectiveness of the 'link' in a more contemporary context of economic success in the emerging countries—India and China—using the ideas developed herein to explain differences in their growth experiences.

Moving from macro to micro, the third part of the book explores the nature and functioning of the relationship between human, institutional and social capital at the firm level. Finally, the book concludes with an elaboration of the implications for theory and policy of incorporating human, institutional, and social capital as crucial variables in explaining the economic evolution.

Notes

1. A standard exercise in economics is to decompose the observed growth of a national economy into its sources. How much can be attributed to the growth of the labour force; to the improved quality of labour; to the accumulation of capital in the form of factories, machines, computers; and so on? After all this is done, almost always there is a 'residual' left over, some part of observed growth that cannot be credited to a measured factor of production (Solow 1995). The challenge was clearly to refine both understanding and measurement of the residual. The work of Edward Denison (1962) was a much more influential approach to accounting for the residual. This developed an explicit measurement of the contribution of labour quality, in particular through the effect of education on earnings. Denison also suggested that economies of scale were responsible about half of the remaining residual though he had no way of justifying what was no more than an assumption. Shortly thereafter, Denison (1967) applied his methodology to early post-War European economic growth to downsize the contribution of technical change to labour productivity growth rather sharply.

2. The idea that economic activity is 'socially embedded' has received widespread attention since the publication of Mark Granovetter's seminal essay (Granovetter 1985). For Granovetter, the term 'social embeddedness' refers to the fact that people are social beings whose attributes and actions are conditioned by their location within networks of 'concrete, ongoing personal relations' (p. 490). These ongoing personal relations are significant as they are the motives that drive people's actions.

3. At the outset, it is important to clarify that the author acknowledges that thinking of knowledge as an economic good in its own right is challenging, given that there is natural tendency to assimilate what is unknown to what is known. In this regard, the concept of knowledge is problematic in itself, and the author does not delve in the various reflexive and dialectical relationships between institutions, social capital and knowledge—now part of the business studies' discourse. Knowledge has come to be viewed as an asset in its own right and not simply as an enhancement of other kinds of assets. Knowledge assets are coming to constitute the very basis of post-industrial economies (Boisot 1998). Knowledge includes expertise and skills acquired by a person through experience or education—the theoretical or practical understanding of a subject; familiarity and awareness—what is known in a particular field. For Adam Smith, wealth was a consequence of the specialization of knowledge, which was a function of the division of labour as determined by the extent of the market. Drucker (1993) argued that knowledge is the only meaningful resource today. Reich (1991) contends that the only true competitive advantage will reside

among those who are equipped with the knowledge to identify, solve, and broker new problems. Nonaka (1994) considered the creation of knowledge as the essence of building competitive advantage by firms. According to Gibbons et al. (1994), in the domain of production of knowledge, the transformation can be considered as marking a shift towards a new mode of knowledge production that is replacing and reforming established practices, policies. Loasby (2001) suggested that the driving mechanism in the wealth of nations is imaginative enterprise in the application and growth of knowledge.

4. Several scholars believe that there is fundamental shift in the regime of growth, towards a new phase called 'knowledge-based economy'. A knowledge-based economy is an economy where the role of knowledge, as compared with natural resources, physical capital, and low-skill labour, has taken on greater importance (OECD 1996). Abromowitz and David (1996) have described the twentieth century as one characterized by increasing knowledge intensity in the production system. Their conclusions are supported by the OECD's structural analysis of industrial development. The sectors that use knowledge inputs, such as research and development (R&D) and skilled labour, most intensively have grown most rapidly (OECD 2000).

5. Intangible capital is not an input needed to create output, but is like a catalyst which is not consumed in the process. A process moulds an intangible capital and hence the process is paramount.

6. Yet efforts have been made to broaden the scope of application of economic principles by encroaching upon the subject-matter of the other social sciences. These generally incorporate different traditions and methods that are incompatible with neoclassical economics because of their concern to address the social directly and on a much broader canvas than utility maximization. It has been acknowledged under the rubric of 'economic imperialism' (Fine 1999).

7. More than economists, other social scientists across various disciplines seem much better at: (a) identifying issues concerning the behaviour of people, whether as rational individual choice-makers, households, consumers, savers, investors, etc., as well as of (b) collectives such as societies and nations, which largely comprise (c) the institutions whether formal, informal, and of an infinite variety, determined by purpose, organization, rules, processes, structures that constitute and bind them into functioning collectives such as nations.

8. The cumulative characteristic of knowledge implies path dependence and the progressive creation of barriers, as established in given technologies, accumulates a differential advantage over potential entrants (Amin and Cohendet 2004).

9. Synthesis is generated through convergence or integration between previously independent pieces of knowledge (Amin and Cohendet 2004).

10. The main tenets of the Austrian school of thought that were adopted into mainstream economic theory were: methodological individualism (individual actions must serve as the basic building blocks of economic theory); methodological subjectivism (questions of value, expectations, intent, and knowledge are created in the minds of individuals and must be considered in this light); marginalism (all economic decisions are made at the margin); tastes and preferences (individuals' demands for goods and services are the result of their subjective valuations of the ability of such goods and services to satisfy their wants); and opportunity costs and time structure of consumption and production (decisions about how to allocate resources for the purposes of consumption and production across time are determined by individuals' time preference). In addition, Kirzner (1963) believed two additional tenets were adopted by the mainstream, that is, the notion of markets and competition as learning and discovery processes, and that uncertainty pervades all actions and choice is made in this context. The Austrian position with regard to macro-economic theory was that for macro-economic problems (unemployment, inflation, and business cycles), there are only micro-economic explanations and solutions. After the collapse of the Soviet Union, the modern Austrian focus on the importance of institutions in providing the incentives for the acquisition and use of information and entrepreneurial innovation had merged considerably with the work of the New Institutional Economics of Ronald Coase, Douglass North, and Oliver Williamson.

11. Solow (1956) developed the idea that economic growth is an outcome of capital accumulation. Countries that experience per capita growth have increasing capital–labour ratios, which in turn result from high enough rates of savings (capital accumulation) to compensate for the cost of capital depreciation and population growth. The concept of capital was later broadened to include human capital (Barro and Sala-i-Martin 1995; Lucas 1988). Based on the hypothesis of diminishing returns to capital, the Solow growth model predicted that growth in per capita income eventually ends in the long-run. This was in contradiction with empirical data on a number of countries that displayed positive growth rates for more than a century. Given that long-term growth in the Solow growth model is determined by an exogenous rate of technological progress, the contradiction was later explained as being due to the absence of an endogenous process of technological innovation in the model. The theoretical foundation of technological change and its impact on growth was laid by Arrow (1962) and Sheshinski (1967). However, in the late 1980s Romer (1986, 1987) and Lucas (1988) developed a framework where sustained R&D, in a context of imperfect competition, lead to positive per capita GDP growth in the long term. Determination of long-run growth within the growth model led to the so-called endogenous growth model.

12. Sociologists may refer to social capital as 'bad' or 'good' depending on whether it is useful to humans in a given context. The economist probably would not refer to a 'bad' social arrangement as social capital, although it might qualify as an economic institution (Castle 1998).

13. As in the past, economists had avoided treating humans as capital because

> the mere thought of investment in human beings is offensive to some... Hence, to treat human beings as wealth that can be augmented by investment runs counter to deeply held values. It seems to reduce man once again to a mere material component, something akin to property. And for man to look upon himself as a capital good, even if it did not impair his freedom, may seem to debase him. (Schultz 1961)

I
Theoretical Framework

This part of the book contains the theoretical framework that outlines the concepts of human capital, social capital, and institutions, together with their definitions, and existing theories that have been used for this study. This part consists of pertinent literature survey of theories, the analytical model and its appropriateness. The theoretical framework provides the basis for hypotheses postulated in Chapter 5 of this book.

1 Analytical Framework

Growth of knowledge is responsible for the progress of societies. New knowledge is discovered through trial and error. These ideas are tested and some are found reliable. Others are rejected, and then regenerated, usually as a variation of the rejected idea. This new knowledge is used to solve problems, and the economy evolves as an ever-changing structure of opportunities and constraints. Economic evolution is thus broadly a process involving a myriad of multiple disturbances and a corresponding number of transient equilibria being reached in different areas of activity, through the generation of novelty and selective retention of some of the novelties that are generated (Loasby 1991, 1999). This creative disturbance is subject to forces of variation, selection, adoption, and adaptation. The process occurs repeatedly with new equilibria being reached and disturbed continually. All novelties that challenge existing practice make prior knowing obsolete and require new thought frames in which the implications of such novelties can be understood (Foster and Metcalfe 2001).

The nature of all evolutionary processes (economic, political, and social) that transforms economies and societies at large is knowledge driven. '[E]conomic evolution is basically all about how knowledge is acquired, deepened, widened, accumulated, transformed and applied, as well as how it grows and evolves' (Potts 2003). Knowledge and its application facilitated through human capital, is the fuel that drives economies and societies. The principle of the division of labour as the means of developing knowledge became the foundation of Smith's (1776) theory of economic growth. This division of labour creates dependence on other people's knowledge in production, in consumption, and in decision making, necessitating informal networks, trust, and common understanding among individuals (social capital). Ability and willingness to learn from others often lead to the spread of best practice or received wisdom (which once established may be resistant to change). These are what are often called institutions, they emerge as aids to the solution of individual problems and prove useful in helping to co-ordinate human interaction (Choi 1993).

To say that economies and societies comprise considerable complexity[1] whose dimensions and scope are as yet inadequately and imperfectly understood, would be an obvious understatement. The properties and behaviour of these processes cannot be predicted by understanding the behaviour of component parts (especially that of different types of capital) alone. The interconnections and boundaries between them matter greatly. A study of the link between human capital, social capital, and institutional capital provides an understanding of those connections and boundaries. The framework employed in this book is aimed at understanding the evolving connections between these three variables.

The intuition underlying the evolutionary process is that economic system emerges from human behaviour and interaction with respect to knowledge necessitated by the limitations and the potential of human cognition. Knowledge build-up and its expression produce dynamic and unpredictable effects. It is axiomatic that knowledge exists in the mind. Yet the mind is not the limit of the concept of knowledge. A plausible corollary to the axiom is that knowledge also exists in the structure of interactions between agents of knowledge. Social knowledge (such as networks) is pivotal to the dynamics of economic knowledge (Choi 1993; Granovetter 1985; Nelson 2000). Therefore, knowledge consists of rules that exist as connections between ideas; rules that are internal to the mind are trial and error methods as cognitive mechanisms. When these rules become behaviours with a measurable frequency in a population of agents, they emerge as institutions either in the form of organizational rules or laws. Each agent is continually engaged in problem solving, resulting in the construction and maintenance of complex systems of rules. The process through which new rules originate, and are adopted and diffused (with modification) into an economic system, constitutes the driving force of economic evolution (Dopfer et al. 2004). The growth of knowledge, and therefore the evolution of the economic system and its components, is a process driven by the origination, adoption, and diffusion of rules.

Competencies, capabilities, exchange, routines, and institutions comprise the elements and structures of knowledge. It is through competencies and capabilities that value is generated from economic resources, while it is through economic routines that such resources are allocated and utilized. It is the mobility of resources, that is, their exchange that creates knowledge. The knowledge process also involves adapting intelligently to new circumstances and creating new opportunities by developing a repertoire of routines that are stored in institutional memory and drawn upon as circumstances change (Dopfer and Potts 2004).

The evolution of the economic system therefore depends on the exercise of imagination, exchange, choice, and coordination. Adam Smith first established that markets are perhaps the optimal mechanisms that trigger, structure, and restructure the growth of the knowledge process. The wider and more organized the markets, greater are the possibilities for exchange, specialization, and, by implication, growth of knowledge to drive the wealth of nations. The premise of economics to this day rests on the idea that wealth results from the coordination of specialized knowledge and that this coordination works best when organized as a decentralized process of exchange. In a knowledge-driven evolution process, the notion of capital translates itself into a temporal store of knowledge that can be valued, measured, and applied in some operational form. Labour (human capital) is knowledge applied in one physically active form. Money and finance (financial capital) are means of valuing, intermediating, and undertaking knowledge-driven transactions. Money and finance also provide a convenient (albeit highly imperfect) means of translating different types of capital (human, social, and physical) into a common standard of value and permit the 'storage' (and reciprocally, dissipation) of accumulated value over periods of time.

Evolutionary economic analysis[2] sets out three analytical domains—micro, meso, and macro—through which the evolution of the economic system as a growth of knowledge process is traced. These three analytical domains provide the basis for using the combination of the three forms of intangible capital to respond deterministically to discrepancies faced by different societies in their growth experience.

This book employs the analytical framework of micro–meso–macro architecture. With this approach, both bottom-up and top-down operational models of the economy emerge. This approach incorporates fundamental notions of imagination, coordination, choice, and change in line with the perspective that economic evolution is a 'growth of knowledge' process. A multi-level framework that integrates three levels of analysis and elucidates the cross-level linkage, offers a more complete picture of the knowledge transformation process. The most immediate benefit of the micro–meso–macro framework is its capacity to synthesize disparate parts into a unified framework.

At the micro level, economic evolution proceeds as new knowledge enters into the economic system and diffuses across it. But as this occurs, the capabilities of agents change with the interaction amongst agents, at the meso level. Markets and institutions are mechanisms for finding knowledge by identifying the building blocks. They help

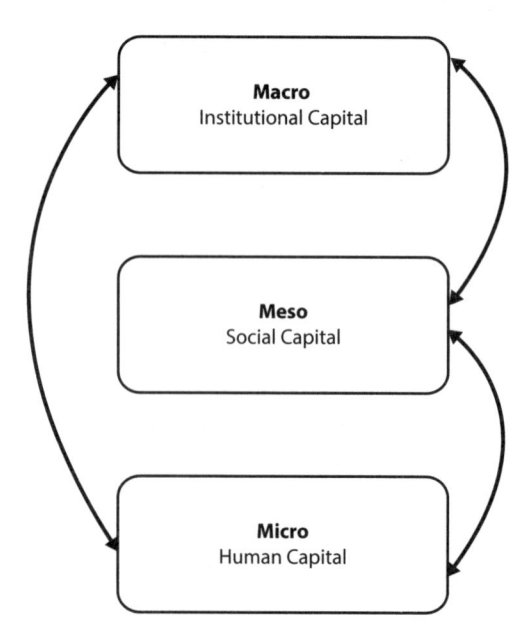

Figure 1.1 The Link between Human, Social, and Institutional Capital

apply knowledge in myriad ways that add value, the combined effect of which result in economic evolution. The meso level (social capital of agents) of an economy is never still because of the opposing forces of ongoing degeneration in knowledge structures versus inherent human curiosity and experimentation (Dopfer and Potts 2004). Macro involves a change in coordination among meso units and is about order.

This analytical framework provides the conceptual underpinning for a combination of human capital, social capital, and institutional capital as the essential interacting variables in the process of growth of knowledge, and therefore of economic evolution: human capital in the micro domain, social capital in the meso domain, and institutional capital in the macro domain (see Figure 1.1). The micro–meso–macro approach provides a framework for integrating the major questions in economics: those concerning change, choice, and coordination.

Notes

1. An economic system is a rule-based system in the sense that there are many ideas involved in an economic system, and what happens depends upon their frequency and structure. Evolutionary economists intuitively capture this with the concept of the 'economic system' as being a structure of knowledge and 'economic evolution' as being the growth of knowledge (Loasby 1991, 1999). The economic system is a complex system of knowledge, and so the complexity of an economic system is a result of the complex structure of knowledge (Potts 2001).

2. Evolutionary economics is a new scientific approach to economic analysis and one that has come of age in the past decade or so. Evolution was first conceived as a process at work in the economic realm in eighteenth-century European and Scottish society by the likes of Voltaire, Montesquieu, Adam Smith, and David Hume. Evolutionary economics is an essential insight into the relation between evolutionary theory, economic theory, and liberalism. It is the study of the mechanisms by which knowledge grows, widens and deepens.

2 Human Capital

The theory of knowledge-based economic evolution and the central role of human capital in proliferating this knowledge, including the development and dissemination of technology,[1] have been given an enormous stimulus by the new endogenous growth theory (Lucas 1988; Romer 1990) and human-capital augmented Solow models (Mankiw et al. 1992). Knowledge is created through three generic processes—discovery, combination,[2] and exchange. Human capital plays an important role in all these processes. In evolutionary economics, economic agents are viewed as reducing the uncertainty that they face and achieving economic goals by adhering to bundles of rules. For evolutionary economists, uncertainty is the precondition of knowledge and human cognition provides the means by which knowledge can be grown from uncertainty. Technological, organizational, and institutional changes are viewed by evolutionary economists as the core drivers of economic growth, inducing innovation diffusion and competitive selection (Foster and Metcalfe 2001). Therefore in a knowledge economy creation, distribution and use of knowledge are decisive factors and making the most of human assets in this process is important.

Causality in explaining economic growth has posed an intellectual challenge ever since the beginning of systematic economic analysis. Adam Smith claimed that growth was related to the division of labour, but did not link them clearly. He included skills and useful abilities of human beings in the category of fixed capital. Until the 1950s, economists generally assumed that labour power was given and not augmentable. The sophisticated analyses of investments in human capital (that is, education and other training) were not integrated into discussions of productivity. Then Theodore W. Schultz and others began to explore the implications of human capital investments for economic growth and related economic questions, with human capital theory conceived by Schultz in 1960. The human capital theory as conceived by Schultz emerged in 1962 when the *Journal of Political Economy* published its supplement volume on 'Investment in Human Beings'. This volume contained the preliminary chapters of Becker's 1964 monograph—'Human Capital', which has served as the key reference point on the subject ever since. Schultz and others emphasized that investments in human capital and the outcomes of those investments were a major contributor to economic growth. But the relationship between human capital and growth was insufficiently explained and economists became discouraged about whether available growth theory gave any insights into the progress of different countries. The revival of more formal models of endogenous growth in the early 1990s brought human capital once again to the forefront of the discussions (Becker 1993).

But well before Schultz and Becker, and before 'modern' human capital theory emerged, economists like Petty, Smith, Say, von Thunen, Bagehot, Walras, Fisher, and others considered human beings or their skills as capital.[3] Most of these economists held that human beings should be included in the concept of capital for three reasons: (a) the cost of rearing and educating human beings was a real cost, (b) the product of their labour added to national wealth, and (c) expenditures on human beings also increased national wealth (Kiker 1966).

Early interest in the field of human capital recognized the importance of a variety of human attributes, including health, as well as a fuller understanding of human capital, and not just skills and knowledge acquired through formal education or on-the-job training. This early interest acknowledged the important contribution of education and human capital more generally to various aspects of human well-being, difficult as these are to measure and incorporate in a comprehensive cost–benefit analysis. Decades later, while the concept of human capital is now firmly established, its operational definition and measurement still remain matters of an ongoing debate. Modern 'human capital' theory, though born in the 1960s, gathered momentum in the 1980s and 1990s with:

- renewed emphasis placed on the role of knowledge as a key factor in the economic growth process—'new growth theory', Lucas (1988), Barro and Sala-I-Martin (1995) and Romer (1990);
- role of knowledge (both collective and individual) in organizations emerged as a key area in analysis of firm performance and capacity;
- emphasis on various types of 'non-market' or 'social' benefits of education and learning (Haveman and Wolfe 1984);
- renewed attention to the social, ethical, and non-cognitive dimension of learning in schools; and
- finally, greater attention to the social context in which learning took place. This is especially marked by the rise of social capital in complementing human capital, stemming from the work of Coleman (1988) and others regarding the powerful influence of social networks and norms on the quality of learning outcomes.

Various studies on understanding the growth process and improving economic competitiveness and performance, declare investment in human capital an essential ingredient for economic evolution to occur. The emphasis on such investment varies ranging from improved schooling, expanded initial education, vocational training, and workplace training to a broader notion of lifelong learning. The general message, however, is pervasive: skills, knowledge, and competencies are key factors in determining whether organizations and nations will prosper in the long run. The combination of policy consensus on the high priority to be given to education and training in creating and expanding 'human capital', as well as the attention being paid to detailed analyses of such investment, suggests that the theory of human capital is approaching a greater level of maturity. But the vexing issues of metrics and measurement remain elusive as does the question of what combinations of human capital are optimal in any specific context at any given time.

Meaning and Definition

In the knowledge era, human capital is considered the main source of wealth: the embodiment of productive capacity within people. Human capital is the sum of skills and knowledge intensity of the labour force in an economy, combined with attributes, motivations, and fortitude, which are essentially acquired through schooling and training. Human capital can be given or rented to others, but only on a temporary basis; its ownership is non-transferable. For Schultz, it was the acquisition 'of all useful skills and knowledge...that is part of deliberate investment'.

Human capital is the productive capacity within an individual that results from a combination of natural capability, behaviours and personal energy which in turn are augmented and enhanced by schooling, on-the-job training, experience, and mobility in the labour market. Expenditures on education and training are investments in capital that influence future real income through the imbedding of resources in people. However, these produce human capital (unlike financial or physical capital) because one cannot separate a person from his or her knowledge, skills or values the way it is possible to move financial and physical assets while the owner stays put (Becker 1993). The individual can leverage this capital asset in an employment relationship, leading to higher wages in the marketplace. Human capital is skilled labour, that is, labour that functions on a higher level and has the ability to create new ideas and new methods in economic activity (Ray 1998). Human capital may be broadly identified as labour skills, managerial skills, scientific and technical skills, as well as creative, entrepreneurial, and innovative abilities, along with such physical attributes as health and strength.

However, human attributes and their enhancement is not enough in itself, what is important is the degree to which he or she is able to put a wide range of knowledge, intelligence, imagination, and skills to productive use. Accordingly, human capital as defined by the Organisation of Economic Co-operation and Development (OECD) is 'the knowledge, skills, competences and other attributes embodied in individuals (combining in different ways according to the individual and the context of use) that are relevant to economic activity'. These attributes are enhanced through schooling and quality education.

Human capital constitutes an intangible asset which has economic and monetary value and supports productivity, innovation, and employability. It may be augmented, or may decline or may be destroyed or become redundant. Thus 'human capital' is a loose catch-all term for the practical knowledge, acquired skills, and learned abilities of an individual that make him or her potentially productive, and thus equip him or her to earn income in exchange for labour.

In the pre-modern period, human capital formation (in the form of labour) was primarily an accumulation of learning by doing. Formal schooling appeared only because the needs of a developing socioeconomic system demanded it. When production was limited to relatively crude agricultural commodities and handicrafts, and labour was the primary input, learning on the job was regarded as all that was necessary for good performance. More formal apprenticeship systems were required in more developed, more affluent pre-modern societies where production of a variety of quality goods had become the norm. Formal schooling for human capital formation became necessary when markets came into existence and the need arose to keep accounts and records, to read instructions on how better to conduct's one's business, and to communicate and trade at a distance rather than via face to face contact (Nakamura 1981).

In practical terms, human capital essentially deals with private and social rates of return to individuals from investments in different levels of education and training. Human capital is what drives the economic behaviour of individuals, especially their accumulation of knowledge and skills that enables them to increase their productivity and their earnings, and in so doing, to increase the productivity and wealth of the societies they live in.

Human Capital Framework

In the simplest framework, individuals are characterized by an ability vector – vector a, which is transferred into a skill and a capabilities vector – vector s through an educational production matrix – matrix E. Skills are transferred into outputs – q by a productivity matrix – matrix Q, and with output prices – p, productivity determines standard earnings or wages – y.[4]

Where,

Vector a = natural ability, family background, general health status, stature, strength, stamina

Matrix E = schooling, training, experience, informal learning processes

Vector s = learned abilities, professional skills, entrepreneurial skills

Human capital theory 'conceptualises workers as embodying a set of skills that can be "rented out" to employers' (Ehrenber and Smith 1994). This process also allows enlarging a person's functionings and capabilities, that is, the range of things a person can do and be in his/her life (Sen 1989).

Ability

Any study of human development cannot be pursued without taking into consideration the three important, empirically established observations about 'ability' Cunha and Heckman (2010). The literature finds that ability matters and they are multiple in nature. Abilities can be created and not solely inherited. Accordingly, traditional ability–skill dichotomy no longer exists and the 'nature' versus 'nurture' distinction is also obsolete. Moreover, some cognitive (except IQ) and many non-cognitive skills can be upgraded at different stages of life. Family plays a very important role in shaping abilities of the children. Genetic factors and family environment determine the ability and talent of a child. A sufficient number of studies shows that adverse environment can be partially compensated by adequate supplements made in the earlier part of a child's life. People with the same economic background may end up with different levels of schooling and innate ability and some other variables may be responsible for this.

Capabilities and Skills

There are four kinds of knowledge. The principal dimension is defined by Gilbert Ryle's (1949) distinction between 'knowing that' and 'knowing how'. 'Knowing that' is knowledge of facts, relationships, and theories—the primary subject matter of formal education—which may be subdivided into 'knowing what' and 'knowing why'. 'Knowing how' is the ability to perform the appropriate actions to achieve a desired result and includes skills both in performance and in recognizing when and where this performance is appropriate. Individuals may possess the relevant knowledge themselves or know where they can find it, they may know how to do something or know how to get it done. Capabilities are know-how—both direct and indirect. Capabilities aid in the application and integration of competences whereas, competences help in achieving a certain level of performance.

The development of knowledge is a path-dependent process in which the acquisition of certain kinds of 'know-how' facilitates the acquisition of further knowledge of the same kind and impedes the acquisition of knowledge of incompatible kinds. This principle applies both to the performance of productive operations and to the procedures by which individuals seek to develop new 'knowledge that'. Capabilities may be of varying quality and applicability. They may be realized in many ways, and through the exercise of intelligence, they may be developed in ways not foreseeable (Loasby 1999). Capabilities are an indication of the potential of an individual: the mental and physical characteristics of an individual that determine potential proficiency in human performance. Skill is the actual proficiency in a specific mental or physical activity. Schooling is an input–output system where an individual's qualities are upgraded and developed into skills that are valued in the labour market. Differences in length of schooling definitely increase the differences among individuals in levels of skill and hence in earnings (Hartog 2002). Cognitive skills are related, amongst other things, to both the quantity and quality of schooling. They may be developed in formal schooling and they may also come from family and peers.

Six specific capabilities, it is argued, are needed in particular for a 'knowledge economy' to develop at a rapid pace. These five capabilities are: (a) the capacity for inquiry or research, (b) the capacity for creativity, (c) the capacity to use high technology, (d) the capacity for entrepreneurial leadership, (e) the capacity for moral leadership, and (f) the capacity for complex task management and flexibility. Technical skills[5] are an example of know-that capability whereas behavioural skills,[6] cognitive capabilities,[7] and procedural capabilities are examples of know-how capabilities. Procedural capabilities are further distinguished into four kinds: (a) the attributes of creativity and innovativeness; (b) more routine qualities, such as problem-solving abilities, complex task management, and leadership; (c) flexibility (being able to perform multi-task activities readily and also to absorb re-training easily); and (d) social capabilities or non-cognitive skills[8] (a set of specific personal qualities such as diligence, loyalty, cooperativeness, and the capacity for discerning trust in other individuals). Although these various classes undoubtedly overlap and interact, it is useful to proceed with qualifications as if each class has a special set of attributes. There comes a point, however, at which this reductionist approach is misleading, because human beings possess hierarchies of integration among abilities (Schultz 1975). Knowledge of a person's capabilities consists of inferences drawn from his or her performance and skill is perceived as the efficiency with which particular acts are performed.

At the macro level, individual capabilities are transformed into a general human capital stock determined by entrepreneurs[9] and professionals.[10] Entrepreneurs provide the economy with new ideas, products, and ways of doing things, while professionals utilize their accumulated knowledge to facilitate economic transactions.

Human Capital and its Micro and Macro Implications

The impact of human capital accumulation on economic evolution stems from its potential benefits in terms of enhancing micro, meso, and macroeconomic productivity, efficiency and the long-run distribution of incomes, once some basic conditions are met. Human capital turns labour from a homogenous factor of production into a differentiated and mouldable input of production (Cypher and Dietz 1997). On the other hand, sociologists and modernization theorists highlight the fact that human capital acquired through schooling is often associated with the loosening of traditional and religious norms and transforming of individual values, beliefs, and behaviour. The sequence therefore is: schooling → modernity → economic growth. This section highlights how human capital facilitates social interaction by influencing attitudes, values, and how it facilitates rationality by making people more open to new ideas, by augmenting the knowledge and ideas on which individuals base their behaviour, and by influencing the way individuals reason. Schools as institutional environments favour informal associability among peers and fellow members. Human capital enables people to appreciate the advantage of overcoming collective action problems through 'self-interest rightly understood'.

Impact on Values and Attitudes

Schooling is about the transmission of cultural capital and it increases in importance when social hierarchies based on descent are challenged[11]

(Bourdieu 1996). Persistent underdevelopment in many countries is due to poor schooling. Initial conditions (the poor distribution of human capital endowments) result in certain political constituencies entrenching and maintaining their power for long periods of time to the detriment of overall welfare. Augmenting human capital through education policy is the only way to change the adverse initial conditions. Exposure to 'modernizing institutions' inculcates modern values and attitudes such as openness to new ideas, independence from traditional authority, a willingness to plan and calculate future exigencies, and a growing sense of personal and social efficacy. These normative and attitudinal changes continue throughout life, permanently altering an individual's relationship to the social structure. The compounding effects of this process are crucial: the greater the number of people exposed to modernizing institutions, the greater is the level of individual modernity attained by the population (Inkeles 1978). Once a critical mass of the population changes in this way, the pace of societal modernization and economic evolution quickens. Thus, education, through its effect on individual values and beliefs, sets into motion the necessary building blocks for a more productive workforce and for sustained economic growth.

The personal benefits of human capital, including non-economic returns, learning in the form of enhanced personal well-being, and greater social cohesion, are as important as the impact on labour market earnings. These personal and social goals of learning are consistent with the goal of promoting economic performance.

Differentiating between learning that individuals undertake as consumption and as investment is difficult in theory and impossible in practice. Attitudes to team work, enthusiasm, motivation and openness to new ideas are as important in this regard as cognitive abilities directly concerned with knowledge. Human capital generates benefits in many other distinct ways: by changing individuals' outlooks and preferences, by influencing their values and therefore, by changing the constraints individuals face, or by augmenting the knowledge or information on which individuals base their behaviour.

Human capital empowers people by giving them a chance to consider a wider array of choices because of the skills, information and ideas it provides, making the workforce more adaptable to change, and includes spillovers at the plant and economy wide level. It allows people to interact socially and to essentially interact and engage in the larger society (Heckman 2001). Intellectual development is dependent on the role of social interactions and in the intergenerational transfer of cognitive ability. The new understanding of the role of social interactions in cognition suggests that cognitive development is a lifelong activity. Cognition occurs within the context of a mental model that is built by the individual in response to learning and to experience in the world. The individual and the way in which all these experiences are interpreted make up the rest of the difference. In this way, the growth, development, and transformation of human capital are heavily influenced by social capital because the learning and experience that influence change in human capital are usually facilitated through interaction with other persons in a network.[12]

Additional benefits accruing to the better-schooled individual comes in the form of increased knowledge and 'savvy' regarding market transactions, referred to as 'consumer efficiency'[13] (Michael 1982). Human capital enhances the ability to perceive new classes of problems, to clarify such problems, and to learn ways of solving them that arise as a consequence of economic changes (Schultz 1975). Studies conducted in the US also suggest that schooling is associated with 'better' choices regarding marital partners (Becker et al. 1977) and with lower rates of divorce (Martin 2002). Human capital helps people to be more successful in securing desired family sizes. Evidence of this relationship also exists for developing countries. Parents with more schooling appear to have greater efficiency in producing higher quality children in terms of health and intellectual development (Haveman and Wolfe 1984).

The impact of human capital on civic participation has been analysed by political scientists for a long time. It enables people to more fully enjoy life, appreciate literature and culture, and be more informed and socially involved citizens. The correlation between education and voting is strong; persons with more schooling may make more informed choices when voting and may participate more fully in their communities. They may contribute to the common good in other ways; for example, higher education is also associated with greater charitable giving and more volunteerism.[14] Education also increases certain measures of civic engagement and knowledge: the frequency of newspaper readership and support for free speech by anti-religionist, communists, and homosexuals (Dee 2004). Those with more education are less likely to rely on public transfers, even when eligible for benefits (Wolfe and Haveman 2001).

Impact on Productivity

Growth driven by human capital has the potential to be substantial and sustainable due to the increase in productivity, technological innovation and diffusion (Aghion and Howitt 1998; Lucas 1988; Nelson and Phelps 1966; Romer 1990). Work in the early 1960s focused on assessing the contribution of human capital on individual productivity as measured by observed earnings increments and on aggregate economic growth as measured by national income. In the 1980s, human capital work looked at how growth was affected through total factor productivity. This takes place through two channels. First, given social capital and institutions, human capital influences productivity directly by determining the capacity of nations to innovate new technologies through entrepreneurial activities (Romer 1990). Second, human capital levels affect the speed of technological catch-up and diffusion, that is, the ability of a country to adopt and implement new technologies from abroad as a function of its domestic human capital stock. As the World Bank (1993) concluded with regard to the East Asian growth experience that higher levels of labour cognitive skills permit better firm-level adoption, adaptation, and mastery of technology.

Human capital enhances productivity and, therefore, earnings, but part of that enhancement comes from its role in changing individual's preferences, values, and beliefs; in augmenting and transferring the knowledge on which people base their behaviour; in making efficient choices in terms of occupation, location, skills matching, etc.; in leading to a greater efficiency in consumption and hence, greater utility through an improved market basket of expenditures; in securing a job which allows for interaction with other skilled workers; in augmenting the ability to deal with problems of economic disruption; in making people more rational; in making people better citizens; and in allowing people to interact socially.

***

Economic, social, and technological change requires constant flexibility and adaptation. Consequently governments, organizations, enterprises, and individuals alike are increasingly aware of the importance of lifelong learning and share a common interest in renewing and increasing the skills base of the population. Human capital investment encompasses not only the skills and knowledge acquired in the course of formal education, but also includes what is learned at work as well as informally, in the family and elsewhere. The frequently used definition of human capital as 'skills and knowledge acquired in the course of initial education' and other non-cognitive or 'cross-curricular' abilities acquired outside formal settings are relevant to, for example, teamwork, problem solving, and civic responsibility. The creation of knowledge, skills, and abilities relevant to economic activity affects not only performance at work but also social behaviour.

There are important social benefits associated with higher human capital acquisition in terms of better public health, lower crime, the environment, parenting, political and community participation, and social cohesion. Schools that impart good standards of behaviour help to socialize young people and also enable them to engage in society by virtue of being better informed. Human capital has a positive impact on individual attitudes, values concerning personal and social relations, and the psychological propensities of individuals to be more inclusive and tolerant. Human capital not only equips well-trained workers with knowledge and skills, it also creates well-balanced citizens, and encourages active participation in a democratic society. Human capital thus aids in the formation of social capital as information, which yields knowledge, gains significance from its connections, and enables individuals to understand the importance of greater civic and social engagement.

Notes

1. If knowledge includes expertise and skills acquired by a person through experience or education and familiarity, awareness of a subject, then technology is about the application of knowledge to useful objectives. Education creates the simple basic capacities to acquire basic knowledge to utilize technology and learn on the job which adds to knowledge.
2. Combination is the process viewed by Schumpeter as the foundation for economic development, 'to produce means to combine materials and forces within our reach'.

3. Their motives behind treating human beings as capital and valuing them in money terms were to: (a) demonstrate the power of a nation; (b) determine the economic effects of education, health investment, and migration; (c) propose tax schemes believed to be more equitable than existing ones; (d) determine the total cost of war; (e) stir public awareness to the need for life and health conservation by underlining the significance of the economic life of an individual to his/her family and country; and (f) aid courts and compensation boards in making fair decisions in cases dealing with compensation for personal injury and death (Kiker 1966).

4. Heterogeneous labour, differentiated by level and type of human capital, determines a country's comparative advantage. Cross-country differences in human capital are systematically related to patterns of production and trade. The technology for human capital accumulation is differentiated between the private human capital of individuals and the stock of knowledge of the society as a whole. An individual accumulates human capital by investing—such as going to school when young. The level of human capital upon leaving school and entering the workforce depends on the length of the investment period, which he/she chooses and on the effectiveness of the time spent, which is determined by the social stock of knowledge available. His/her choice about the length of the investment period is made by balancing the opportunity cost of later entry into the workforce against higher wage rate paid to more skilled labour (Stokey 1991). His/her level of human capital upon entering the workforce determines his/her wage rate. Human capital literature assumes that the human capital once acquired will determine a person's wage rate over the rest of his/her life, which he/she spends working. There is no doubt that the initial wage rate is determined by the acquired human capital, subsequent wages over a long period of time is to a large extent dependent on other skills like behavioural and non-cognitive skills.

5. Those skills which are associated with the purchase of labour on the open market (such as recognized trade or professional skills).

6. Behavioural skills are personal skills associated with the worker's ability to perform in the context of particular authority relations on the job.

7. Cognitive capabilities are the foundation of general skills possessed by any worker (such as, literacy, numeracy, general educational competence). Cognition has at least two main aspects. On the one hand, cognition refers to the mental processes that people use to acquire knowledge, and on the other hand, cognition refers to the knowledge that has been acquired using these mental processes. All human intellectual activities such as thinking, communicating, problem solving, and learning require both processes and knowledge. The contexts in which people work affect the type of knowledge they develop and how well they are able to perform tasks. Society and culture

provide the most important resources for human cognitive development. Social groups direct a person's cognitive development through the value placed on the learning of certain skills, thereby providing the all-important motivation for engaging in learning and behaviour that lead to an individual's cognitive development beyond that resulting from untutored experience in the world. Initially, a child has no way of understanding or communicating his or her experiences. It is through the teaching of parents and other members of the community that children come to understand the world they inhabit. The knowledge and values that caregivers have to pass on to their offspring reflect their particular social and cultural groups. Early learning takes place through the internalization of this interpretation of the world.

8. It is common knowledge outside of academic journals that motivation, tenacity, trustworthiness, and perseverance are important traits for success in life. Most discussions on skill and skill formation focus on cognitive ability and ignore non-cognitive skills. The signalling literature emphasized that education was a signal of a one-dimensional ability usually interpreted as a cognitive skill. Much of the neglect of non-cognitive skills in analyses of earnings, schooling and other life-time outcomes is due to the lack of any reliable measures of them. Cognitive ability alone cannot contribute to achievement. In addition to language and other cognitive tools transmitted to new members of society, there are important motivational conditions transmitted as well. Cognitive sociologists have referred to the motivational aspect of social communities as social capital. People learn information that corresponds to their view of the world—and they learn skills that will be meaningful to them. Children who are born into poverty whose parents' lives and communities are characterized by unemployment may not see the value of formal education. In addition to messages that help them determine whether or not they are capable of learning. They learn well or not depending on their view of their own ability to learn. An example of this motivational condition is the way culture responds to failure and errors. There are culturally transmitted attitudes about the probability of learning successfully after one has initially failed to learn. These attitudes can greatly affect future learning.

9. Entrepreneurial human capital may be more productive in the development of technology than professional human capital. Thus, entrepreneurship determines the level of technology because entrepreneurial skills generate new ideas, innovations, and products. These unique skills contribute to the development of technology in a way that is potentially different from skills accumulated through education. Entrepreneurs may also indirectly influence the level of technology by starting new businesses that put competitive pressures on existing businesses to innovate. Even if an entrepreneurial venture serves only to increase the variety of goods produced and does not directly

enhance current technology, its existence spurs others to invent. There is wide agreement among economists that entrepreneurship is a crucial factor in the diffusion of new technologies, international competitiveness, and the creation of new jobs. Entrepreneurship offers the decisive link between the technological system and the exploitation of business opportunities. Entrepreneurial skills are accumulated through a more work-intensive process, and as a result, are distinct from those accumulated through an education-intensive process. Yet entrepreneurs differ from more skilled labour in that entrepreneurial activity is risky. Entrepreneurship is also associated with an opportunity cost in terms of foregone income from alternative occupations (Naudé 1999).

10. Professionals may be more productive in the utilization, adoption, and diffusion of existing technology. Professional skills help to facilitate economic transactions, to organize efficiently the transformation of inputs into productive outputs, and to monitor and evaluate the inputs. Professionals are capable of creating improvements in the level of technology like aiding with the administration of new technology. This form of capital is also called occupation or industry-specific capital (Sherer 1995) and is mainly developed through a body of knowledge and experience gained through informal learning and from observing actual workplace leaders at work. For example, lawyers, medical doctors, accountants, and psychologists generate occupation-specific human capital at law school, medical school, and a university, and then continue to apply and create further human capital as associates or interns. The cost of development of this form of capital is incurred both by the individual and the industry. Knowledge therefore comprises an explicit body of both theoretical as well as tacit knowledge developed through the practice of a profession.

11. Education tends to increase the political participation of the poor and threatens to subject the rich to redistribution.

12. Becker finds that there are anomalies in predictions of economic actions and measures which are not explained on his existing model of exchange amongst rational individuals. He uses two new concepts for him, personal capital and social capital to fill the gap (Becker 1996). He sees these terms as important for completing the picture of calculating the stock of human capital for the individual.

13. Benham and Benham (1975) find that persons with more schooling tend to pay less for glasses than those with less schooling; Morton et al. (2001) report similar findings for the price paid for new cars. Rizzo and Zeckhauser (1992) find that the charge per unit of time that a physician spent with a patient was lower for better-educated individuals than for those with less education.

14. A study in the US found that college graduates volunteered nearly twice as many hours and donated 50 per cent more of their income than high school graduates (Hodgkinson & Weitzman 1988).

3 Social Capital

It is generally recognized that a high percentage of knowledge is not readily codifiable and is transmitted through direct interaction between individuals. Evolutionary economics does not follow the standard assumption of uniform agents interacting with other agents through an anonymous market place. Instead, networks play an important role as an underlying assumption of how agents interact. These networks are further used for the effective social enforcement of rules and norms for undertaking economic transactions (Birke and Swann 2005).

It is slowly being accepted in economics literature that the well-known concepts of financial and human capital should be supplemented by social capital when attempting to explain human action. A person's actions are shaped by his or her social context, not simply by the financial and human resources available to him or her. Several scholars have underlined the increased importance of social capital as societies have transformed from manufacturing/industrial economies to knowledge economies. For a society to be capable of stimulating the emergence of, and then supporting the workings of, a knowledge economy, it must be organized to foster economic and social exchange between people. Social interactions matter in this context as they create social networks, foster trust and values, sustain norms, create communities, and influence economic and social outcomes. To realize the potential of their human capital, individuals must integrate their knowledge and this integration requires both cooperation and coordination. Collective norms and values significantly influence the success of human interaction. Thus, knowledge and its individual bearers and their social infrastructures are some of the key elements of the knowledge economy.

While these ideas have roots in the early writings of such diverse authors as Karl Marx, David Hume, Adam Smith, Antonio Genovesi, Emile Durkheim, Talcott Parsons, and Thorstein Veblen, they have taken place of pride in the recent literature on social capital. The concept of social capital has been applied to explain a wide variety of social and economic phenomena, ranging from the growth tragedy in Africa (Easterly and Levine 1997), to successful group lending programmes in Peru (Karlan 2003), and to flourishing township village enterprises in the People's Republic of China (PRC) (Weitzman and Xu 1994). This concept highlights the importance of non-market social interactions to fill a lacuna in the traditional neoclassical economic framework. As has been argued by sociologist Granovetter (1985), the neoclassical framework posits an 'under-socialized conception of man' that views man as atomized, anonymous, and bereft of any social influence through social relations. The neoclassical framework ignores the role of non-market social interactions in determining individual and collective behaviour and shaping economic and social outcomes. In the real world, however, individual and collective behaviour is shaped by non-market social influences in the form of norms and social structure (Quibria 2003).

The sense in which the term social capital is used today dates back more than 80 years to the writings of Lyda J. Hanifan, a state supervisor of rural schools in West Virginia. Hanifan (1916) invoked the idea of social capital to urge the importance of community development for successful schools. The same idea was independently rediscovered in the 1950s by a team of Canadian urban sociologists (Seely et al. 1956), in the 1960s by an urban scholar (Jacobs 1961), and in the 1970s by an economist (Loury 1977). In the 1980s, French sociologist Pierre Bourdieu (1980, 1986) underlined the social and economic resources embodied in social networks. However, the researches of the sociologist James Coleman (1988, 1990) on education, and of the political scientist Robert Putnam (1993, 1995, 2000) on civic participation, institutional performance, and American communities, have provided the basis for most of the current work.

All human communities confront collective action problems.[1] Collectively, societies are better off when their members cooperate with one another to achieve common goals. Individuals, however, have incentives to behave selfishly, seeking the benefits of cooperation without paying the costs (that is, free riding). Well-known solutions to the inescapable conflict between the interests and desires of individuals and requirements of society include Hobbes' *Leviathan*, Marx's concept of ruling class, Weber's Protestant ethic, Parson's idea of normative consensus, and Freud's concept of superego (Elster 1989; Wrong 1994). In the last decade, scholars in sociology, economics, and political science have converged on the concept of 'social capital' as a comprehensive explanation for why some communities are able to resolve collective problems cooperatively, while others are unable to bring people together for common purposes.

Initial insights into the origins and effects of 'social capital' retrieved from the classical sociology literature contend that there are four different sources of social capital: 'bounded solidarity' from Marx and Engles—that adverse circumstances can act as a source of group cohesion; 'reciprocity transactions' from Simmel—the norms and obligations that emerge through personalized networks of exchange; 'value introjection'[2] from Durkheim and Parsons—values, morals, and commitments precede contractual relations; and 'enforceable trust' from Weber—formal institutions (legal/rational mechanisms) and particularistic group settings (substantive/social mechanisms) use different mechanisms for ensuring compliance with agreed upon rules of conduct (Woolcock 1998). These theoretical evolutions allowed economists to communicate and find common ground with other social scientists of development. With the study of Putnam (1993) on the differential development performance of northern and southern Italy attributed to differences in the stock of social capital, social capital theory has become a popular approach to development studies.

Meaning and Definitions

Social capital is a broad term encompassing reciprocity, sanctions, trust, and networks facilitating collective action for mutual benefit. Social capital in its contemporary form was initially identified by Jane

Jacobs, Pierre Bourdieu, Jean-Claude Passeron, and Glenn Loury but has since been developed most extensively by James Coleman, Ronald Burt, Robert Putnam, and Alejandro Portes. It now assumes a wide variety of meanings and has been cited in a rapidly increasing number of social, political, and economic studies.

A meaningful categorization of the theories of social capital classifies them into four groups:

1. Theories that consider social capital as an individual resource (Bourdieu 1986; Glaeser et al. 2002; Lin 2001);
2. Theories that consider social capital as a characteristic of the social structure (Dasgupta 1998; Granovetter 1985);
3. Theories that identify social capital with inherited social norms (Bowles & Gintis 2002; Fukuyama 1995; Putnam 1993); and
4. Theories that concentrate on the productive and achievement-enhancing nature of social capital (Coleman 1984).

These four basic traditions in social capital are, in turn, internally heterogeneous. The first is based on the work of Bourdieu, who defined social capital as

> the aggregate of the actual or potential resources which are linked to possession of a durable network of more or less institutionalized relationships of mutual acquaintance and recognition—or in other words, to membership in a group—which provides each of its members with the backing of the collectivity-owned capital, a credential which entitles them to credit, in the various senses of the word. (Bourdieu 1986)

This definition highlights the network aspect of social capital, that is, the opportunities and advantages that accrue to individuals from group membership. In his writings, Bourdieu focuses on the instrumental value of social capital in deriving economic and social benefits from group membership and the impetus for individual investment in such membership.

This definition has many variations, the most important being the one developed by Portes (1998), who defined social capital as the ability to secure benefits through membership in associations and other social structures. Group-level social capital in a network is a 'function of individual-level actions and attributes'. The economic approach to social capital was therefore '...an individual's social capital is an individual's social characteristics—including charisma, status, and access to networks—that enable that person to extract private returns from interactions with others'.

Another variation developed by Lin, suggests that the decision of establishing social relationships and being part of a certain social network is a decision of investing to obtain social, political, or economic advantages. Social networks are the foundation of social capital and a resource embedded in social relations within various types of egocentric networks (Lin 2001). This model contains three segments. The first represents an individual's structurally conditioned position which facilitates or limits the investment of social capital. The second accentuates the process of mobilization, and the access to and use of contact resources. The third is related to the effects of social capital in terms of instrumental and/or expressive returns. Such operationalization allows a clear distinction between causal variables (position within network), processes of mobilization of embedded resources (contacts, support, information) and outcomes (better jobs, social promotion, etc.) (Lin 2001). The network approach is micro-oriented; its focus is on individuals and their ability to secure benefits by virtue of membership and position in a social network.

The second group of theory sees social capital as a characteristic of the social structure and interpersonal relations and is represented by trust and trustworthiness. In the context of rational agents' behaviour, the first kind of trust is the one built on reputation. People offer trust to people who have reputation of trustworthiness. Personal relationships are the central point of such a network, where trust and cooperation reinforce each other reciprocally. Reputation is an asset by which people can invest—renouncing current profits in order to enjoy durable benefits. In a social network, it is in everyone's interest to behave according to the norms. Trust as reputation of trustworthiness, together with cooperation, is Dasgupta's (1988) definition of social capital. This social capital is an alternative way for the market to allocate resources, typical of a pre-market phase in developing countries. When such a trust network comes in contact with the market, the cost of punishment falls, and as a consequence, the capacity of that network in determining a cooperative behaviour weakens.

A second type of trust is based on 'disposition': a planned decision of trustworthy behaviour. If the rationality of trust as reputation is measured on the basis of a single act, the rationality of trust as disposition refers to the whole class of situations in which the individual will behave in his life.

On the other hand, for Granovetter, trust exists because every individual is embedded in his natural social network: family, school, workplace, neighbourhood, etc. He considered a kind of trust that is neither reputational nor institutional accords (that substitute trust), nor natural conduct (rooted in a generalized morality). The creation of trust is the normal consequence of natural human involvement in social relations. Albeit in different ways, these theories are based on individualistic and instrumental rationality of behaviour.

The third type of social capital theory is based on social norms as capable of producing cooperation and consequently benefits, '... social capital is an instantiated informal norm that promotes cooperation between two or more individuals' (Fukuyama 1999). These social norms are arational (not necessarily irrational); they are based on inherited ethic habits and reciprocal moral obligation. For this reason, behaviour and choices may not be rational because they are consequences of norms that have not been freely chosen. Social capital differs from other forms of human capital since it cannot be acquired through a rational decision of investment, but rather is built on and handled through transmission channels: beliefs, values, religion, tradition, and customs. Fukuyama recognizes that prosperity depends on rationality, but he affirms that it is not sufficient. Rationality erodes social cohesion and trust and, as a result, it cannot take advantage of its potential benefits. Economic rationality damages the social cohesion through which societies exploit the economic opportunities. Efficiency depends on reason, trust depends on cultural capital, and prosperity depends on striking the right balance (Hollis 1998). Putnam, who is considered the father of the third group of theories, offers the following definition of social capital: 'those features of social organization such as trust, norms, and networks that can improve the efficiency of society by facilitating coordinated actions'.

A fourth school has been formed on the basis of Coleman's approach. Studying educational outcomes, Coleman (1988) asserted that

> social capital is defined by its function. It is not a single entity, but a variety of different entities having two characteristics in common: they all consist of some aspect of social structure and they facilitate certain actions of individuals who are within the structure. Like other forms of

capital, social capital is productive, making possible the achievement of certain ends that would not be attainable in its absence.

The three specific forms of social capital are levels of trust, information and norms, and sanctions (Coleman 1988). Social capital is inherently functional, and is whatever allows people or institutions to act. Social capital is neither desirable nor undesirable; it simply allows actions to take place by providing the needed resources (Coleman 1990). This definition is a shift from individual outcomes which predominated the approach developed by the first two groups of theorists.

In the social capital literature, authors therefore argue for three major elements: a structural dimension (network ties, network configuration, and patterns of linkages in terms of density, connectivity, hierarchy, and appropriable organization); a cognitive dimension (shared representations, interpretations, and systems of meanings among parties); and a relational dimension (trust and trustworthiness, norms and sanctions, obligations and expectations, and identity and identification). Nahapiet and Ghoshal (1998) made a distinction between these three dimensions of social capital. The first dimension refers to the overall pattern of connections between actors, that is, who you reach and how you reach them (Burt 1992). The cognitive dimension comprises more subjective and intangible elements, such as generally accepted attitudes and norms of behaviour and shared values. This dimension refers to resources that provide shared representations and values, interpretations, generally accepted attitudes and norms of behaviour, and systems of meaning. The relational dimension describes the particular relations that people have such as respect and friendship that influence their behaviour. It is through these ongoing personal relationships that people fulfil their social motives like sociability, approval, and prestige.

Given the diverse interpretations of social capital, a good approach to trying to settle the issue of defining social capital is the one provided by Knowles (2005) who states that 'although everyone has their own favorite definition of social capital, most researchers would not object too strongly to a definition that incorporated the notions of trust, networks (or group memberships), and cooperative norms'.

This book defines social capital as *the extent to which people are engaged in co-operative relationships, social engagement and mutual trust*. Social capital therefore includes obligations of personal and social norms necessary to maintain interpersonal relationships, reciprocal altruism, and implicit codes of conduct. These cooperative relationships among individuals behaving both arationally and rationally are characterized by many aspects of the social context, such as norms of reciprocity, trusting relationships, sanctions, and mutual interests. When a cooperative relationship takes the form of a network, social capital acts as the glue that forms the structure of networks and as a lubricant that facilitates the operation of networks. Social capital thus not only facilitates the attainment of collective goals and cooperation, but also the reproduction of class, status, and power relations. This consequently implies that someone's 'good' social capital is automatically someone else's 'bad' social capital.

Social Capital Framework

In the simplest framework, social interaction takes place by a ties vector – vector t, which is sustained by a cognitive and relational element – vector c through an economic system – matrix E; vector c reflects the strength of vector t. When cognitive and relational elements are transferred into production and distribution processes, they influence the efficiency of economic activities. Finally, with output prices, the value of overall economic output is determined.

Where,

Vector t = Bonding, Bridging, Linking

Matrix E = means, ends, order, rationality, or arationality

Vector c = reciprocity, sanctions, trust, networks

To develop, sustain, and support a knowledge economy, a society must be capable of organizing and cultivating exchange between people. Human interactions take the form of bonding, bridging, and linking. Bonding occurs among family members and ethnic groups and facilitates sharing of resources under the constraints of the norms and values defined by family, friendships, or ethnic groups. Bonding is a social adhesive that promotes solidarity, trust, and confidence. Bridging, which occurs among distant friends, colleagues, and associates, promotes transcendence of one's narrow traditional focus to that of broader society. Bridging social capital refers to links between people who differ on key personal characteristics such as race, ethnicity, socioeconomic status, age, and political affiliation. Bridging creates the social adhesive that promotes intergroup connectedness and communal stability, that promote resource exchanges for economic and community development. These ties help different kinds of people in the community to get to know each other, build relationships, and share information. These ties can be useful in linking work and other life opportunities. Linking is a broader concept of relationships based on institutional arrangements that promote the exchange of power, wealth, and status among different social groups (Putnam 2000; Woolcock and Narayan 2000). Linking social capital refers to relationships between people who are interacting across power or authority social structures (Szreter and Woolcock 2004). In a sense, linking is the relationship between members of the community and the agents of the state.

Social interaction needs to be complemented with structures having strong cognitive elements, such as common values, norms, and mutual trust. Values define what a society assigns as priority. Norms deal with the provision of social order and stable processes of exchange, and includes constraints on behaviour in conventions and laws adopted by people and are the guidelines in which behaviour is evaluated. Sanctions consist of punishments as well as rewards that help maintain the norms. They are not just formal, such as punishments for breaking the law. Most are informal, but are nonetheless effective in maintaining social norms (Luzzati 2000).

Having a society with clear values expressed in the allocation of power and assets, and with clear norms expressed in most people's behaviour most of the time, does not guarantee material progress and the expansion of wealth either. This requires agreeing on what is to be achieved and having the organizing ability to coordinate the assets and efforts to achieve it—a combination of the formation of ends and means.

Societies achieve a form of order across these four arenas of norms, values, ends, and means through 'system integration' and 'social integration'. System integration is concerned with how power is allocated and used. In contrast, social integration is the way individuals connect themselves to the surrounding social fabric by such features as a sense of class or status and membership in certain roles. Authority and identity are then the underlying sources of structure for vertical and horizontal order in a society.

The concepts behind what drives the capacity to organize, manage, produce, and consume are—rationality[3] or arationality. Arational behaviour is one according to inherited cultural values that have been passively learned in the traditional community. An important aspect of this approach is the resulting exclusion of outsiders and as an implicit outcome, the instrumentality of the relationship to those not belonging to the community.

Trust, Reciprocity, Sanctions, and Networks

Trust

Trust can be defined as 'a bet on the future contingent actions of others' (Sztompka 1998). When people put their trust in an individual or an institution, people are not entirely sure or confident about what will happen (that would be blind faith). Even if people did not calculate the risks every time they decided whether or not to trust, absolute certainty would make a concept such as trust unnecessary. Hardin argues that people trust a person because they have reason to expect that the person has an interest in acting in their interest on the specific matter on which they decide to trust him or her. 'To say that I trust you means that I have reason to expect you to act, for your reasons, as my agent' (Hardin 1999).

Trust is an individual forming expectations about the actions of others which have a bearing on that individual's choice of action, when that action must be chosen before the individual can observe the actions of the others. This account of trust presumes that trust depends on information and experience. If two people do not know each other, they would have no basis for trusting each other. A single encounter will not suffice to develop trust. Even when they get to know each other better, their mutual trust will be limited to what they know about each other. The decision to trust another person is essentially *strategic*. Strategic (or knowledge-based) trust presupposes risk (Seligman 1997). Beyond the strategic view of trust is another perspective. Moralistic trust is a moral commandment to treat people as if they were trustworthy. The central idea behind moralistic trust is the belief that most people share your fundamental moral values (Fukuyama 1995). Moralistic trust is based upon 'some sort of belief in the goodwill of the other' (Yamigishi and Yamigishi 1994). Strategic trust can only lead to cooperation among people you have gotten to know, so it can only resolve problems of trust among small numbers of people. Moralistic trust is needed to get to civic engagement. Trust is of importance because its presence or absence can have a bearing on what people choose to do, and in many cases what people can do (Dasgupta 2001). Trust reduces transactions costs, promotes cooperation, and increases economic efficiency.

There is a huge debate on how and how far one can foster trust and other features of social capital. Can it be done directly; is it emergent or a byproduct of other activities? The literature cites two main mechanisms for engineering trust. The first relies on material incentives and is exemplified by the legal and regulatory system, which enforces contracts with a monopoly of coercion-threatening fines, imprisonment, and the like. The second relies on emotional forces that are manipulated by social bonding and moral rhetoric. The disadvantage of the legal system is that it requires a monitoring mechanism to detect defaulters and a legal system to weigh the evidence against them. Its advantage is that it is a relatively impersonal mechanism and, therefore, it works well when people may not know each other very well. The advantage of the moral mechanism is that it does not require monitoring like the legal system because people effectively monitor themselves. Its disadvantage is that being dependent on emotions, it works best in a localized environment where face-to-face contact is possible, and may prove unreliable where communication is remote. Given these two mechanisms, trust can be considered both arising as a result of social capital, and also constituting social capital itself. For both these mechanisms, repeated interactions among agents are important, helping in nurturing norms of reciprocity.

Reciprocity

Reciprocity is a social rule that maintains, among other things, that people should return favours and other acts of kindness (Gouldner 1960). Adherence to this rule allows for smooth and fair social exchanges. However, the norm can also be exploited by those who seek to gain an unfair advantage. People adhere to this social rule that tells them to return favours because individuals may return favours out of a concern for what the other person will think of them. The reciprocity norm is widely understood, and people who violate the norm may be seen as ungrateful or as 'freeloaders' (Cialdini 2001). Moreover, people enjoy the rewards that come from showing others that they return favours and chastise themselves when they fail to live up to the reciprocity rule. The second explanation for returning favours points to internal standards of behaviour (Perugini et al. 2003). The widespread acceptance of the reciprocity norm may lead individuals to adopt the rule as a personal standard for evaluating their own behaviour.

Once the occurrence of reciprocity has been established, there is room for reputation building by individuals. Even those who would otherwise not act cooperatively, might do so in order to increase the probability of being reciprocated. Hence, reciprocity provides an explanation for cooperative behaviour of individuals, for whom it is not in their (short term) interest to cooperate. As a consequence, it provides necessary conditions for cooperative behaviour to be stable in the long run and is therefore seen as an important mechanism in the evolution of cooperation in human societies (Axelrod 1984). Much of the existing literature has focused on 'direct' reciprocity, that is, a reaction to the acts of individuals one has interacted with before, requiring repeated encounters between the same two individuals. However, many authors have stressed that reciprocity does not need to be restricted to two individuals. In 'indirect' reciprocity, individuals use not only information from their own experience, but also from the interactions they observe between other individuals within their group. Cooperative action in this case is reciprocated by a third actor, not involved in the original exchange. Indirect reciprocity plays a central role in human societies and the link between actors is made through 'reputation' or 'social status' (Alexander 1987). Individuals in society are continuously being evaluated and reassessed with respect to how 'cooperative' they are. This gives them a reputation that may be used by others when deciding on how cooperatively to act towards them.

Sanctions

Neighbourhood living is associated with certain kinds of sanctions on good and bad behaviour. These often appear very mild in form but are still effective. Neighbours find ways of communicating their disapproval of acts that violate the unwritten codes of the neighbourhood. Sanctions can be direct or indirect and subtle. They can also be positive (Halpern 2005).

Social capital amalgamates incommensurable objects—trust, reciprocity, and sanctions—as the essential inputs in forming networks and in solving collective action problems. 'Virtually every commercial transaction has within itself an element of trust, certainly any transaction conducted over a period of time. It can be plausibly argued that much of the economic backwardness in the world can be explained by the lack of mutual confidence' (Arrow 1972). The importance of the ubiquitous relational element called trust is acknowledged as the lubricant necessary for economic efficiency. Sanctions are part of the tools that structure social interaction and economic exchange, enabling people to act collectively and to receive opportunities to use other forms of capital, thereby avoiding 'prisoners' dilemmas' in social choice. They are informal means that emerge from social evolution,[4] and are characterized by the fact that they derive their acceptance from an integrated system against which individuals have to judge their own actions no less than the deeds of others and hence need no third-party enforcement. They complement other formal and legal tools in their objective towards creating trust that is developed in an iterated interaction process. Through repeated play, individuals tend to converge on strategies of cooperation that improve joint well-being. Social capital therefore encompasses both an end (trust) and the means (informal) to achieve the twin objectives of economic efficiency[5] and collective action.

Networks

Networks are 'any collection of actors that pursue repeated enduring exchange relations with one another and at the same time lack a legitimate organizational authority to arbitrate and resolve disputes that may arise during the exchange' (Podolny and Page 1998). Networks describe links among individuals in a group. A closed group with finite members is often known as a club. The term network has been used to describe both the entire set of links among individuals in a group and the set of links around a specific individual. Networks can be groupings, extended kinship, lobbying organizations, and hierarchical relationships associated with patronage. Networks encompass relationships between and within horizontal and vertical associations, that is, intercommunity, intracommunity ties.[6] A characteristic of the network is the relative uniformity of its members in terms of competence, optimism, and aversion to risk. This reinforces the uniformity that prevails in the moral dimension. Social interactions depend on network structure; the type of network that performs best and the best locations within a network come from an individual's perspective. The volume of social capital embedded in a network is dependent on the size of the network as well as on the capital of other agents in the network. Networks are governed by trust, social and behavioural norms of society, such as sanctions, reciprocity, traditions, and codes of conduct. Table 3.1 summarizes the discussion in this section.

Table 3.1 Social Capital and Its Elements

Elements	Category	Types	
Trust	Relational	Disposition	Reputation
Reciprocity	Cognitive	Direct	Indirect
Order/Sanctions	Organizational	Identity	Authority
Networks	Structural	Vertical	Horizontal

Source: Author's own compilation.

Social Capital: Micro and Macro Implications

In all its micro, meso, and macro perspectives, social capital is the social structure which facilitates coordination and cooperation. The usefulness of the concept of social capital begins with the observation that recurring and patterned social interactions within a well-defined boundary form a local 'social structure', and that the characteristics of this social structure will affect many economic decisions of individuals within that boundary. Specifically, the local social structure may affect economic decisions and outcomes through five main mechanisms: information sharing, transaction costs, the reduction of collective action dilemmas, mitigation of risk, and voluntary compliance with rules.

Social structures can affect information sharing among agents. When agents interact frequently in local networks and in the observance of local norms, they are more likely to observe each other's behaviour and to exchange information about their daily lives. Social capital thus facilitates and promotes economic actors' acquisition of knowledge and useful information (Landry et al. 2002; Maskell 2001). Social capital is a key factor in understanding knowledge creation. Social capital and knowledge creation have a positive relationship because social capital directly affects the combine-and-exchange process (Nahapiet and Ghoshal 1998).

These social interactions can affect the level of transaction costs associated with many market exchanges because when agents frequently and regularly interact in social settings, they establish patterns of expected behaviour and build bonds of trust. Social capital can improve economic performance by reducing transactions costs through trust (Sako 1992), providing better information than markets (Sako 1992) and allowing actors to adjust more quickly to environmental changes (Powell 1990). Coordination based on informal norms remains an important part of modern economies, and arguably has become more important as the nature of economic activity has become more complex and technologically sophisticated. Social capital plays a role in reducing the transaction costs associated with formal coordination mechanisms like contracts, hierarchies, bureaucratic rules, and the like. It is of course possible to achieve coordinated action among a group of people possessing no social capital, but this would presumably entail additional transaction costs of monitoring, negotiating, litigating, and enforcing formal agreements. No contract can possibly specify every contingency that may arise between the parties; most presuppose a certain amount of goodwill that prevents parties from taking advantage of unforeseen loopholes. Contracts that do seek to try to specify all contingencies become very inflexible and costly to enforce (Fukuyama 1999).

Combined with the possibility of social sanctions, social capital lowers the likelihood of opportunistic behaviour by agents that are in the same social structure. Frequent and regular interactions in social settings lead to the development of institutions that can serve as such constraints, thereby lowering the incentives of individual agents to free ride. Without selective constraints, agents in many settings will not have an incentive to participate in mutually beneficial collective action. Established networks and norms can also help those who are suddenly in need, thereby mitigating risk. For example, household–household transfers and informal credit institutions can ensure consumption smoothing for most members of poor communities, particularly those who do not face contemporaneous exogenous shocks[7] (Isham 2002). Social capital also facilitates better synergy with outside actors, including government, civil society organizations, and enterprises (Vaessen and Bastiaensen 1999). Social capital transforms individuals from self-seeking agents with little sense of obligation to others into members of a community with shared interests, a common identity, and a commitment to the common good (Adler and Kwon 2002).

At the firm level, social capital aids in transforming tacit knowledge[8] to codified knowledge.[9] Transforming tacit knowledge to codified knowledge is an attempt to institutionalize a capital that originally is social and non-institutionalized. Not all tacit knowledge is social capital since some of the tacit knowledge is strictly personal. However, most tacit knowledge must be regarded as created in social interactions, which makes it a part of the social capital. Social capital fosters learning by acting as conduits for pieces of information (Burt 1992) or by creating learning synergies (Fountain 1998).

Social capital is important not only to the firm's internal knowledge production but also to knowledge exchange between firms that have some kind of production-related links. Social capital helps cut expenses and reduces time needed for knowledge exchange between firms. A firm's costs for knowledge and information are influenced by social capital through the degree of trust and the climate of cooperation prevailing both in individual workplaces and between firms. Social, non-formalized links, between a firm (and its co-workers) and other firms, with which it has production relations, increase the flows of knowledge and information between the firms. Feedback, from the firm to its suppliers and to the firm from its customers, is increased and speeded up. These links of acquaintance and trust are of obvious importance in R&D projects, aimed at developing new products or production methods. By creating relationships with customers in diverse ways and by building networks with suppliers a firm attempts to shut out competitors from the network it has established. Apart from customers and suppliers, it is in the interest of the firm to establish social relations with public decision makers directly and indirectly, as firms depend on a predictable political-institutional infrastructure and the need for favourable political decisions. Firms tend to emerge in such areas where there is tacit knowledge and information (including gossip and rumours), potential partners, co-workers, and competitors, as it is easier to watch and learn from them.

A country's economic development is dependent upon its social organization. Social capital affects economic evolution through four main channels. The communitarian perspective equates social capital with such local organizations as clubs, associations, and civic groups. Communitarians, who look at the number and density of these groups in a given community, hold that social capital is inherently good, that more is better, and that its presence always has a positive effect on a community's welfare. But when communities and networks are isolated, parochial, or working at cross-purposes to society's collective interests, productive social capital is replaced by perverse social capital (such as sectarian interest groups, crime syndicates, or ethnic mobs) (Rubio 1997).

A second perspective on social capital and economic evolution stresses the importance of vertical as well as horizontal associations between people and of relations within and among networks or groups. This perspective recognizes that not only strong intra-community ties give families and communities a sense of identity and common purpose (Astone et al. 1999; Granovetter 1973), but also the need for inter-community ties, such as those that cut across various social divides based on religion, class, ethnicity, gender, and socio economic status. Strong horizontal or bonding ties can become a basis for the pursuit of narrow sectarian interests. The networks' view of social capital considers it to be a double-edged sword: it can provide a range of valuable services for network members, but it can also place considerable non-economic claims on members' sense of obligations and commitment with negative economic consequences.

The institutional view on the relationship between social capital and economic evolution posits that the political, legal, and institutional environments are the main determinants of the strength of community networks. It also suggests that for social capital to flourish, it needs to be embedded in, and linked to, formal political and legal institutions. The capacity of citizens to develop cooperative ties and establish social trust is heavily influenced by formal institutions (Levi 1998; Tarrow 1996). There are two types of institutional arguments in relation to the concept of social capital: an attitudinal approach and an institutional-structural approach. In the attitudinal approach, scholars examine the relationship between institutional/political trust and generalized trust. The institutional-structural approach generally centres on the role of the state as a source of social capital generation. Tarrow (1996), for example, argues that the 'state plays a fundamental role in shaping civic capacity'. But that is possible if citizens consider the state itself to be trustworthy such that it has the capacity to generate trust (Levi 1998).

The synergy view focuses on the relationships between and within governments and civil society (Grootaert and van Bastelaer 2002). Evans (1996) concludes that synergy between government and citizen action is based on complementarity and embeddedness. Complementarity refers to mutually supportive relations between public and private actors and is exemplified in legal frameworks that protect the rights of an association. Embeddedness refers to the nature and extent of the ties connecting citizens and public officials. Often when citizens are deprived of services and benefits, informal networks substitute for the failed state.

Successful development of modern market economies requires a departure from trade restricted to traditionally closed groups and an expansion of interaction to include anonymous others. Traditional societies had features rendering them more able to undertake the monitoring, information flow, and repetition of interaction required to make fulfilling promises possible, but such traditional structures cannot provide the basis for the development of successful modern production. Traditional societies, though characterized by pervasive intra-group trust, do not typically extend this trust, and the reciprocal notion of commitment, to outsiders and hence to anonymous interactions (Platteau 2000). When only able to trust traders with whom one is previously familiar, the functioning of market institutions is severely restricted because the domain of viable business relationships remains small. Entrepreneurs end up in scrupulously avoiding transactions that may result in a breach of agreement and resort to a flea market mode of behaviour: 'inspect the goods on the spot, pay cash, and walk away with them' (Platteau 2000). Anonymous interaction takes place only when there is a fairly widespread belief that one party does not see the interaction as an opportunity for it to take advantage of the other (Francois and Zabojnik 2005). Thus both social capital and institutions are necessary in mitigating that risk of expropriation.

Social capital can lead to both positive (norm observance, family support, network-mediated benefits) and negative (restricted access to opportunities, restrictions on individual freedom, excessive claims on group members, downward levelling norms) outcomes. There can be negative normative associations as well as positive ones; some networks embody the 'dark side' of social capital to the detriment of the wider society and even of its own members. Good and bad social capitals go together as the so-called benefits of social capital derived by some are exclusionary of others (Fine 2010). Strong ties can become dysfunctional by excluding information and reducing the capacity for innovation. Voluntary cross-cutting networks, associations, and related norms based in everyday social interactions lead to the collective good of citizens, whereas networks and associations consisting of primary social groups without cross-cutting ties lead to the betterment of only those groups.

Primary social group solidarity is the foundation on which societies are built. The impact of primary social groups depends on their resources and power. But when power between groups is asymmetrically distributed, it is the cross-cutting ties between social groups that become critical to both economic opportunity and social cohesion. While primary groups and networks undoubtedly provide opportunities to those who belong, they also reinforce pre-existing social stratification, prevent mobility of excluded groups, and become the bases of corruption and co-option of power by the dominant social groups (Narayan 2002). In addition, the trust implied in many social networks may lead to a decrease in vigilance and monitoring of information that is received (Szulanski and Jensen 2004). Network ties may entail needlessly burdensome obligations for the involved parties as individuals may not recognize the private bad character of the tie as strong bonds prevent realization of the negative impact of these ties and individuals are pressured to conform through network ties (Gargiulo and Benassi 2000).

* * *

The term 'social capital' has found its way into economic analysis in the recent past, although various elements of the concept have been present under different names for a long time. In political science, sociological, and anthropological literature, social capital generally refers to the set of norms, and networks, through which people gain access to power and resources, and through which decision making and policy formulation occur.

Social capital is created from the myriad of everyday interactions between people. It is not located within the individual person or within the social structure, but in the space between people. Social capital refers to values, norms, and trust between people which establish networks, associations, and facilitates reciprocity, coordination, and cooperation for mutual benefit. Through this capacity to create societal cooperation, existing contexts of action are made more productive and the creation of new ones takes place more easily. By participating in these networks, people combine short-term altruism with their long-term self-interest. Although human capital encourages engaging with others to form social networks and to invest in social capital irrespective of on religion, class, ethnicity, gender, and socio-economic status, social capital can be used for both positive and negative outcomes.

Networks are formed when people identify with one's own group or community, which acts as a powerful motivational force leading to forms of solidarity bounded by the group identity. Solidarity can be maintained within a community through repeated exchanges between close parties that have good information available about each other's behaviour. While groups can use solidarity as a weapon to wield against social injustice and to further the interests of the group, it can also be used to exclude others or to establish dominance over other groups.

Exchanges between two communities individually bound by their own local norms, values, and trust relationships are, however, necessary for the economic growth process. Institutions reduce uncertainty, support the formation of social capital in intercommunity exchanges, and thereby establish conditional rules of credibility. The problems of collective action are often solved by an institutional actor external to the interests of subjects involved in a cooperation project. Institutions help to prevent failure of cooperation between two communities through their mechanisms of regulation, communication, and reciprocal knowledge.

Notes

1. Collective action involves use of norms and networks in situations where individuals might otherwise be reluctant to be co-operative or socially engaged. Thus, norms of reciprocity and networks help ensure compliance with collectively desirable behaviour. In the absence of trust and networks ensuring compliance, individuals tend not to co-operate because others cannot be relied on to act in a similar way. Many social scientists refer to such co-ordination problems with various labels including 'the prisoner's dilemma' or the 'free-rider problem'.

2. Internalization of the standard in order to act in conformity with it becomes a need-disposition in the actor's own personality structure, relatively independently of any instrumentally significant consequences of that conformity (Parsons 1951).

3. Two features of rationality can be selected for purposes of introducing an 'idea'. The first is objectivity in analysis and the second calculability in decision. They are of course connected. Max Weber saw, in analysing the growth of the West that it was not only the economic sphere but the entire modern western culture which had become suffused with a specific form of rationalism. Effects were very clear in science, but also in music and in the worlds of officialdom and law. Order, procedure, principle, calculation, analysis and above all personal influence, had grown to become motifs of the social structure.

4. Evolution is understood as a class of trial and error processes, which comprise three elements: the generation of variety, the reduction of variety, and some persistence both in the characteristics of the variants and in the environment within which they are selected (Loasby 1999).

5. Economists agree in that implicit contracts play an important role in real world economic life. At the core of these contracts lies the notion of trust. As implicit contracts are not enforceable by a court, the parties have to trust each other that the contract will not be reneged on.

6. Woolcock and Narayan (2000) and Putnam (2000), among others, have delineated three types of the nature of human interactions: bonding, bridging, and linking. Bonding occurs among family members and ethnic groups and facilitates sharing of resources under the constraints of the norms and values defined by the institutional agreements defined by family, friendships, or ethnic groups. Bonding is a social adhesive that promotes solidarity, trust, and confidence. Bridging, which occurs among distant friends, colleagues, and associates, promotes transcendence of one's narrow traditional focus to that of broader society. Bridging creates the social adhesive that promotes intergroup connectedness, communal stability, and expanded configurations of trust that promote resource exchanges for economic and community development. Bonding

fosters denser social networks while bridging creates larger networks. Linking is yet broader a concept of relationships based on institutional arrangements that promote the exchange of power, wealth, and status among different social groups. A primary example of linking activities can be seen in national, transnational, and global interaction of commercial activities. Sharing Granovetter's thought, Putnam (1993, 1995) affirms that weak links are more important than familiar relations (strong links) in order to create cohesion inside the community and in the solution of dilemmas of collective action.

7. Poor people in developing countries often face risks that are systematically different and greater than those faced by other people around the world. Rural areas in these countries are often agriculturally oriented and hence production and consumption are susceptible to weather, health, crop-related, and other income shocks (Rosenzweig 1988; Townsend 1994). As a result, households often incur relatively large and unforeseen expenditures, such as medical costs, or are faced with the prospect of significant losses in income and consumption possibilities. Faced with such uncertainty, people adopt risk-mitigating strategies. This is corroborated by the empirical evidence that although household income in developing countries varies greatly, consumption is relatively smoother (Fafchamps and Lund 2003; Jacoby and Skoufias 1997; Townsend 1994). The presence of consumption smoothing, despite the lack of formal insurance options, points to the existence of informal options. In the literature, these options have taken the form of labour market arrangements such as sharecropping, informal credit and insurance arrangements, and social networks among others (Chadha 2011).

8. Tacit knowledge is defined as knowledge that cannot be obtained by a mere sum of codified (digitalized) information. It can be generated through personal knowledge through particular experiences and/or due to inherently personal qualities and competence; therefore it cannot become immediately available in open markets (Aoki 2001).

9. Codified knowledge can be defined as formalized, stored, written, or digitized information, which can be used or tested by another actor than the one who formalized the information.

4 Institutional Capital

Economic growth and evolution depends on human interaction by which knowledge is effectively generated, used, reused, and transformed. The generation of knowledge is channelled by institutions that allow knowledge to be repeatedly reused (Loasby 2001) and transformed. Institutions shape the direction of the acquisition of knowledge and the production of goods and services; that direction is the decisive factor for the long-term evolution of any society. Institutions also structure the incentives of exchange in the economic, political, and social spheres. Institutions typically offer a framework of reference—they constitute 'the environment', an autonomous reality that exists independently from the consideration of individuals. They guide the behaviour and the process of knowledge creation. North (1990) argued, in this regard, that institutions form a rescue anchor for individuals, they can greatly simplify the choice between the options, narrowing the number of possible alternatives. Institutions also offer a stable equilibrium and the knowledge of routine within which the problem of the choices appears regular, repetitive, and evident. In evolutionary economics, economic agents are viewed as reducing the uncertainty that they face and achieving economic goals by adhering to bundles of rules. The basic role of institutions in a society and an economy is, therefore, to reduce uncertainty by establishing a stable structure of human interaction, although not necessarily efficient. Formal organizations and informal institutions are both consequences of the human dependence on patterns to guide understanding and action, and they have their own consequences for understanding and action.

It is now generally recognized that 'institutions matter' and that the determinants of institutions are at least partially susceptible to analysis by the tools of economic theory. The idea that the prosperity of a society depends on its economic institutions goes back at least to Adam Smith—such as with his discussions of mercantilism and the role of markets—and was prominent in the work of many nineteenth-century scholars, such as J.S. Mill, who said societies are economically successful when they have 'good' institutional capital.

Similarly, the institutional tradition may be traced back to the writings of Thorstein Veblen in the US at the end of the nineteenth century, to the German Historical School, which was represented by authors such as Schmoller, and in the early writings of development economists (Hirschman 1970). The old institutionalism of Thorstein Veblen, John R. Commons, Wesley C. Mitchell, Clarence Ayres, and their followers reflected several common themes, mostly criticism of orthodox economics, characterized by a focus on collective rather than individual action, a preference for an evolutionary rather than a mechanistic approach to the economy, and an emphasis on empirical observation over deductive reasoning.

This earlier institutionalism was dominant in economics departments in American universities between 1920 and 1930, after which the 'old' institutionalism was repeatedly written off and dismissed for failing to provide a systematic and viable approach to economic theory.

However, it took Williamson's (1975) and North's (1974) formulation on the role of transaction costs, imperfect information, and a variety of cultural and legal constraints for the institutional tradition to be fully integrated into the analytical framework of mainstream economics. This 'new institutional economics' (NIE), now in widespread use, is associated with a vast literature and has gained increasing adherents and influence in economics, strategy, history, and other disciplines. It began to develop as a self-conscious movement in the 1970s, tracing its origin to Coase's analysis of the firm, Hayek's writings on knowledge, plus contributions of Arrow (1962), Alchian and Demsetz (1972), and Simon (1959). The new institutional economics differs from mainstream neoclassical economics in insisting that policy analysis be guided by what Coase (1964) calls 'comparative institutional analysis'. NIE is an interdisciplinary enterprise combining economics, law, organization theory, political science, sociology, and anthropology to understand the institutions of social, political, and commercial life. Its goal is to explain what institutions are, what role they play in economic evolution and growth, how they arise, what purposes they serve, how they change, and how—if it all—they should adapt, adjust and be continually reformed in responses to continual change in their external environments which pose challenges and threats to them.

As human beings have incomplete information and limited mental capacity by which to process information, individuals require cognitive frameworks within which to act, or even to think. These frameworks and procedures are influenced by assumptions, conventions, categories, practices, routines, and programmes by which individuals are surrounded from birth (Hodgson 1998). Likewise, for any human interaction, general regularities, guidelines, frameworks, and constraints are needed to structure and order exchange, social behaviour, environment, and everyday life. These procedures embedded in durable structures (institutions) help individuals to frame problems, define and limit the set of choices, and offer guidance on action, thereby allowing them to function (Hodgson 1998; Loasby 1999; North 1974).

The role of institutions in economic development made a revival in the early 1990s when the World Bank undertook a serious exploration of how the East Asian 'growth miracle' occurred and was reinforced in the late 1990s when the 'transition' process in central and eastern Europe and in parts of Central Asia preoccupied and challenged academia. What distinguished these reforms from the earlier stabilization and structural adjustment policies was their systemic character, which aimed to change not only relative prices but the entire set of economic, legal, and social incentive structures governing human economic behaviour. Successful transition was therefore considered to be critically dependent on a redesign of the institutional setup. Economic theory has accordingly credited institutional capital as being one of the most significant determinants of the growth process.

Meaning and Definitions

'Institutions' are formal structures that facilitate human action and interaction, from framing problems, to: simplifying and approximating infinite representations of reality, providing a set of categories to which all phenomena can be assigned; defining a set of choices; making logical deductions and processing; making decisions, to making connections, to aiding communication and knowledge sharing, to permitting competitive collaboration; increasing compatibility of thought; providing patterns to individual behaviour; governing agreements made by specific individuals, and so on. Institutional structures offer continually evolving guidance on problem solving and resource allocation. These structures are knowingly or unknowingly formed and changed by individuals in an evolutionary process. In other words, institutions provide rules, constraints, and incentives instrumental to the governance of human exchanges, whether of knowledge, goods, services or economic transactions of any sort. These institutions and their adoption and practice in the real world are what constitute institutional capital.

A meaningful categorization of the theories of institutions classifies them into three groups:

1. the old institutionalism which offered a different perspective on the nature of human agency based on the concept of habit (Thorstein Veblen, John R. Commons, Wesley C. Mitchell, Clarence Ayres);
2. theories that consider institutions as a framework in which human action takes place (Greif 1992; Greif et al. 1994; Milgrom et al. 1990; North 1990); and
3. theories that identify institutions as governance structures (Alchian and Demsetz 1972; Grossman and Hart 1986; Hart and Moore 1990; Jensen and Meckling 1976; Williamson 1975).

John R. Commons defined an institution 'as collective action in control, liberation, and expansion of individual action'. Collective action, according to Commons, ranged from unorganized custom to the many organized going concerns, such as family, the corporation, the trade association, the trade union, and the state. The principle common to all of them was greater or less control, and expansion of individual action by collective action.

Institutionalism, according to Commons (1931), was a relation of man to man and the transaction, a basic unit of observation in institutional economics, with three social relations implicit in every transaction: conflict, dependence, and order. Transaction costs arise from the coordination of exchange among different actors and include the costs of obtaining and processing market information, negotiating contracts, monitoring agents, and enforcing contracts. Therefore, transactions may be reduced to three economic activities, distinguishable as bargaining transactions, managerial transactions, and rationing transactions. The four economic issues arising out of a bargaining transaction are competition,[1] discrimination,[2] economic power,[3] and working rules[4] (Commons 1931).

One of the most useful definitions of an institution was provided by another old institutional economist Walton Hamilton (1932). He saw an institution as, 'a way of thought or action of some prevalence and permanence, which is embedded in the habits of a group or the customs of a people'. This elaborates Veblen's (1919) definition of an institution as 'settled habits of thought common to the generality of men'. These early institutionalists saw habit as the basis of human action and belief. Habit was defined as a largely non-deliberative, self-sustaining, and non-reflective propensity to engage in a previously adopted pattern of behaviour. For the early institutionalists, habit—implicitly, the repetition of particular types of behaviour—was linked to knowledge and belief. All ideas, including beliefs, preferences, and rational modes of calculation, were regarded as evolutionary adaptations to circumstances established through the acquisition of habitual propensities. For the 'old' institutionalists, habit was considered crucial to the formation and sustenance of institutions. Habits also formed part of cognitive abilities of individuals; the individual relied on the acquisition of such cognitive habits, reason, and communication. Learned skills became partially embedded in habits. When habits became a common part of a group or a social culture, they grew into routines or customs (Commons 1931). Habits and routines thus preserved knowledge in relation to skills and institutions acted through time as their transmission belt. Institutions were regarded as imposing form upon human activity, partly through the continuing production and reproduction of habits, thought, and action (Hodgson 1998).

Old institutionalism was partially disabled by a combined result of the profound shifts in social science in 1910–40 and the rise of the mathematical discipline that dominated neoclassical analysis in economics in the depression-stricken 1930s and beyond. With their use of formal statistical techniques, mathematical economists caught the imagination of both theorists and policymakers. In comparison, institutionalism was regarded as qualitative, conceptual, technically less rigorous, and, thereby, inferior in terms of 'science'.

On the other hand, the new institutional economics and its two strands have been influential. They deal with what Davis and North (1971) distinguished as 'institutional environment' and 'institutional arrangements'. The former refers to the 'set of fundamental political, social, and legal ground rules that establish the basis for production, exchange and distribution' (Davis and North 1971). These can be both formal, explicit rules (constitutions, laws, property rights), and informal, often implicit rules (social conventions, norms). These rules and customs that make up the institutional environment are primarily economy-side phenomena. While these background rules are the product of—and can be explained in terms of—the goals, beliefs, and choices of individual actors, the social result is typically not known or 'designed' by anyone. This strand of literature is associated primarily with North (1981, 1990) and Greif (1992, 1997) and it concentrates on comparative historical analysis of development processes (mainly in western Europe and North America).

Institutional arrangements, by contrast, are specific guidelines—what Williamson (1985, 1996) refers to as 'governance structures'—designed by trading partners to mediate particular economic relationships. Business firms, long-term contracts, public bureaucracies, courts and legal systems, non-profit organizations, and other contractual agreements are examples of institutional arrangements. Table 4.1 provides information on what constitutes the different strands of New Institutional Economics.

The functioning of institutions and their performance depends on both the institutional environment and arrangements. The first aspect is the overall environment which fosters the rule of law, citizen rights, and the freedom to associate, since these create the societal norms which influence the emergence, and subsequent performance, of a range of societal institutions. The second aspect concerns the competence, authority, objectivity, resources, regulation, and accountability of organizations working within the overall environment.

In the new institutionalism, institutions are regarded as general regularities in social behaviour, 'the rules of the game in society or... the humanly devised constraints that shape human interaction.

Table 4.1 Different Strands of New Institutional Economics (NIE) and Their Components

Institutional Environment	Institutional Arrangements
Deals with macro-economy side phenomena	Deals with micro-economy side phenomena, essentially with theory of the firm
1. Legal Environment—design of legal rules and the legal system itself, character and effects of law, mechanisms by which legal rules change.	1. Transaction Cost Economics (TCE)—The emphasis is on governing transactions. TCE holds that all but the simplest transactions require some kind of mechanism—governance structure—to protect the transacting parties from various hazards associated with exchange. The governance approach is distinguished by its emphasis on incomplete contracts. TCE also holds that all complex contracts are unavoidably incomplete exposing the contracting parties to certain risks.
2. Norms and social conventions	
3. Economic history and growth—understanding how economies develop through time. Development is seen as a response to the evolution of institutions that support social and commercial relationships.	2. The moral hazard or agency-theoretic approach, which begins with Berle and Mean's identification of the separation of 'ownership and control' in the large firm.
4. Positive political theory—political institutions have also received much attention in NIE. The rational choice approach to politics as outlined in public choice and positive political theory holds that political institutions can be explained in terms of purposeful human choice. The rational choice perspective is also used to explain the effects of political institutions on public policy, including macroeconomic policy, welfare policy, budgets, regulation, and technology policy.	3. Capabilities and the core competence of the firm—the capabilities view, which traces its roots to Alfred Marshall and Schumpeter was first stated by Edith Penrose in her work, *The Theory of the Growth of the Firm* (1959). The capabilities view regards the firm not as a nexus of contracts or as a set of residual control rights but as a stock of knowledge. In the field of strategic management, organizational capabilities have been examined from within the 'resource-based' view of the firm. In the resource-based view, competitive advantage comes from having unique factors of production, resources that are not easily imitable or transferable. The evolutionary theory of production is based on differential capabilities, embedded in the personal and

(Cont'd)

Table 4.1 (*Cont'd*)

Institutional Environment	Institutional Arrangements
5. Complexity and cognitive science—recent work has focused on the relationship between the institutional environment and cognitive processes in forming a framework for decision making under uncertainty.	organizational structure of firms. Skills on the personal level, and routines at the organizational level form the repository of knowledge, which, in turn, defines the production possibilities of firms.

Institutional constraints include both what individuals are prohibited from doing and sometimes, under what conditions some individuals are permitted to undertake certain activities' (North 1990). Organizations are defined as the players in the game; they are the agents that play by the rules to win the game (North 1990). Organizations include political bodies, such as governmental departments and political parties; economic bodies, such as firms and family farms; social bodies, such as clubs and churches; educational bodies, such as schools and universities; and also non-governmental organizations (Table 4.2). Adams and Neal (1993) consider institutions as 'sets of opportunities' rather than as a set of constraints. When people are interdependent, one person's opportunity to act is another's exposure to that act or even obligation to act in a certain way. From this notion, it follows that institutions are never simply constraints in general, but also enablement—enablement, not only in the sense that the rights holder has an opportunity with which others may not interfere, but also that the holder may achieve something not possible to achieve alone. In contrast, Hodgson (1998) believes that within institutions, individuals are not merely constrained and influenced, but also are constituted by institutions. Institutional capital is institutions as rules of the game, players of the game, practice of the game and adoption of changes in the rules of the game.

Institutional Framework

In the simplest framework, economic and social interaction is facilitated by the institutional environment – vector I, in an economic system

Table 4.2 Types of Institutions

Type of Institution	Public/State-owned/State-related				Private		Mixed
	Supranational	National	Sub-national	Local/Municipal	Commercial	Non-commercial	Quasi-Public/Pvt.
1. Constitutional	Core UNO	Constitutional Authority Monarchy/ Republic/ Autocracy Elected/ Appointed Legislature Independent/ Appointed Judiciary	Provincial Authority	Local/City Authority			
2. A. Bureaucratic—[Administrative]	Global and regional, organizations/ agencies such as, WB, IMF, WTO, MDBs, EU, etc.) Legal System	Federal/Unitary Governments and their respective ministries, sub-ministries, agencies, and instrumentalities Legal System Institutions	Provincial or State level governments and their respective ministries, sub-ministries, agencies, and instrumentalities Legal Institutions	District or Municipal Governments, corporations/ agencies and their respective sub-divisions, agencies, and instrumentalities			Quasi-Governmental organizations and agencies (quangos)

2. S. Bureaucratic—[Security]	UN or Regional Military Forces	Army, Navy, Air Force, Coast Guards, Marines and Central Police Forces and Intelligence Agencies	State-level Police Militias Territorial Armies	Local Police and security forces	Private Security Firms	Neighbourhood Watches and voluntary security organizations	Public–Private Security related partnerships
3. Theocratic	Various Global Religions and Churches: Christian (Vatican, Anglican, Mormon, etc.) Islamic, Judaic, Hindu, Buddhist, Shinto, etc.	National religious authorities, entities and institutions (bishoprics, etc.)		Local churches, temples, mosques, synagogues, etc.	Church-owned profit making organizations	Church-owned non-profit organizations, charities, homes, schools, clubs, addiction centres, etc.	Church–state joint initiatives in education, welfare, poverty alleviation initiatives, etc.
4. Commercial	Multi-State (such as, EU) owned multinational or global corporations in any area of activity	SOEs/PSUs in any area of activity	Sub-sovereign entities and agencies with commercial orientation	Local/Municipal corporations and entities aimed at revenue generation	Company or Firm Sole Proprietorship Partnerships Other Legal Entities	Foundations, Charities, Trusts	Public–Private Partnerships Private Finance Initiatives

(*Cont'd*)

Table 4.2 (Cont'd)

Type of Institution	Public/State-owned/State-related				Private		Mixed
	Supranational	National	Sub-national	Local/Municipal	Commercial	Non-commercial	Quasi-Public/Pvt.
5. Voluntary NGO	Various types of aid agencies, charities, educational orders (Jesuits, Anglicans, ICB schools, etc.) operating globally: such as, Oxfam	National NGOs in all areas of activity	Sub-national NGOs in all areas of activity	District/City-based NGOs in all areas of activity	Political Action Committees and Various Industry or Private Interest Lobby Groups	Non-commercial Political Action Committees and Various Industry or Private Interest Lobby Groups	Mixed: NGO–State funded initiatives in various areas of service delivery and welfare activity
6. Social	Lions & Rotary Clubs Alumnus Associations	National clubs of various types: for sports, music, art, drama, etc.	Sub-national clubs of similar types	Local/city clubs of various types	Professional or Vocational Associations, Societies, Accreditation Agencies of various types	Non-commercial Professional or Vocational Associations, Societies, Accreditation Agencies of various types	

7. Cultural	UNESCO or Regionally promoted initiatives/agencies	National Cultural Agencies, Museums, Opera, Ballet, Dance, Drama, Literature, etc. (e.g., BBC in UK, etc.)	Sub-National/Ethnic Cultural Agencies, Museums, Opera, Ballet, Dance, Drama, Libraries/Literature, etc.	Local/City-based Cultural Agencies, Museums, Opera, Ballet, Dance, Drama, Libraries, etc.	Commercial privately promoted cultural organizations in the performing arts	Non-Commercial privately promoted cultural organizations in the performing arts	Joint Public–Private promoted cultural organizations in the performing arts
8. Academic	UN or Regional (EU) Universities, Research and Policy research Organizations	National Universities Colleges Schools Vocational Training organizations, Pure & Applied Research Institutes, Policy-Oriented and Policy-Influencing Institutes (e.g., Brookings, Hudson, Rand, Cato, Adam Smith, etc.)	Provincial Universities Colleges Schools Vocational Training organizations, Pure & Applied Research Institutes, Policy-Oriented and Policy-Influencing Institutes (e.g., Brookings, Hudson, Rand, Cato, Adam Smith, etc.)	Local/City Universities Colleges Schools Vocational Training organizations, Pure & Applied Research Institutes, Policy-Oriented and Policy-Influencing Institutes (e.g., Brookings, Hudson, Rand, Cato, Adam Smith, etc.)	Universities Colleges Schools Vocational Training organizations, Pure & Applied Research Institutes, Policy-Oriented and Policy-Influencing Institutes (e.g., Brookings, Hudson, Rand, Cato, Adam Smith, etc.)	Universities Colleges Schools Vocational Training organizations, Pure & Applied Research Institutes, Policy-Oriented and Policy-Influencing Institutes (e.g., Brookings, Hudson, Rand, Cato, Adam Smith, etc.)	Universities Colleges Schools Vocational Training organizations, Pure & Applied Research Institutes, Policy-Oriented and Policy-Influencing Institutes (e.g., Brookings, Hudson, Rand, Cato, Adam Smith, etc.)

Source: Mistry.

– matrix E; vector I requires a vector g of governance structures to create credible commitment.[5] The institutional vector I defines the opportunity set and influences investments in physical capital, human capital, and technology—the production and distribution of resources in the future. Vector g, on the other hand, when transferred into production and transaction processes,[6] provides an incentive structure for efficient performance, and finally with output prices – p, the level of overall economic output is determined.

Where

Vector I = rules of the game, players of the game,[7] referees of the game, effectiveness of rule enforcement

Vector g = play of the game – transaction costs, core competence, capabilities

Matrix E = means, ends, order, rationality, or arationality

As individuals make decisions, they increase their knowledge by making connections. Knowledge essentially grows by combination, exchange, division and specialization; individuals can increase their knowledge only by accepting limits on what they know. All knowledge requires a framework and these frameworks must be imposed. Actions are taken within a framework, whether it is supplied by a precisely specified model, a familiar procedure, a novel vision, or some other means. A loosely defined framework of scope and methods is necessary for all to increase their understanding, and a framework that is shared with others permits a kind of competitive collaboration in the development of knowledge (Loasby 1999).

All decisions, like knowledge, depend on frameworks and methods by which to handle them.[8] People cannot cope with an unlimited decision space and information; partial closure is essential. The achievement of sufficient closure is necessary to make logical deductions. Closure limits an individual's attention and procedures to what is manageable.

The assumptions, criteria, categories, and procedures that people employ for achieving closure are usually representations of the reality that they believe exists. A mental model is developed by which people construct their experience through their perception and interpretation of events by a mixture of unconscious accumulation and deliberate thought (Kelly 1963). The way by which the mind processes information is not only the basis for the existence of institutions, but is also a key to understanding the way they play an important role in the makeup of the choice set (North 1990). However, it is highly likely that problems are inappropriately defined and wrongly closed; and closures which are effective for one purpose are likely to be ineffective for others. There can be no universally valid framework. Choices differ between people and these differences continually generate variety, but there are strong pressures to limit this variety within any cohesive group. Such limits facilitate communication within a group and thereby promote the development of certain kinds of knowledge.

The frameworks and procedures in common use within any group are the institutions of that group. In an interdependent society, widely shared rules help people to predict the behaviour of other people and thus help people to interact effectively and to avoid conflict. They help individuals frame problems and offer guidance on action, thus allowing them to function (Loasby 1999). Rules and routines provide an institutional setting for each individual's use of knowledge by converting tacit knowledge into knowledge that is public, unambiguous, and readily transferable. These common frameworks and procedures increase the compatibility of thought and action between people who use the same categories and procedures. Agreements are made between such people to govern their relationships; this is necessary as there is an amount of uncertainty about the future and about other parties' actions, the complexity of their arrangement, strategic abuse, bilateral dependence, the costliness of information,[9] and the frequency with which any transaction occurs. But it takes resources to define, protect, and enforce agreements. These agreements or governance structures help provide an order, allay conflict, and help achieve mutual benefits in resource allocation.

Institutions, together with the technology employed, determine the cost of transacting and the cost of transformation. How well institutions solve the problems of coordination and production is determined by the motivation of the players (their utility function), the complexity of the environment, and the ability of the players to decipher and order the environment (measurement and enforcement) (North 1990). Institutions change under the interactive pressure of changing opportunity costs as well as evolving individual and social perceptions. While individual and household actions are 'locked in' the dynamics of the inherited institutional context, human beings, perceiving and reacting to changes in the opportunity set, contribute to transform the institutional environment (North 1990) and governance structures.

Formal and Informal Institutions

Institutional capital encompasses rules of the game, players of the game, referees of the game, effectiveness of rule enforcement, and the play of the game itself, all of which guide how people within societies live, work, and interact with each other. Within the universe of what we know to be institutions, there are two broad types: formal and informal. Formal institutions refer to the official rules of society as defined by law. This includes the political ground rules as laid down in the constitution and the laws and procedures governing the political system and the state and economic transactions. Formal institutions are also institutional arrangements structured and defined by the formal institutional environment.

On the other hand, the whole array of norms, beliefs, values, shared meanings, customs, religious precepts, conventions, and patterned ways of behaving that constrain and facilitate individual behaviour constitutes informal institutions. By defining the difference between the relevant and the irrelevant, the acceptable and non-acceptable, the desirable and non-desirable, and so on, informal institutions exert a strong influence on people's behaviour. While informal rules are generally not codified, it is normally widely accepted as legitimate and are therefore 'rules in operation' (in use) rather than just rules on the books, or what Ostrom terms 'rules in force' (Ostrom 2005). Informal rules are:

(i) extensions, elaborations, and modifications of formal rules outside the official framework;
(ii) socially sanctioned norms of behaviour (attitudes, customs, taboos, conventions, and traditions);
(iii) enforcement characteristics are self-enforcement mechanisms of obligation, expectations of reciprocity, internalized norm adherence (standard operating procedures), gossip, shunning, ostracism, boycotting, shaming, threats, and the use of violence (Ostrom 2005).

'Culture', as an aggregate term, encompasses this array of informal institutions. Culture means the whole complex of traditional behaviour that has been developed by constituent ethnicities and is successively learned by each generation. Culture is learned, is associated with groups of people, and its content includes a wide range of phenomena including norms,[10] beliefs, values, shared meanings, and patterned ways of behaving (Axelrod 1997). Recent definitions take into account a shift in meaning to culture that is the socially transmitted knowledge and behaviour shared by some group of people (Peoples and Bailey 1997). Earlier authors defined culture in the following ways as cited in Brumann (1999):

- Culture...refers...to learned, accumulated experience. A culture... refers to those socially transmitted patterns for behaviour characteristic of a particular social group (Keesing 1981).
- Culture, or civilization, ...is that complex whole which includes knowledge, belief, art, law, morals, custom, behaviour and any other capabilities and habits acquired by man as a member of society (Tylor 1871).
- The culture of any society consists of the sum total of ideas, conditioned emotional responses, and patterns of habitual behaviour which the members of that society have acquired through instruction or imitation and which they share to a greater or less degree (Linton 1936).
- A culture is the total socially acquired life-way or life-style of a group of people. It consists of the patterned, repetitive ways of thinking, feeling, and acting that are characteristic of the members of a particular society or segment of a society (Harris 1975).

All these definitions agree that culture consists of an intricate combination of something shared and/or learned by a group of people, but the content of the culture varies in different definitions. The content of the culture includes a set of traits, which can refer to behaviour, knowledge facts, ideas, beliefs, norms, etc. Bourdieu (1986) maintained that culture shares many of the properties characteristic of economic capital. In particular, he asserted that cultural 'habits and dispositions' comprise a resource capable of generating 'profits'; they are potentially subject to monopolization by individuals and groups, and, under appropriate conditions, they can be transmitted from one group to another and from one generation to the next (Lareau and Weininger 2003).

Some cultures are considered 'stronger' than others, in that the rules are more clearly understood and more widely accepted (Redding 2001). Peter Berger's *The Social Construction of Reality* and Geert Hofstede's concept of 'the collective programming of the mind' suggest a social process that shapes shared mental frameworks of meaning and in which people come to accept a particular way of doing things as appropriate. The way of doing things includes ways of defining and thinking about things, ways of behaving, ways of relating, and ways of assigning value or priority. How the process works, and the reason why it is so powerful and persistent, is based on two underlying instincts of human beings: the instinct to belong and the need to establish some form of productive social order. The second is needed if cooperation is to be built across society such that small groups are not constantly fighting other small groups for resources. Because both membership and general cooperation bring benefits to individuals, and especially because membership is more or less essential to normal existence, people pay the price of having those benefits: They conform, learn the rules, and practice them. Those who best exemplify what a particular culture sees as ideal traits are given status and respect.

Formal rules are an important part of the institutional framework, but only a part. To work effectively, rules must be complemented by norms of behaviour that supplement them and reduce enforcement costs. Together, rules and behaviour establish a minimal level of security and trust between the individual actors, provide self-sustaining contract enforcement, and support efficient third-party enforcement from the state, all of which lower transaction costs of economic contracts and facilitate cooperation and collective action within the community. Informal institutions can supplement, modify, and reinforce formal rules in both the polity and the economy. Informal institutions are very important because they form the base for the intentional development of formal institutions which organize and influence economic and political life (Knight 1992).

Formal institutions alone do not shape human behaviour, but that much of what goes on can be explained also by informal institutions. This aspect however has been fairly neglected. The reasons are that informal institutions are difficult to identify, measure, quantify and often relate to dimensions of a society's culture that economists and other social scientists prefer to shy away from. Informal institutions interact with formal institutions as they affect outcomes in four stylized ways: complementary, accommodating, competing, and substituting (see Table 4.3).

In terms of the first, informal institutions are complementary with formal ones when they converge and the formal institutions are effective. Second, the informal institutions may accommodate the formal ones when they diverge and formal institutions are effective by not violating the letter of the law but violating its spirit. Third, informal institutions compete with formal ones when formal institutions are ineffective and the two diverge. This is true where formal law is poorly enforced, or simply ignored by authorities.

People in both rich and poor countries rely on informal institutions to varying degrees to facilitate transactions, but these institutions are relatively more important in poor countries and small, traditional communities where formal institutions are less developed and the reach of formal law and state power is relatively weak (Bardhan 2001). Moreover, poor people in developing countries are often ill-served by the limited formal institutions available. In poor countries, and poor regions in particular, informal institutions substitute more frequently for formal institutions (Bardhan 2001). The effectiveness of formal law, even in rich countries, however, may depend to a large extent on how well the law corresponds with norms, making enforcement less costly, thus norms and attitudes matter for how well even formal institutions can work (Posner 1997).

Fourth, informal institutions matter because they substitute for law in complex economies given that every aspect of interaction between people cannot be governed by a written law (Cooter 1994). While there is a tendency for some informal institutions to be replaced by formal rules as the division of labour becomes more complex, informal

Table 4.3 Typology of informal institutions

Outcomes	Effective Formal Institutions	Ineffective formal Institutions
Convergent	Complementary	Substitutive
Divergent	Accommodating	Competing

Source: Helmke and Levitsky (2004: 728).

institutions continue to exert a strong impact on institutional performance. But even in more advanced market economies, the replacement of informal institutions by more formal coordinating mechanisms is far from complete. At a practical level, whether informal institutions are considered constraints or parts of a society's opportunity set is probably less important than the recognition that informal institutions fundamentally influence human behaviour while not being directly amenable to policy. The direction and form of economic activity in an economy reflect the opportunities thrown up by the basic institutional framework of customs, religious precepts, formals rules, and the effectiveness of enforcement.

Micro and Macro Implications of Institutional Capital

Institutions within each community channel the processes by which that community develops its knowledge. Institutions emerge to minimize transaction costs, to facilitate market exchange, to make risk management easier, to create order, and to decrease risk or improve and enhance the flow of information. The evolution from personalized exchange to impersonal or anonymous exchange, supported by legal systems that enforce contracts, is central to the process of growth (North and Thomas 1973).

Institutions (such as cognitive maps, decision premises, procedural rules) anchor the definition of problems and the repertoire of responses and inhibit the range of experimentation. The need for rules and patterns arises from the inescapable limitations of individual human knowledge. 'People decide and act in a given situation based on a paradigm identified as appropriate for that situation. Without a paradigm there will be no decision and no action' (Choi 1993). Institutions embrace and enshrine patterns acquired from others which guide individual actions, they constitute a stock of other's reusable knowledge. They help individuals cope with complex decisions and help form a shared set of mental models possessed by groups of individuals. These mental models are 'the internal representations that individual cognitive systems create to interpret the environment' (Denzau and North 1994). For each individual, the combination of internal connections and external institutions economizes on the scarce resource of cognition, first by allowing many operations to be performed without thinking about them, and then, when thought is required, by providing both cognitive maps, with which to make sense of novel situations, to which logical reasoning may be applied (Eden 1992). Individuals do this by drawing on the stock of previous examples of successful performance and of previously successful ways of making sense. Furthermore, each individual has reason to believe that as long as they observe these helpful conventions, their behaviour, even when reacting to situations that have some novel characteristics, will be acceptable to other people within the group and compatible with their actions. Firms encourage similar representations, similar possibilities, and similar procedures among its members, and thus reduce the costs of transacting ideas. The strong influence of institutions upon individual cognition provides significant stability in socioeconomic systems by constraining diverse and variable actions of many individuals (Hodgson 1998).

In addition to supplementing cognitive capabilities, institutions give people support and confidence. People's readiness to act, whether based on explicit reason or implicit routine, is frequently supported by a belief that other, successful, people rely on similar representations and procedures. The personal value of rules and conventions is an important factor in explaining how institutions come to be accepted as aids to the solution of coordination of problems, and thus form part of the explanation of the development of institutional arrangements. It is institutions that help explain why and what physical factors are present and combined in a particular way and time and it is institutions that make one person's interests a cost to others (and thus a source of income).

Institutions contribute towards innovation by opening up one segment of the institutional framework, or by intelligently seeking to apply rules and conventions outside familiar limits (Loasby 1999). Innovation originates with individuals. It depends on differences between individuals, first in their perceptions of a situation, and second in the responses to that situation that arise in their imaginations. Different situations are likely to lead to differences in behaviour, including different ideas for innovation. This is the basic principle of Adam Smith's (1976) theory of economic development as a consequence of specialization. Therefore, diversity helps achieve progress at a rate and of a kind that no single individual can even imagine.

Institutions stabilize economies and influence the structure of economic incentives in a society. Without institutions, individuals will not have the incentive to invest in physical or human capital or adopt more efficient technologies. Economic institutions are also important because they help to allocate resources to their most efficient uses, and determine who gets profits, revenues, and residual rights of control. Societies with institutions that facilitate and encourage factor accumulation, innovation, and efficient allocation of resources will prosper. Institutions also reduce uncertainty in human exchange.

Institutions channel the evolution of economic activities and are themselves subject to evolution. The continuous interaction between institutions and organizations (firms) in the economic setting of scarcity results in institutional change. Therefore, competition which induces innovation is the source of institutional change. Competition forces organizations to continually invest in skills and knowledge to survive: the kinds of skills and knowledge individuals and their organizations acquire; shape-evolving perceptions about opportunities and choices that incrementally alter institutions (North 1990).

Competition, however, does not affect macro institutions which change relatively slowly. Institutions are determined as collective choices of the society, in large part for their economic consequences. There is typically a conflict of interest among various groups and individuals over the choice of institutions. When there are two groups with opposing preferences over the set of institutions, the political power of the two groups determines which group's preferences will prevail. Whichever group has more political power is likely to secure the set of institutions that it prefers. A group has political power depending on its social capital and its resources, which determine both their ability to use (or misuse) existing institutions.

***

Institutions consist of formal and informal rules, organizations, monitoring, distribution and enforcement mechanisms, and systems of meaning that define the context within which individuals, corporations, labour unions, nation states, and other organizations operate and interact with each other. Institutions are settlements born from struggle and bargaining. They reflect the resources and power of those who made them and, in turn, affect the distribution of resources and power in the society. 'Good' institutions are viewed as establishing an incentive structure that reduces uncertainty and promotes efficiency. They play a complementary role in intra-community and extra-community exchanges. In the latter, they aid in the creation and maintenance of longer-term relationships and reputations. In societies with good governance and high levels of bridging social capital, there is a complementarity between state and society and economic prosperity and social order are likely.

Societies need effective, impersonal contract enforcement because personal ties, voluntary constraints and ostracism are ineffective when more complex and impersonal forms of exchange emerge. As an economy matures, a system of laws, rules, and regulations replaces the 'community' as the guardian of social, business, and personal contracts. But it is unlikely that institutions can remove entirely the risk of malfeasance and, therefore, legal apparatus can never serve as a substitute for trust. So even when an economy has reached a stage of maturity, trust-based exchange will still exist. Trust-based exchange relations are valuable in developing countries where institutional mechanisms needed to facilitate the transactions between individuals or groups are lacking.

Notes

1. The bargaining transaction derives from the familiar formula of a market, which, at the time of negotiation, before goods are exchanged, consists of the best two buyers and the best two sellers in that market. Out of this formula four relations of possible conflict of interest arise: The two buyers are competitors and the two sellers are competitors, from whose competition and guided by custom, the courts have constructed the long line of rules on fair and unfair competition.

2. One of the buyers will buy from one of the sellers, and one of the sellers will sell to one of the buyers and out of this economic choice of opportunities, both custom and the courts have constructed the rules of equal and unequal opportunity, which, when reduced to decisions of disputes, become the collective rules of reasonable and unreasonable discrimination.

3. At the close of the negotiations, one of the sellers, by operation of law, transfers title to one of the buyers, and one of the buyers transfers title to money or a credit instrument to one of the sellers. Out of this double alienation and acquisition of title arises the issue of equality or inequality of bargaining power,

whose decisions create the rules of fair and unfair price, or reasonable and unreasonable value.

4. Decisions on disputes, and on the rules prescribed to guide the decisions, may be called in question, on the grounds that property or liberty has been taken by the governing or judicial authority without due process of law. Due process of law is the working rule of the highest court for the time being, with changes in custom and class dominance or with changes in the customary meanings of property and liberty.

5. A commitment is credible in either of two senses, the motivational or the imperative. A commitment is motivationally credible if the players continue to want to honour the commitment at the time of performance. In this case it is incentive compatible and hence self-enforcing. It is credible in the imperative sense if the player cannot act otherwise because performance is coerced or discretion is disabled.

6. The total costs of production consist of the resource inputs of land, labour, and capital involved, in both transforming the physical attributes of a good (size, weight, colour, location, chemical composition, and so forth) and in transacting—defining, protecting, and enforcing the property rights to goods (the right to use, the right to derive income from the use of, the right to exclude, and the right to exchange) (North 1990).

7. Institutions determine the opportunities in a society. Organizations or the players of the game are created to take advantage of those opportunities and as organizations evolve, they alter the institutions.

8. Because individuals are boundedly rational, they do not calculate a complete set of strategies for every situation they face. Individuals tend to use heuristics that they have learned over time regarding responses that tend to give them good outcomes in particular kinds of situations (Ostrom 1999). These heuristics are inherited, historically satisfactory solutions to problems as they are culturally perceived. Cultural perceptions and inherited rules of thumb make up heuristic models, composed of recognized problems and validated solutions, which structure household behaviour by defining the subjective set of viable strategies and interactions.

9. It is the key to the costs of transacting, which consist of the costs of measuring the valuable attributes of what is being exchanged and the costs of protecting rights and policing and enforcing agreements (North 1990).

10. A norm is '…a rule that is neither promulgated by an official source, such as a court or a legislature, nor enforced by the threat of legal sanctions, yet is regularly complied with' (Posner 1997). Schotter (1981) calls norms as, 'a regularity in social behaviour that is agreed to by all members of society, specifies behaviour in specific recurrent situations and are self-policed'.

5 The Relationship between Human Capital, Social Capital, and Institutional Capital

One of the most interesting puzzles in contemporary economic growth and evolution debates revolves around why individuals in some countries, regions, cities, or villages are able to join together, trust each other, and solve many of their collective action problems while others cannot. Traditional neoclassical growth models explained cross-country differences in terms of different paths of factor accumulation. In these models, differences in factor accumulation are due to differences in either saving rates, preferences, or other exogenous parameters, such as total factor productivity growth. More recent growth models endogenize steady state growth and technical progress, but their explanation for country-wise differences is similar to that of older theories. Though this theoretical tradition is still vibrant in economics, it has long seemed unable to provide the fundamental explanation for cross-country differences in growth experiences. Factors like innovation, economies of scale, capital accumulation, etc. are not causes of growth; they are growth (North and Thomas 1973).

However, recent tendencies in growth theory have increasingly focused on capabilities rather than resource endowments as the main factors of development. This represents a shift from a perspective in which people are passive recipients of the fruits of development to one in which they actively participate in shaping development. Another tendency is to regard knowledge as perhaps the most important resource in growth; the role of knowledge, the problems of knowledge transfer, and knowledge utilization are increasingly being recognized as having been underestimated in development theory and policy. Accordingly, in a bid to understand persistent differences in economic growth and other measures of well-being, social scientists are increasingly broadening their analysis beyond traditional variables to include human capital, social capital, and institutional capital. The potential impact of these three components (individually) on economic growth has attracted a great deal of attention. This chapter provides an explanatory framework of the simultaneous interaction between the three components of human capital, social capital, and institutional capital.

The intrinsic link between human capital, social capital, and institutional capital in a knowledge economy rests on the fact that knowledge creation, transfer, sharing, and use are processes that take place between individuals within social and institutional contexts. A dynamic relationship links knowledge, with human capital and social capital, and institutional capital; in that, changes in knowledge and economic activity require a change in framework. Different societal and economic outcomes depend on different possible combinations of these three factors (human capital, social capital, and institutional capital) in different interlinked contexts.

The strength of such an analysis linking the three broad variables is the inclusion of micro, meso, and macro levels of knowledge process. Such an analysis also allows for important effects of complementarity and substitution between the three levels. For example, generic human capital needs institutions, such as firms, to create value. Human interactions are bound by a variety of institutional arrangements that can be either informal or legalistic. Social capital facilitates interactions within these institutional structures.

Assumptions

1. Accumulation of human capital in one form or another is the main aim in the personal development of human beings.
2. Human capital formation is facilitated by a social process. For example no one goes to school in isolation of the context in which that school is located, administered, or funded (institutional characteristics). Other than schooling, some skills and knowledge can only be formed in an organizational context and embodied only in a team of individuals. Individual productivity crucially depends on the education of co-workers, mutual information-sharing, skill

complementarity, and informal training by co-workers (Barron et al. 1997).
3. Human capital provides the ability and the understanding to allow people to essentially interact and engage in larger society while yielding information, facts, ideas, rational thought, and behaviour. It gives people the mental skills to foresee the consequences of their actions and develop a more complex sense of enlightened self-interest. Education instils common norms that increase social cohesion and establish a common set of understandings that help people to cooperate with one another (Gradstein and Justman 2001). In addition, higher educational attainment helps greater civic and voluntary engagement, as well as larger and more diverse social networks (Dworkin et al. 2003).
4. Social capital facilitates and promotes economic actors' acquisition of knowledge and useful information (Landry et al. 2002; Maskell 2001). Social capital is a key factor in understanding knowledge creation. Social capital is the social structure which facilitates coordination and cooperation.
5. Besides pure complementation, there is trade-off relationship between human and social capital. Almost all people are equipped with some form of human and social capital; individuals tend to maximize their benefit by making some combination of their 'capital portfolio', that is, to utilize different amounts of capital of each type, based on their endowment.
6. Human and social capitals are acquired through a form of effort that puts a limit on accumulation. Both can generate large positive or negative externalities.
7. Multiple institutions nurture the habits and values that give rise to social capital, including the community and other voluntary associations, families, religious organizations, and cultural patterns (Brehm and Rahn 1997).
8. Institutions and their legacies structure preferences, interests, and values in society. The origins or internal workings and the performance of institutions largely depend on the wisdom of their founders or subsequent leaders and their values, commitments, resources, and choices. Institutions are reasonably permanent or durable.
9. Institutional outcomes (the rule of law) depend to a large extent on human and social capital endowments (Djankov et al. 2003). Each

community faces a set of institutional opportunities, determined largely by the human and social capital of its population. The greater the human and social capital of a community, the more attractive are its institutional opportunities. Human and social capital shape both institutional and productive capacities of a society.[1]

10. Institutions matter for economic growth because they shape the incentives of key economic actors in society and are responsible for an array of economic outcomes, including the future distribution of resources.
11. Trust is a value involving the interpretative, moral, emotional, and motivational characteristics of social values and is an element of economic and social transactions. Trust depends on the context of the community in which it is shared. Mutual trust increases with more intense use. Generalized trust indicates the potential readiness of citizens to cooperate with each other and the abstract preparedness to engage in civic endeavours with each other. Trust increases the desire of people to take risks for productive social exchange (Tyler 2001). Attitudes of generalized trust extend beyond the boundaries of face-to-face interaction and incorporate people who are not personally known, going beyond the boundaries of kinship and friendship, and the boundaries of acquaintance. Social capital and institutions are informal and formal tools required for the creation of trust, respectively.

How Human Capital, Social Capital, and Institutional Capital Operate in Economic Evolution (Explanatory Framework)

The link between human capital, social capital, and institutions embodies the move from 'having' knowledge and skills to 'using' that knowledge. The 'using' of knowledge implies that trust, mutual confidence, processes, and relationships (social capital) are needed to transform knowledge (which is owned by the individual and the society at large) into a product or service that is of value to the society and its members (Swart 2005). An individual's extended utility function includes not only the goods consumed, but also his/her human capital and the social network of which the individual is a part.

The latest equipment and most innovative ideas in the hands or mind of the brightest and fittest person amount to little unless that person also has access to others to inform, correct, assist with, and disseminate his/her work (Woolcock 2002). As young people spend long periods of time growing up in the same institution of education and training, they build strong bonds with one another, social skills to get along, and cooperative skills to engage in peer- and community-based activities. People well-endowed in human capital realize that it is in their own best interest to engage with others in a constructive and trustworthy manner in order to overcome certain constraints (like cognitive limits of individuals) that they cannot overcome on their own and to deal with uncertainty. At the same time, social capital can be stronger and more pronounced among less-educated people who need to rely on trust because of their limited understanding of the world around them.

Young people's social skills acquired at schools and universities are a resilient and transferable form of social capital. Human capital therefore facilitates intra- and inter-community interaction and exchange (even between those with unequal power and resources) that have good information available about each other's behaviour. People endowed with human capital engage with others to form social networks and invest in social capital because they see the rationality of doing so, while uneducated people do so to overcome their personal disadvantages. Although the reasons behind social networks may be based on rational thought, they still encourage people to engage with each other. Human and social capital are therefore complements, in that literate and informed individuals are better able to organize and evaluate conflicting information, and express their views in constructive ways (Woolcock 2002). If human capital facilitates social networks, there are certain values and behaviours that characterize a network.

It is these values and norms of behaviours (social capital and informal institutions) that bind people from within the communities and across different communities in viable and lasting social networks. Social capital and informal institutions therefore direct attention to the relationships that shape the realization of human capital's potential for the individual and for the network. The relationship between human capital, social capital, and informal institutions essentially reconciles the conflicting desires of individual choice and the longing to be tied to others in a community.

Networks derive strength from the capital they possess, and they can accomplish far more per unit of time devoted to a joint activity and are more productive with whatever physical, financial, and human capital they draw on.[2] In addition to productivity and efficiency, the other economic argument supporting group activities involves bargaining power. Bargaining strength flows from the ability of people to influence the terms and conditions of an arrangement in their own favour due to their possession of unique and valuable resources.[3] The ability to influence depends critically on having skills and assets that can be applied elsewhere easily.[4] Human capital embedded in the network plays a crucial role in building that bargaining power. The bargaining power of the network or the group[5] is dependent not only on the relative number of connections in the network, the integrity and competence of their members, the intensity and quality of connections (internal composition), and the effective use of capital resources that the network can draw upon, but also on the way group members will coordinate activities and credibly commit themselves to a sequence of future actions (Ostrom 1999).

When networks are structured and bound by rules to achieve particular objectives they evolve into, change,[6] and reinforce (formal) institutions. Each person gains from interacting with others in the network, in particular through their coordinated activities. The learning that takes place within the network also contributes towards the evolution of institutions. Institutional emergence and change arise from a structured bargaining between actors who agree to a self-organizing governance system when they organize themselves into groups and networks.[7] But once created, institutions become powerful external forces that not only help determine how people make sense of their world and act in it, but also prevent networks based on (bonding) social interaction from rent-seeking. When different networks are disconnected from one another, the more powerful groups dominate to the exclusion of others. These networks may use their power[8] to extract resources from society, giving undue or disproportional advantages to its members at the cost of the rest of society by colluding or unduly influencing the rules of the game, shaping the institutions, policies, regulations, and the laws for their own private benefits (Lewin 1992; Olson 1982). The existing networks (adapted to a certain economic structure) do not support the restructuring of the economy and the emergence of new actors, when economic changes demand new industries with new actors. If the networks of the old economic structure are too strong, they may retard or prevent the emergence of new actors, new networks and economic restructuring. The new actors then need to build new, competing networks that distribute and reproduce norms, values and behaviour in conformity with the new economic actors' demand.

If human capital encourages rational thought and reason, trust and social norms (social capital) are easily damaged by individually driven rationality. In this context, institutions play an important role: They disseminate among the participants the disposition to cooperation. Institutions, through incentives and sanctions, serve as the anchor for complex trust relationships.[9] Compliance with institutional rules affects an actor's beliefs about the propensity of others to cooperate in similar settings, which, in turn, affects that actor's willingness to cooperate at some subsequent point in time in that same social setting. But it is unlikely that institutions entirely remove the risk of malfeasance and therefore legal apparatus can never serve as a substitute for trust.[10]

Efficient institutions are 'universal' or 'impartial' or 'open access orders' (North et al. 2006; Rothstein 2005; Rothstein and Teorell 2008) and they increase the likelihood that agents will trust that others do not behave in a treacherous way. If institutions that would make treacherous behaviour an exception are lacking, market agents would come to believe that most other players cannot be trusted in economic transactions. If such trust is lacking, creation and strengthening of networks could increase because of the necessity to counteract the individual disadvantage against weak, ineffective, under-developed, entirely missing institutions or institutions which fail to adapt to the needs of changing conditions (Addison and Baliamoune-Lutz 2004; Baliamoune-Lutz 2005). The effect of social capital in this case will be to substitute for the weak institutions. The absence or weakness of formal institutions is often compensated for by the creation of informal organizations (Narayan 1999). Thus, the development of networks does not occur in isolation, but in the context of institutions upholding the principles of impartiality, universality, and objectivity. The bargaining power that networks possess is then used to change the 'efficient' institutions to become 'redistributive' so they will support specific agents' position in the market. As in the words of Adam Smith (1976), the networks' 'interest is, in this respect, directly opposite to that great body of the people'.[11] Although, strong bonding ties give networks or groups a sense of identity and common purpose, without bridging ties that human capital facilitates—which can transcend various social divides—bonding ties can become a basis for the pursuit of narrow interests.

***

Institutions and social capital can be complementary, substitutive, and mutually convertible. While social capital can promote efficiency by coordinating people's activities, it has counter-efficiency properties as well, like boundedness and peculiarism. Social capital, in accordance with the spirit of law, may induce cooperation, develop trust among people, and complement the legal system, and it can also be used to seek self-interest at the price of justice and legal order. In effect, the functioning of social capital is heavily contingent on the stability and certainty of institutions. When institutions provide the basic level of justice and predictability, social capital may help to build mutual trust and cooperation as a complement to the legal system. When institutions cannot provide stable and reliable prediction, mutual distrust will make agents worse off. To overcome the distrust of institutions, market participants depend on private mechanisms that reduce the general level of social efficiency, pushing the social order into an inefficient path. Social capital is probably even more valuable in developing countries where institutional mechanisms needed to facilitate the transactions between individuals or groups are lacking. Nevertheless, the dynamic aspect of social capital, ironically, points to its inherent limitations. In the absence of certain complementary conditions, social capital remains a necessary but insufficient resource at best.

There is a strong relationship between social capital and human capital, as social capital emphasizes the importance for individuals and communities to integrate themselves into formal and informal institutions to achieve coordination of collective actions and the achievement of shared goals. A society well-endowed in human capital is highly interconnected, sharing information and strengthening knowledge through a never-ending web of connections. The networks they form, as Tocqueville says, serve as 'schools of citizenship' where individuals learn the habits of cooperation that would eventually carry over to other parts of economic life. But the prospects of networks and their efficacy in shaping the willingness and ability of the state to act in a developmental manner rests squarely on the institutional framework as it can either strengthen or undermine the networks' capacity to organize in their own collective interest.

The role of the social factors is important. However, it is not clear whether they have an impact on economic growth through capital accumulation or through facilitating the adoption of technologies.

Notes

1. More recently some scholars have begun to question the relevance of property rights for developing countries where entrepreneurship is weak or discouraged. According to Colombatto (2004), the origins of success in the fight among competing civilizations are identified by two major notions; the principles of entrepreneurship and of individual responsibility, with geography and ideology, having significant impact on these two principles. Clearly specified and enforced property rights—private property rights in particular—are of course also necessary. But without entrepreneurship and self-responsibility property rights per se do not generate growth. An ideological or cultural environment that is hostile to individual responsibility means that individuals are reluctant both to develop new knowledge and to take advantage of their talents, irrespective of the potential for high monetary rewards. Furthermore, such an environment tends to discourage outsiders, who may indeed be willing to take responsibilities, but are afraid that free riders or rent-seekers would be morally justified in interfering, if not explicitly encouraged to do so. Stagnation and poverty are the obvious results.

2. Networks and groups are important to individual well-being because network membership and group achievements affect people's sense of well-being and networks influence values and choices and, hence, the extent to which individuals choose to pursue valuable capabilities for themselves and for others (Stewart 2004).

3. In bargaining theory, the ability to walk away from a deal is captured by the concept of 'outside options' and the outside options of bargainers define the bargaining space within which the outcome will be found. Between otherwise identical individuals, those with better outside options can more credibly threaten to walk away from a deal unless it is tilted towards them. This is not entirely the story about power, because it also depends on who gets to make the

first offer, how patient people are, or less easy to pin down, norms of fairness, as well as ability to manipulate or persuade others.

4. Even marginalized groups, if they possess unique resources, can use them to overcome exclusion from political and economic institutions (maintained by vested interests), and to help forge access to these institutions.

5. Heyer et al. (2002) divide groups with economic functions into three types: *efficiency* functions, aimed at overcoming market failures; *claims* groups, which are intended to improve the share of resources or power of their members; and *pro bono* groups, aimed at providing benefits for others (usually among the poor) in society. Groups with primarily efficiency functions are likely to have positive impact on their members' incomes. They may overcome externalities or market failures in a variety of ways, notably by coordinating activities where information is imperfect and by overcoming problems of the commons by internalizing externalities. Groups with primarily claims functions may have a positive impact on the incomes of their members, but a negative impact on that of others, by increasing the bargaining power of their members and thereby improving their conditions. Whether such groups have a positive impact on society at large depends on how one evaluates the change in income distribution. If claims groups are formed among the better off (such as business lobbies that persuade politicians to reduce higher level taxation), the result may be more inegalitarian, which might be evaluated negatively. But where such groups are formed among poor people, they may improve income distribution and reduce poverty.

6. Institutions are not necessarily created to be socially efficient; rather they, or at least the formal rules, are created to serve the interests of those with the bargaining power to devise new rules. In a zero-transaction-cost world, bargaining strength does not affect the efficiency of outcomes, but in a world of positive transaction costs, it does and, given the lumpy indivisibilities that characterize institutions, it shapes the direction of long-run economic change. If economies realize the gains from trade by creating relatively efficient institutions, it is because under certain circumstances the private objectives of those with the bargaining strength to alter institutions produce institutional solutions that turn out to be or evolve into socially efficient ones (North 1990).

7. Institutional change will likely occur as a result of changes in the power relationships between actors or in the outcomes desired by actors who are powerful enough to prevail in bargaining with weaker ones. Such institutional changes may have implications for trust between actors, insofar as they affect the willingness of actors to behave in a trustworthy fashion or the availability of information about the trustworthiness of actors. In turn, changes in trustworthiness and in trust between actors are likely to lead to changes in the extent and form of cooperation between actors.

8. Power is also a fundamental aspect of networks, flowing from the exchange relations among network members and facilitating the achievement of results. Coalition-building, negotiation, and the direct exercise of power through command over resources are integral to network operations (Granovetter 1973).

9. By knowing the content of institutional rules, social actors can establish stable expectations about how others are going to act in common social situations. When the content of the rules dictate cooperative behaviour, social actors can use this information to develop expectations about the likelihood the others will cooperate and then make a decision to act accordingly. The fact that existing institutions militate against certain kinds of opportunism which may be damaging—remove one major source of insecurity in certain relationships and allow people to trust and cooperate with each other more easily in other matters. In this way, social institutions generalize social expectations. As Granovetter (1985) contends, formal institutions 'do not produce trust but instead are a functional substitute for it'.

10. There is near—unanimity that complete contingent claims contracting is impossible. Contractual incompleteness poses added problems when paired with the condition of opportunism—which manifests itself as adverse selection, moral hazard, shirking, sub goal pursuit, and other forms of strategic behaviour. Because human actors will not reliably disclose true conditions upon request or self-fulfil all promises, contract as mere promise, unsupported by credible commitments, will not be self-enforcing (Williamson 2000).

11. Similar concerns were raised by Weber in 1925, his criticisms went beyond exclusions and monopolizations to stress that such trust-based networks further distort and hamper growth within the economy by inviting free riders from within the relationships not to work as hard as they might, or have to, if they were not connected.

II
Case Studies

This part of the book deals with macro case studies, in the form of qualitative-descriptive research that has been used to look at country experiences. Data have been collected for the case studies from secondary research sources. The objective of this part is to show how the relationship established between human, social, and institutional capital in Chapter 5 has played out in different contexts and at different time periods. The case studies look intensely at the historical and contemporary growth experiences of Britain, America, Japan, China, and India, drawing conclusions only in that specific context and time period. Although the focus of these case studies is on exploration and description, the objective is to carefully separate particular facts dealing with the simultaneous interaction between human, social, and institutional capital, to provide a universal, generalizable truth, and cause–effect relationships.

The historical growth experiences of Britain and America deal with how the Industrial Revolution (IR) took place in these countries and the concurrent role played by human, social, and institutional capital. Celebrated as a watershed, IR was a major discontinuity or inflexion point in human history. IR was the largest and first example of a 'knowledge economy' entering consciousness. Apart from transforming dramatically the nature and use of human capital, it brought about unprecedented changes in the concept of 'work' and in human and social behaviour. In addition, IR triggered dramatic changes in formal and informal institutions, in organization, and in output that, until then, had been embedded in rigidly hierarchical social class structures with the landed aristocracy at its apex.

The case study of Japan charts the growth experience of the country post-WWII and also the slow growth experience since the 1990s, by analysing the above reasons through the lens of the relationship between human, social, and institutional capital. Japan's historical links to other countries in East Asia, helped these countries to refine and perfect 'Japan's Model' and achieved remarkable economic growth and development in a short span of time—this phenomenon was a 'miracle' for some, such as the World Bank. However, this book does not deal with the growth experiences of other countries in East Asia. The case study goes to explain further how those institutions and social networks in Japan, which served her well for many years, are now proving to be impediments to changes and reforms that the economy needs.

Japan's extraordinary economic growth since 1945 was orchestrated by the Japanese government and achieved through Japanese companies and their employees. After the defeat in the Second World War, Japan was left with a quarter of its national wealth depleted. With its already-possessed crucial initial conditions—mainly high education attainment and low degree of economic inequality, by the late 1950s, Japan experienced economic boom with higher industrial production with the government declaring that Japan's post-War (the Second World War) reconstruction period was almost over. Academics and policymakers in the West described Japan's high economic growth in the 1960s and the 1970s as a 'miracle'. The Japanese gained both economic and social well-being during this time. After the exceptional growth phase, since the early 1990s the Japanese economy has experienced a decline in macroeconomic performance and stagnation—successive financial crises, price deflation, rising public debt, while growing at a very slow rate.

Chapter 8 looks at the growth experience of Japan post-WWII and also the slow growth experience since the 1990s analysing the above reasons through the lens of the relationship between human capital, social capital, and institutional capital. The chapter shows how the same relationship has created impediments to change and reforms that the country has so required since the mid-1990s.

The case studies of China and India provide their contemporaneous growth experiences, especially the role of human, social, and institutional capital in contributing to the current success that the countries have achieved in their manufacturing and services sectors respectively. The two chapters, 9 and 10, explain the growth patterns in China and India from the time that these countries broke out of their insulation from the world economy and ushered in market-oriented reforms and liberalization. Specifically, the two chapters look at how human, social, and institutional capital contributed to that growth process. The chapters also argue that in the absence of effective economic institutions during the countries' early reform period, it was the combination of two intangible capitals that more than compensated for the lack of institutions. As the reform period progressed, the economic outcomes achieved in the absence of institutions forced the state to create formal economic institutional capital to sustain those outcomes.

6 Industrial Revolution in Britain

The Industrial Revolution (IR) was the result of an economic expansion that started in the sixteenth century as agrarian economies transformed into semi-industrial ones. But, it was the eighteenth century that brought a decisive break in the history of technology and the economy with the invention of the steam engine to displace animal and human power. The era marked a decisive turning point between 'a world of slow economic growth, in which population, output and real incomes were rising slowly (or not at all), and a world of much faster economic growth, in which population increased at an almost frightening rate, and in which there have been sustained increases in output and in per capita real incomes' (Hartwell 1971). Prior to the IR, four features characterized the general society: high fertility and mortality rates, low education, the dominance of physical over human capital (in particular land), and low rates of productivity growth (Clark 1986). IR marked the point in time during which 'technology' assumed an ever-increasing weight in the generation of economic growth and when economic growth accelerated dramatically as a consequence of applying scientific knowledge.

The IR resulted in knowledge-induced economic growth, based on technological breakthroughs and their application to production by a class of industrial entrepreneurs. Both the breakthroughs and their applications revolutionized the formation and application of human capital, while inducing concomitant transformation of social capital and institutional capital. Without the rapid evolution of new kinds of institutions to organize 'work' and to diffuse and sell factory output around the world, IR would have stalled had innovations been limited to technology alone. Taken together, they explain first British and later American leadership in the early and later stages of IR respectively.

The IR started in Britain with inventions that enabled factory textile production, the shift to coal and coke in the iron industry, and the continuous improvement of technologies for motive power. These provided the knowledge-based technological foundations for a continuous stream of innovation, spurred by institutional competition that, along with the advent of electricity, radio, the telegraph, telecommunications, and computers in the nineteenth and twentieth centuries, carried the world to unprecedented mass prosperity in the twenty-first century.

Several theories have attempted to explain how the IR took place and why it occurred when it did. They fall into three types. First, exogenous growth theories claim that some feature outside the economy, such as institutions of the society (changes in the institutions governing the diffusion of knowledge, or the security of all property) changed the relative scarcities of different inputs in production and induced investment in expanding the production techniques by potential innovators. The arrival of constitutional monarchy in England in 1689 was the key political innovation that ushered in modern economic growth (North and Weingast 1989). The Enlightenment, an intellectual movement among the elite of Western European society in the eighteenth century, was the exogenous shock that changed the fundamental dynamic of the economy (Mokyr 2003). These theories assert that around 1760, an institutional or some other innovation occurred in England which was not seen earlier. Second, multiple equilibrium theories state that shocks—disease, war, conquest of new lands—led the economy to jump from the stagnant equilibrium of the Malthusian population trap to the dynamic equilibrium of the modern world. And third, the endogenous growth theories are based on the premise that knowledge and ideas comprise a significant source of economic development. These models raise fundamental questions about the nature of human capital, what knowledge, skills, and other personal characteristics are conducive to extraordinary creativity, and how those factors vary over time and with the field of endeavour.

This chapter looks at how human, social, and institutional capital worked in creating and diffusing new technology, and in applying new knowledge profitably during IR. It provides a decomposition of growth into a human capital–driven technology component and social and institutional capital component and takes into account simultaneous interactions between these two components which facilitated the IR in Britain and America.

Human Capital

The IR was preceded by a Scientific Revolution that facilitated the process of new knowledge creation. The Scientific Revolution had three distinct phases: the Renaissance, 1440–1540; the Wars of Religion, 1540–1650; and the Restoration, 1650–90 (Bernal 1971). The first phase challenged the world-view that the Middle Ages had adopted from classical times. This opening phase of the Scientific Revolution was one of description and criticism. The second period saw the first great triumph of the new observational, experimental approach. In the third and definitive phase, competent men of independent means carried out scientific research on their own. As these men became numerous, they tended to gravitate to each other for discussion and interchange of knowledge. This also was the time when the first well-established scientific societies were formed, turning science into an institution.

Scientific method, scientific mentality, and scientific culture, all played a part in giving birth to IR. Mokyr (2002) coined the term Industrial Enlightenment to describe the features of the Enlightenment that linked the Scientific Revolution of the seventeenth century to the IR of the following centuries. Intellectual changes during Industrial Enlightenment affected the sphere of knowledge and its interaction with the world of technology. They were part of a movement that insisted on asking not just 'which techniques worked' but also 'why techniques worked;' such questions and their answers held the key to continuing progress. The Industrial Enlightenment emphasized on the application of scientific and experimental methods to the advancement of technology, the belief that all natural phenomena could be subject to systematic investigation, and the expectation that scientific study of the natural world and technology would improve human life (Allen 2006). In this new mode, more and more people rebelled against the idea protected by religious institutions that knowledge was 'forbidden' or a better-kept secret (Eamon 1990). Instead they kept an open mind and embraced a willingness to abandon conventional doctrine when confronted with new evidence. This mentality imbued engineers and inventors with a faith in the orderliness, rationality, and predictability of natural phenomena.

These ideas were consciously popularized until they eventually permeated social culture. The channels through which this was done included professional societies like the Royal Society that was the embodiment of the free dissemination of useful knowledge, and the publication of books like the Encyclopedia that described manufacturing processes. Popular scientific lectures also played a role in disseminating new approaches to technology and nature (Allen 2006). In the eighteenth and early nineteenth century Britain, popular lectures on scientific and technical subjects by recognized experts drew eager audiences. These lectures were given at scientific society meeting places, coffeehouses and masonic lodges. Audiences watched experimental demonstrations illustrating the application of scientific principles to pumps, pulleys, and pendulums (Inkster 1980). The formal meetings were secondary to the networking and informal exchange of technical information among members.

Scientific culture placed applied science at the service of commercial and manufacturing interests (Jacob 1997). Scientific culture led to the gradual emergence of engineering science and the continuous accumulation of orderly quantitative knowledge.

Much of the practical knowledge in the eighteenth century was unsystematic, and informal. Yet formal and informal knowledge complemented in the development of new techniques. The spillovers from scientific endeavours affected not only the way in which new knowledge was created, but also the culture of access to information. Scientific knowledge became a public good, communicated freely rather than confined to an exclusive few.

By 1790, Britain had acquired an advantage in the execution and economic application of new techniques. The British advantage in application came from its comparative advantage in micro-inventions and in the supply of the human capital that could carry out the new techniques. Britain may not have had more propositional knowledge available for its invention and innovation process, but its workers possessed higher levels of competence which helped new techniques that emerged to find their first applications there. The country's successful system of informal technical training, through master–apprentice relationships, created workers of uncommon skill and mechanical ability (Humphries 2003). Britain could draw on three types of human capital to sustain its scientific advancement—artisanal, entrepreneurial, and innovative. This human capital endowment helped Britain to adapt ideas and techniques that could be applied in new and more industries, improve and refine earlier inventions, and extend and deepen their deployment.

Artisans were people who made things they did not design, not once but several times, leading to some improvements. They were an indispensable complement to inventors for building designs to specification and making complex mechanisms work. While artisans had been around for centuries, IR did not take place earlier than the eighteenth century because there was no infusion of new useful knowledge. Artisans were not inventors who came up with the revolutionary insights, but they could read a blueprint, understand practical technicalities and had experience with the qualities of iron, wood, leather, and other materials (Mokyr 2007). They were the craftsmen who could accurately produce the parts, use the correct dimensions and materials, and understand the interdependence of mechanical parts. Their human capital was instrumental in creating competence rather than useful knowledge itself, and in teaching how to carry out instructions rather than writing them. These mechanics and technicians made IR possible by generating a stream of micro-inventions that accounted for the actual productivity gains when the great breakthroughs or macro-inventions created the opportunities to do so (Mokyr 2007).

The apprenticeship system in Britain supplied it with a layer of skilled artisans (Humphries 2003). Apprenticeship helped in transmitting tacit artisanal knowledge which was the essential component of competence. Apprenticeship took place within a 'traditional network of friends, neighbours, co-religionists, and next of kin' (Humphries 2007).

As a result, British innovations toward the end of the eighteenth century and at the start of the nineteenth century were largely produced by workers who had little formal education, but who had benefited from apprenticeships and on-the-job learning. Britain's technological success relied on the large contingent of skilled artisans and mechanics. Even the great inventors took the route of apprenticeship, including some who came from privileged backgrounds. Apprenticeship was a flexible source of human capital acquisition, which did not preclude social mobility or further education (Mokyr 2007).

The second type of human capital was that of the entrepreneurs who were a small but significant economic elite who helped carry the IR forward. Entrepreneurship and technical skills were complementary inputs. The coupling of individuals with technical skills and those with commercial acumen created the great advantage that Britain enjoyed in this dimension. The complement was symmetric: those with technical ability, whether creative or supportive, needed people who could run a business, understood markets, knew about the recruitment and management of workers and foremen, had access to credit and other technical consultants, and, above all, were ready to accept the uncertainties of innovation. Some of the most remarkable inventions made on the continent were first applied on a wide scale in Britain (Humphries 2003).

The third source of human capital was that of the inventors who were more educated than the general population, but still not beyond the primary or secondary school levels. Formal training was not a prerequisite for important inventions in the early period of industrialization. More formal scientific endeavours of the day were owed to aristocratic amateurs, whose efforts were directed to impractical pursuits and general principles of astronomy, magnetism, mathematics, botany, and chemistry, rather than to useful knowledge (Khan and Sokoloff 1993). Inventors did not necessarily have an exposure to scientific training but drew on apprenticeships and on-the-job training that enhanced their individual abilities. The kind of knowledge and ideas that produced significant technological contributions during British industrialization seems to have been rather general and available to all creative individuals, regardless of scientific training (Mokyr 2006).

For inventions to be successful, inventors needed to communicate not only with other like-minded people, but also with those who wanted to apply their inventions. Inventors needed to communicate with other inventors to tap their knowledge to improve their existing knowledge. Institutional setups facilitated this exchange of knowledge. For example, the Lunar Society in the eighteenth century and the Surrey and London Institutions, the 'X-Club', the Society of Arts, the Royal Institution, and the Mechanics Institutes in the nineteenth century.

Prior to 1780, most of these societies were informal and ad hoc, but they eventually became more formal. These societies served as communication networks and clearing houses for technological information. By the middle of the nineteenth century, there were 1,020 associations for technical and scientific knowledge in Britain with a membership estimated conservatively at 200,000 persons (Inkster 1991). This personal and informal contact was necessary as the diffusion and circulation of knowledge was dependent on the movement of people who came to teach or to learn when knowledge could not be codified and had to be seen to be copied (Mokyr 2005).

The working class tended to gravitate toward mutual improvement societies to gain human capital. These societies were formed by institutions, such as the church, trade unions, and temperance associations. They set up libraries which enabled members to educate themselves and acted as centres of sociability.

Britain slowly became well-endowed in traditional human capital—apprenticeships that not only imparted skills but allowed naturally gifted mechanics to teach themselves from whatever source[1] was available and learn from their masters as well.

Role of Institutional Capital in the Industrial Revolution

'A few decades after stable and nationwide government had been established in Britain, the Industrial Revolution was on its way' (Olson 1982). Formal institutions mattered largely because written formal rules and the court system established the second layer of economic cooperation and resolved conflicts. A technologically dynamic society of the eighteenth century needed institutional capital that encouraged creative destruction à la Schumpeter. What helped the British economy grow and sustain its growth was more than having the kind of institutions conducive to economic development; it also meant having the kind of agility that allowed institutions to change when the environment changed.

Before 1750, economic progress of any kind tended to run into negative institutional feedback. One of the features of the pre-modern world was that whenever a society managed, through enterprise or ingenuity, to raise its standard of living, a variety of opportunistic parasites and predators used their power, influence, and violence to appropriate this wealth. Such rent seekers, who distributed wealth rather than created it, came either from within the economy in the form of exclusive coalitions or thugs, or they came from outside as alien pillagers and plunderers. Exclusive coalitions that sought rent were local monopolists, guilds with exclusionary rights, or nobles with traditional rights. The most costly form of negative institutional feedback before 1815 was war (Mokyr 2006).

The Glorious Revolution of 1688 helped create a set of constraints that solved the predatory ruler problem (Dam 2005). The Bill of Rights of 1689 was followed by a string of laws that established the British Parliament as the institution that wrote the rules and had the power to change other institutions. The Parliament acquired legitimacy in the sense that when it changed the rules, even the losers could not deny its right to do so and had a responsibility to comply with them. By 1714, the Parliament had acquired a position of legitimacy and power and was gaining more and more in reliability (Mokyr 2006). The Parliament was also the body that had the capacity for being receptive to both the changing needs of the economy and the changing ideology and beliefs of its elite, and could change the rules of the economic game accordingly. Parliamentary power meant that changes occurred increasingly from top-down, even if the initiative came from below. Eventually, changes in beliefs at the top affected the entire country (Mokyr 2006).

The Parliament supported entrepreneurs and innovators against technologically conservative interests and protected their rents. It awarded pensions and prizes to inventors who solved a problem of national importance.

The ascent of the Parliament helped Britain in developing an institutional strength and agility that provided it with a considerable advantage over its continental competitors (Mokyr 2005). The system of relatively secure property rights emerged in Britain in the seventeenth century, which aided investment and entrepreneurship required for large scale diffusion and implementation of the new knowledge.

British institutions not only created an environment in which inventors and entrepreneurs could operate and cooperate freely, but also stimulated and encouraged technological progress and informal private institutions. Britain cultivated institutions that encouraged technological progress, and encouraged innovation and the dissemination of useful knowledge. In Britain, three kinds of institutions were important in facilitating the sustained technological progress central to economic growth:

1. those that provided for connections between people concerned mostly with knowledge and those on the production side;
2. those that set the agenda for research to generate new knowledge that could be mapped into new techniques; and
3. those that created and safeguarded incentives for innovative people to actually spend efforts and resources in order to map this knowledge into techniques and specifically that weakened the effective social and political resistance against new techniques.

The formal institutions that created bridges between prescriptive and propositional knowledge in late eighteenth and the nineteenth century were scientific societies, universities, polytechnic schools, publicly funded research institutes, museums, agricultural research stations, and research departments in large financial institutions. The professionalization of expertise increasingly meant that anyone who needed some piece of useful knowledge could find someone who knew, or knew someone who knew (Mokyr 2005).

During IR, Britain provided many incentives to inventors. Institutions gave signals to natural philosophers for problems to be solved, indicating there might be money or honour to be gained from doing so; these natural philosophers should focus their efforts on searching for solutions to real-world problems. In 1852, the British patent system was reformed towards the American system in ways that increased access to patent institutions and strengthened the security of property rights in patents. Significant aspects of the institutional overhaul included lower patent fees and a rationalized administration. Inventors responded to the decrease in monetary and transactions costs by increasing their investments in patented invention (Khan and Sokoloff 1993).

What mattered further to the would-be innovators was access to credit and markets to turn ideas into business ventures, both of which were especially strong in Britain. Even at the early stages of IR, some institutions that emerged in Britain were favourable to venture capital.

One such institution was the country bank. In 1750, there were no more than a dozen such banks, while in 1800, there were 370 of them. In addition, other institutions were recognized which aided in the generation of new techniques. Among those were relatively easy entry and exit from industries, the reduction of uncertainty by assured demand for a new product or technique, and the existence of agencies that coordinated and standardized the networked components of new techniques (Mokyr 2005).

Although Britain successfully created formal institutions, their contract enforcement in eighteenth-century Britain left a great deal to be desired. If a large number of economic agents decided to renege on contracts and engage in blatantly opportunistic behaviour, it was highly doubtful that the courts and law-enforcement agencies would have been able to dissuade them. Eighteenth century Britain passed a myriad of draconian laws for protecting property, by imposing ferocious penalties on those who infringed on them. Those who resisted enclosures and new machinery were threatened with execution and deportation. Britain depended on the deterrent effect of draconian penalties because it had no official mechanism of law enforcement; prosecution was mostly private and crime prevention was largely self-enforcing with more than 80 per cent of all prosecutions carried out by the victims. The country's capacity for enforcement was weak because the prevailing court system at the time was expensive, cumbersome, inadequate, and took a long time to settle cases (Mokyr 2007).

Similarly, civil laws that applied to patents could easily be circumvented through minor changes to inventions. Technological change and industrialization created new situations that were not covered by statutes and led to uncertainty about legal rights and liabilities. Consequently, within the circles of commerce, innovation, finance, and manufacturing, trust relations and private settlement of disputes seem to have prevailed over third-party enforcement (Mokyr 2007).

In terms of its institutional make-up, Britain possessed several features which aided and encouraged IR. Barriers to entry and exclusionary arrangements in the British manufacturing and service sectors were lower because of non-compliance. In the decades around 1750, many redistributive arrangements like guilds, monopolies, and grain price regulations were gradually weakening in Britain. Institutions in Britain changed more easily and at a lower cost because the Parliament acquired the legitimacy to change other institutions and have its decisions accepted even by losers. The other distinct institutional feature that Britain had was the flexibility to adapt its economic and legal institutions without political violence and disruptions. Intellectual property rights and incentives for those who added to the stock of useful knowledge was well organized and society helped to stimulate invention by increasing the social standing of inventors and improving communication between creative and knowledgeable people (Mokyr 2007).

Despite these positive institutional features, there was a growing volume of both domestic and international commerce and credit which was supported less by formal law and order than by social norms. The formal mechanisms of the state were invoked only as a last resort.

Social Capital

The key to successful economic exchange is not only an impartial and efficient third-party enforcement, but also an existence of a level of trust or other self-enforcing institutions within relevant networks of commerce, credit, wage-labour, and other contractual relations that support market activities. During IR, fewer people took recourse to the law and legal action was replaced by common behavioural codes and norms among people belonging to the same class. Eighteenth century Britain was the setting for the emergence of a set of behavioural codes that made it possible to overcome the kind of free riding and opportunistic behaviour that required coercion by formal state institutions. Social norms of cooperation and decency prevailed in the society because of the ineffective formal law enforcement (Ellickson 1991). This happened in tightly knit groups in which reputational mechanisms worked effectively and social norms could be applied. Voluntary compliance and respect for property and rank as social norms were as important as formal property rights in turning the wheels of the British economy. When trust relations were transferred from a social relationship into an economic relationship, they sustained cooperative outcomes in which exchange took place and disputes were resolved without the strict enforcement of contracts by third parties like impartial courts or arbiters. This kind of social capital created the possibility of cooperation even when standard behaviour in finite games would have suggested defection and dishonest behaviour.

Social norms did have an effect on technology, although this is hard to quantify. They contributed toward technological progress by determining the way entrepreneurs interacted with their economic environment, customers, suppliers, workers, and competitors, and these same norms increasingly determined the behaviour of the inventors, skilled craftsmen, financiers, merchants, and the owners of the new mills and mines that defined IR (Allen 1983).

Social norms involved a variety of signalling devices associated with 'gentlemanly' codes described as 'politeness' in a variety of contexts (Langford 2000). Such behaviour was associated with attempts to signal one's trustworthiness to potential partners in the market. The importance of the concept of a gentleman and its economic implication was to act as a constraint on opportunistic behaviour and to support functioning markets. The word 'gentleman' meant a person with some degree of distinction, quite disjoint from the lowest rung of society; and one who was 'always suggesting certain standards of behaviour'. A gentleman behaved with consistency and integrity and, above all, fulfilled his obligations to those who had obligations to him (Mason 1982). By the middle of the eighteenth century, the idea of a gentleman had acquired a meaning of certain behavioural codes that signalled that a person was trustworthy. Agents needed to send out costly signals that indicated to others that they were reliable and trustworthy because they belonged to a class of reliable and trustworthy agents (Posner 2000). For British gentlemen, these signals included dress codes, manners, housing, transportation, speaking styles, and personal behaviour. They also included membership in organizations that helped transmit and filter signals about the trustworthiness of individuals. Politeness was an equally important signal which was widely equated with law-abiding behaviour and it was intuitively sensed that commercial success depended a great deal on politeness. Gentlemanly ideals provided a shared code, based on honour and obligation which acted as a blueprint for conduct in occupations whose primary function was to manage men rather than machines (Cain and Hopkins 1993). People who felt constrained by the gentlemanly code of behaviour acted honourably, kept their word, and did not renege on promises.

Gentlemanly capitalism made opportunistic behaviour sufficiently taboo so that only in a few cases was it necessary to use the formal institutions to punish deviants. An individual who belonged to these circles signalled that he was trustworthy and would not behave opportunistically because, like a true gentleman, he was not primarily motivated by greed. In Britain, during IR, the social norms of what was perceived to be a gentlemanly culture with an emphasis on honesty and meeting one's obligations, supported cooperative equilibria that allowed commercial and credit transactions to be consummated and partnerships to survive without the parties being concerned about possible defections and other forms of opportunistic behaviour. Gentlemen (or those who aspired to become gentlemen) moved in similar circles and faced one another in a variety of linked contexts. Gentlemanly customs, which were observed by the British upper classes, were slowly adopted by the commercial and skilled artisanal classes, which created the kind of cultural beliefs in which two persons expected the other person to behave honourably (Mokyr 2007). These codes of behaviour, when observed by enough people, made it possible to trade with strangers and deal with people with whom there might not be repeated transactions, without the fear that one partner may try to take advantage from the situation (Mokyr 2007).

Gentlemanly codes thus engendered trust. Trust was an essential component of effective markets and a critical ingredient of the environment that created British entrepreneurship and developed British science. The trust that existed within the merchant and artisan classes made it possible to transact with non-kin, and increasingly with people who were not close acquaintances. Gentlemanly behaviour led to cooperative behaviour that made market transactions possible, even at arm's length, and thus encouraged economic evolution. As risk taking was still a scarce resource, the tightly knit network of elites was able to create collective diversification, allowing British entrepreneurs to spread their investments over a substantial number of projects with low cross-correlations, such as insurance, canals, railroads, utilities, and banks (Pearson 1991).

Thus, most business came to be conducted through informal codes of conduct and relied on local reputation (Mokyr 2008). In order to function, a reputation-based system needed good information and communication, and these were provided through the many networks of friendly societies and masonic lodges that emerged across Britain in the eighteenth century (Jacob 1997). The networks established in the eighteenth century were open and accessible to middle class men and were an ideal vehicle for the transmission of the information that supported reputational mechanisms. Britain witnessed an emergence of voluntary organizations that created networks which supported market activity. These organizations created the ideal conditions for the linkages that helped bring about cooperative behaviour (Mokyr 2008). Many of these organizations were purely social, eating and drinking clubs, or devoted to common interests and hobbies, but they functioned as information clearing houses. Many societies that brought together artisans from different trades introduced rules that only one member per occupation could be a member with the understanding that fellow members would get priority in any commercial transaction, thus explicitly linking the commercial business-to-business vertical relations with a social connection (Brewer 1982).

Trust relations and private settlement of disputes prevailed over third-party enforcement within the circles of commerce, finance, and manufacturing. Voluntary compliance and respect for property and rank as social norms were as important as formal property rights in making the wheels of the British economy turn. The shared norms transcended various differences and helped settle disputes and minimize opportunistic behaviour between agents. For agents to be accepted into social networks, reputation was everything. A reputation for solidity, respectability, and probity was considered the key to success. To portray to other agents their credibility, a certain standard was necessary. Behaving like a gentleman became that standard. The British entrepreneur during the IR was very much part of this shared value system. Reputational mechanisms were essential if the kind of contractual environment necessary for entrepreneurs to operate was to be sustained. The culture of gentleman-entrepreneurs and social networks became essential in underpinning the market economy of the eighteenth century. That culture produced not only a private good, but also an externality or network effect for the entire population (Posner 2000). The economics of the culture of gentleman-entrepreneurs is closely related to the ideas associated with 'social capital'.

Interaction between Human Capital, Social Capital, and Institutional Capital

The link between human, social, and institutional capital embodies the move from 'having' knowledge and skills to 'using' that knowledge.

'Using' knowledge is necessary to transform knowledge into a product or service that is of value to society and its members.

Human capital facilitates social networks, yet there are certain values and behaviours that characterize a network.

The British economy in the eighteenth century not only produced the technical acumen to follow up on new ideas and turn them into an economic reality, but also created a group of entrepreneurs to exploit it, people with the ability to take advantage of the opportunities that the inventors and the mechanics created. This relationship appeared in the many pairings of technical ability and businessmen and these relationships were sustained by trust through reputational mechanisms, social networks, and gentlemanly behaviour. This suggests that actors endowed with human capital understood the need to be interconnected, sharing information and strengthening knowledge through connections and once human capital facilitated social networks, trust, gentlemanly codes characterized these networks. A sign of trust-based relationships was the diversified projects in which many of entrepreneurs engaged, investing in local improvements, and subscribing to projects such as roads, bridges, canals, dock works, and, later, railroads. Entrepreneurs could engage in sectors they knew little about because they felt they could trust their partners (Pearson and Richardson 2001). Gentlemanly codes engendered this trust and were helpful in establishing a contractual environment necessary for entrepreneurs to operate. It was this trust development and coupling of individuals with technical skill and those with commercial acumen that was Britain's great advantage.

During the IR, much of the relevant human capital was concentrated within the apprenticeship system. But apprenticeship took place within a social network of extended family, friends, and neighbours. During the eighteenth century, many of the innovations were produced by people who benefited from apprenticeships. But slowly the apprenticeship system became a conservative, rigid force. Skills and experience are acquired over a lifetime, but the ability to learn new skills declines over the life cycle. Workers beyond the student or apprentice stage resisted new techniques insofar that innovation made their skills obsolete and thus irreversibly reduced their expected lifetime earnings. In addition, new technology became inaccessible to them because independent artisans refused to submit themselves to the factory system, which required a willingness to submit to discipline and hierarchy. In order to protect skills and specific human capital, artisans often employed different forms of rent seeking through creation of barriers to entry. Although human capital facilitated bridging ties amongst networks, apprenticeship system in Britain slowly accumulated enough bargaining power which was used as a basis for the pursuit of narrow interests to maintain their status quo. But England was well endowed with institutional capital which effectively resisted entrenched interests.

Institutional capital is a powerful external force that not only helps to determine how people make sense of their world and act in it, but also prevents networks from rent seeking.

An area in which technological innovation and institutional change interacted was in the resistance of vested interests to new technology. Here institutional capital was particularly important. Vested interests used non-market mechanisms to maintain the technological status quo. Non-market mechanisms included the manipulation of the existing power structure, machine-breaking, riots, and personal violence against inventors and the entrepreneurs who tried to adopt their inventions. Groups and lobbies turned to the Parliament requesting the enforcement of old regulations or the introduction of new legislation that would hinder the machinery. When the Parliament refused, extra-legal means were tried, but violent protests were forcefully suppressed by soldiers (Mokyr 2008).

Although networks of the apprenticeship system became rent seekers, after 1780, the Parliament increasingly used its powers to make selected dents in the rent-seeking machinery of the ancient regime under the guise of making the economy more efficient and streamlined. The Parliament became the arbitrator of disputes between special interest groups. As a result, over the course of the eighteenth century, rent-seeking attempts by local and national interests started slowly to run into resistance. The British Parliament brought a certain kind of polity that discouraged rent seeking and diverted the energies and initiatives of the most resourceful individuals toward technology and production and not toward lobbying and redistribution (Mokyr 2008).

The state in Britain did not make many concessions to vested interests groups; it cracked down mercilessly on rioters, siding unilaterally with innovating employers and provided something no other state did, a mandatory outdoor relief system for the poor that remained in force until 1834. The poor law, by providing the poorest workers with a safety net, also contributed to the creation of labour needed for the factories and the railroad (Mokyr 2008).

Landed classes and merchants were also opposed to economic progress before IR because they had large fixed capital invested in the technological and political status quo. In Britain, the land classes had traditionally controlled much of the Parliament, in an informal coalition with the mercantile interests. Both these groups gained from maintaining the status quo in which rents were channelled to merchants and shipping interests, while landlords received rewards on farm exports. The technological innovations of IR transformed the British economy to a degree that was completely unforeseeable in the mid-eighteenth century, and land classes benefited from the development. This old coalition was compensated and bribed to cooperate.

Although the British Parliament has been credited for many of the changes that streamlined the economy, until at least the mid-eighteenth century, the Parliament was in many ways a corrupt body, manipulated by special interests driven by rent-seeking and mercantilist ideology (Rubinstein 1983). But the Parliament gained its legitimacy through a slow process of a protracted struggle and hard-fought bargaining. As its legitimacy increased over time, the Parliament had the power to rewrite the rules that applied to others and it could adapt to changing needs and beliefs about what was good for the nation.

The civil legal system underwent great change during the latter part of the nineteenth century, which did much to raise trust. The law was toughened and the superior and local courts were reformed. Procedures and pleas of the superior courts were simplified, their doctrines were made more systematic, and their relationships with other legal institutions were more clearly defined. So as the nineteenth century progressed, formal law slowly replaced reputation mechanisms and gentlemanly codes of behaviour. Formal law also facilitated deals between the new industrialists and an ever-growing number of people in a market context: suppliers, creditors, subcontractors, employees, customers, and consultants. Formal law also helped in making useful knowledge and best-practice technology accessible, and in dealing with more and more complex contracts (Mokyr 2008).

The IR made the 'great divergence' because of the persistence of technological change. The technological progress was possible because

Britain had a unique combination of human capital which transformed new knowledge to new techniques. The relationship between artisans, inventors, and entrepreneurs was increasingly underpinned by social norms and trust relations and these helped new knowledge to be adapted into production process and incentives provided by Societies and Parliament led to further experimentation and were conducive to further inventions. When technological progress threatened the status quo of entrenched interests of powerful networks of artisans, land classes, and mercantilists, they fought back through legal and extralegal means, but formal institutions were successful in not succumbing to their pressures and co-opting them through various means. Consequently, continued improvement in technology after 1800 became the rule and, by the mid-1840s, the standard of living in Britain was rising for the entire population.

***

The IR of Britain shows how human capital, social capital and institutions together encouraged and aided the rapid growth of knowledge, industry, and productivity. It took place because of a scientific revolution that preceded it. Britain's advantage was in the execution and practical application of its scientific knowledge. This was made possible by Britain's system of on the job training and informal technical training through master–apprentice relationships. The system helped Britain to adapt scientific ideas and techniques to new and more industries. In terms of institutions, Britain possessed several factors that helped and supported the IR. Although IR was propelled by technological progress, to succeed its propagators (entrepreneurs, engineers, merchants, financiers, and technical consultants) needed contracts, credit, and credible commitments. The chain of events during the IR ran from technological success to income, and from there, to institutional change (Mokyr 2005). British institutions created an environment in which inventors and entrepreneurs could operate and cooperate freely. In addition to institutions, common behavioural codes and social norms among people helped in overcoming freeriding and opportunistic behaviour which would have otherwise required coercion by formal institutions.

The IR brought profound changes to the British society. It altered technological paradigms, improved, adapted technology and ultimately raised productivity and introduced new, better, and cheaper goods and services. Improvements in useful knowledge and change in technology inevitably led to an improvement in the welfare of some and a deterioration of others. Innovations were resisted by losers and vested interest groups through legal and extralegal means. British institutions like the Parliament was almost unique in Europe as it acquired legitimacy in the sense that when it changed the rules, even the losers from these actions could not deny its right to do so and had a responsibility to comply. It brought a certain kind of polity that discouraged rent seeking and diverted the initiatives of the most resourceful individuals toward technology and production and not toward lobbying and redistribution. Formal institutions therefore restrained social capital and informal institutions from trapping the society in a technology status quo by hindering and resisting new techniques.

Note

1. In the eighteenth century, the publishing industry supplied a large number of popular science books, encyclopedias, technical dictionaries, and similar 'teach yourself' kind of books.

7 Early Industrial Revolution in America

The transition from an agricultural to an industrial economy took more than a century in the US; such development entered its first phase in the 1790s and lasted through the 1830s. By then the Industrial Revolution (IR) had begun in Britain, but the American colonies lagged far behind the mother country, in part because of the abundance of land and scarcity of labour and capital which reduced interest in expensive investments required for machine production. The period leading up to 1830 was seen as a prelude to the more important time of large-scale, rapid industrial growth beginning from the early 1840s.

American IR started with the adoption of machine methods and factory organization in the production of cotton textiles in southern New England. In America, communication, transportation, finance, marketing and law were collectively more important in reducing costs than were contemporary improvements in the fabrication of goods. If informal networks in Britain determined its comparative advantage in micro-inventions (refining and improving) and diffusion of innovations, in America, it was the abundance of mineral resources, mechanization and the simplification of production, railroads and lowered costs of transportation, and the rise of the managerial firm.

The most significant changes that came out of the American IR were the enormous gains in industrial output accompanied by institutional change, lower transportation costs, increased urbanization of society, and a shift from farm labour to labour in factories and offices (Guest 2005). Technical changes were initiated or imitated in the production of machinery and in the application of water and steam power. Another significant change was new organizational strategies to increase productivity. This had begun with the 'Outwork System', whereby small parts of a larger production process were carried out in numerous individual homes and evolved into the 'Factory System', where work was performed on a large scale in a single centralized location. All the three significant sectors in American development, that is, mining, farming, and manufacturing, helped to develop routine and repetitive patterns of behaviour, which formalized into the quintessential American factory and production line (Cochrane 1998).

Before the 1760s, the role of the mainland North American colonies was to provide raw materials and a captive market for English manufactures. After the Revolutionary War was won, advocates of increased manufacturing argued that national strength required a diversified economy based on neo-mercantilism. Three groups of public organizations promoted such views in the late eighteenth century: mechanic committees and associations, which called for protective tariffs; manufacturing societies, comprising merchant-manufacturers who advocated for government encouragement of capital-intensive enterprises; and agricultural societies, which supported market-based collaboration between farmers and manufacturers, including household producers (Cochrane 1998).

Two regional episodes in American industrialization qualified as revolution. First, the burst of growth of factory textiles in New England and the mushrooming of machinery and machine tool production which created the American system of parts manufacture and assembly. The other was the rapid growth of large-scale coke smelting, steel making, and heavy-machinery construction from Pittsburgh to Cleveland during 1850–80. These two episodes fed into each other after 1860 and created the formidable industrial machine which catapulted America into the twentieth century and which developed further and faster up to 1929 (Cochrane 1998).

This chapter looks at the initial phase of the American IR and how the complementarity between human, social, and institutional capital played a significant role in laying the foundation for rapid industrial growth in America. The chapter provides a decomposition of growth into a human capital–driven technology and skills component and a social-capital-and-institutional capital component, taking into account the simultaneous interactions between these two components.

Human Capital

The most significant source of human capital for the American IR was the immigration of people from many European countries. These individuals brought with them specific technological heritages and sometimes competing technologies. The American IR successfully demonstrated how to use this diverse artisan knowledge from mature European countries to overcome problems associated with a wilderness. Upon arriving, many migrants went to partially settled areas where survival depended on learning different ways of doing things. The ways of life arising from continual migration to new areas led to new ways of doing business and making things. Learning from other people and cultures produced new pools of knowledge (Wallace 1998).

The heterogeneity of workers enabled one to work side by side and learn from a veritable social potpourri. By trial and error, settlers gained knowledge from each other about many fundamental concerns, such as crop production, product shipment, or housing forms for the new conditions. The migration of skilled craftsmen with a variety of urban trades—wood and metal working, shoe making, craft-shop textiles, printing, and mercantile banking—created the conditions for industrial development in America (Wallace 1998).

While, in Europe, artisans tended to become highly skilled at a particular craft, in America, the ever-present need for new construction tended to make the artisan omnicompetent at a moderate level. Consequently, many artisans moved readily from making furniture or hoes to erecting textile machinery and ultimately to fashioning parts for steam engines. Some went from building houses to constructing paper mills or from working for wages to becoming independent entrepreneurs. Americans were short of book learning or artistic craftsmanship but had ample know-how for building crude but effective machines (Cochrane 1998). The American shops also emphasized the acquisition of general technical skills and the perfection of machinery.

The advances made by the English IR offered a distinct opportunity to create a balanced economy in America to eventually replace the colonial economy. Americans exploited their language, family, business, and friendship ties to give them better access to British innovation than any other country. The experience of Americans permitted the easy reception, adaptation, and use of new machines. It even permitted the reproduction of machines developed in Britain with little more information about them than the basic concept. Americans were able to improvise and invent new ways of doing some of the things accomplished by the new machinery (Cochrane 1998). Transmission of technological information from generation to generation was made possible more by observation, demonstration, and practice than by formal apprenticeship or schooling, making for a flexible labour supply with relatively high competence (Cochrane 1998).

Business and political leaders also brought in English mechanics to set up mechanized textile production. But by the time of the American Independence, the English, afflicted by continental as well as American efforts to take over the advantages they had gained in making cheap textiles, had passed laws prohibiting the export of the new machines and the emigration of mechanics who knew about them. Despite the laws, America was successful in gaining the needed knowledge. A few machines were imported by disassembling them into their component parts and packing them in disguised boxes. The prohibition was rendered ineffective as Americans relied much more on immigrant mechanics, visits to England, drawings and descriptions, and the ingenuity of their own mechanics. The most publicized transfer was that by Francis Cabot Lowell, who visited England in 1812 and carefully studied power looms there. He discovered how they worked and brought the information back to America. He was able to translate his knowledge into practice with the aid of an ingenious American mechanic, Paul Moody, who adapted and improvised sufficiently to build a working loom. As Americans modified English machines, they gradually began to invent similar and related devices and put new techniques into use (Cochrane 1998).

The imported knowledge was made increasingly available to people through a broad spectrum of educational, cultural, social, economic, and religious institutions, through a rising volume of books, magazines, and newspapers of British and European origin, through establishment and expansion of both private and public libraries, and through a vigorous press with the capacity to publish books, pamphlets, newspapers, and other reading material. It gave rise to a general expansion of schooling, including more institutions of higher learning (Greene 1999). In addition to the imported knowledge, there was a great interest in improving material objects. For example, the American Philosophical Society in Philadelphia, the largest city at that time, honoured men who worked on practical problems, while the great hereditary landed aristocrat, Robert Livingston of New York, financed experimental steamboats (Cochrane 1998).

By the early nineteenth century, on the foundation laid by improvising imported knowledge, American artisans and upper classes facilitated the emergence of artisan entrepreneurs, who introduced a more advanced division of labour and achieved technological improvements in a wide variety of manufacturing processes.

Social Capital

In the late sixteenth century, England, Scotland, France, Sweden, Spain, and the Netherlands began to colonize eastern North America. These European settlers came from a variety of social and religious groups. In the new land, settlers faced a dilemma of how to reconcile freedom with the need for order. Lacking established traditions that specified the normal functioning of society and its demands, churches, communities and entrepreneurs sought to create norms to bring about a social order.

Missionary societies in the 1790s and early 1800s were instrumental in building a new kind of civil society in which citizens created their own communal norms and social solidarity. They discovered that social capital could develop from below through the voluntary actions of ordinary people in horizontal relationships rather than vertical hierarchical ties. Voluntary religious and moral societies could act in lieu of the established church. These societies hired agents to meet with local citizens to form auxiliaries (Neem 2009).

The spread of mass membership and voluntary associations created a social order fundamentally different from the old one. Ordinary Americans had become active participants in forging social order and communal norms. The new social order was subject to challenges by motivated citizens, as Americans recognized that the social order could be changed by their own actions. The social order, as the Americans discovered, was their own creation, not something inherited and eternal. America's experience with voluntary associations shows how a society discovered 'harmony emerging out of chaos'. Voluntary associations and churches helped shape the moral standards and social capital of America's growing middle class and allowed them to become participants in forging social order. However, the mechanism that formed social capital could also challenge it (Neem 2009).

Networks like voluntary organizations and small communities also played an important role in the promotion of industrialization, technological, and material development. The Franklin Institute held fairs every two years and the American Institute displayed competing products and inventions every year. These fairs proved a successful means for promoting invention and production. Visitors often gained from observing collections of the newest designs in a variety of products. Mechanics institutes also held fairs and introduced lectures and courses to improve the education of the mechanics and actively promoted protectionism for their production. During the 1790s, urban merchants formed associations which advocated tariffs as a means to allow domestic manufacturing to flourish; merchants favoured government's support of their trade. Agricultural societies promoted a harmony of interests between productive agriculture and manufacturing and saw government as a vehicle for supporting better agricultural practices. Voluntary associations ranged from promoting manufacturing to advocating protection for them with the help of politicians (Greene 1999).

Communities also encouraged invention and improvement, including mechanization of household activities. They moved towards technology for answers to human and social problems. Religious communities tried to combine agriculture with industry in a certain social pattern, by actively encouraging invention and by making technology a central part of their life.

Immigrants combined their social capital with labour and investment and transformed their new landscapes into European style spaces complete with concomitant economies, social systems, and cultural arrangements (Greene 1999). As they lost many old-world forms of social capital, it inspired the invention of means for immigrants' social and cultural delivery. Trade, continuing immigration, governmental interaction, and cultural exchanges in science and religion made them a part of an expanding transatlantic information pool. All these made it possible to replenish, expand, and update the social capital in America (Greene 1999).

Institutional Capital

The American continent was inhabited since the sixteenth century by different waves of migrants. Significant among those were people who spoke the Latin languages and brought the social, religious, and economic institutions of the late European Middle Ages. Another wave of migrants consisted of the Anglo-Saxon, Gaelic, and Welsh settlers who were Protestant by religion and predominantly English by political, legal, and literary culture. Out of this rich storehouse of social knowledge, these settlers selected whatever was most useful to their efforts at social reconstruction in the new space. In the process, they discarded much and as they adjusted to the new situations, they simplified or modified everything from economic practices and social organizations to law (Greene 1999). Within these institutions, the settlers moved, took root, and created enterprises.

The dominant Anglo-American culture in general served to explain inventions of the eighteenth century, while the governmental institutions common to the two nations helped by giving entrepreneurs legal security and the freedom to act. The governments provided relatively high protection against war, politics, or other non-market forces and encouraged rapid private investment (Cochrane 1998).

Under pressure by lawyers, the courts became distinctly favourable to entrepreneurial action. Started initially from the colonists' desire to buy and sell land freely, the common law in America grew to favour the operator, sometimes at the expense of absentee investors or the traditional rights of landowners. American land law grew around the facility of improvement and transfer. But the effects stretched beyond the land; business transactions were freed from archaic legal ceremony. Guilds were never powerful in America and cities readily granted artisan's licenses, where necessary, to all applicants. Associations of master craftsmen were never able to exercise exclusive control over their apprentices. Ease of incorporation and protection of contracts against state interference stimulated investment (Cochrane 1998).

The Patent Act of 1790 established the American Patent system, providing 14-year monopolies for patented goods. In 1836, a third patent act was passed which provided for a patent office that awarded patents on the basis of originality, novelty, and utility through a body of patent examiners. The monopoly granted by a patent was intended to reward the inventor, but a secondary purpose was to reverse the monopoly. This was to make the details of the patent available to everyone after the term of the monopoly had ended. The new technology was diffused widely to the benefit of the nation. As a result, visits to the patent office became useful to mechanics seeking to make use of released patent models.

The Constitution gave Congress powers, in addition to the patent power, that permitted further encouragement of manufacturing and industrialization. Congress was given the power to regulate commerce with foreign nations and to impose taxes or tariffs. The tariff became the federal government's most important means for encouraging manufacturing activity.

State and local governments sometimes exercised direct efforts in favour of manufacturing. Some bought stock in desirable enterprises, exempted corporations from taxes, and provided limited liability for investors in certain industries. Others gave premiums to encourage industry. The authority to charter businesses was another important state prerogative. All levels of government were involved in the promotion of internal transportation improvements. In the early nineteenth century, Congress authorized the building of national roads across states. Federal, state, and local governments offered private groups of businessmen franchise rights and privileges of incorporation to establish public conveniences including transportation companies.

Various articles of the Constitution laid the foundation for a national market system. The most important provision was the authority granted to Congress over interstate commerce; the states would be prevented from placing obstacles in the way of the free flow of goods, people, and currency throughout the republic. Congress was given the right to coin money and to regulate its value. The Constitution granted federal authorities the power to assemble militias to suppress insurrections, and thereby offered protection of private property and interests. The Constitution proclaimed that no state could pass laws that interfered with obligations assumed and agreed to in contracts by private parties (Cochrane 1998).

Several entrepreneurs established integrated enclaves encompassing mills, workshops, stores, cottages, and boarding houses. These enclaves helped employers and employees teach themselves how to respond to one another. They created the rules of the game for being industrial employers and employees. In the beginning this social structure depended on the personal character and involvement of the entrepreneur. They intervened frequently to establish wage guidelines, evaluate work turned out, set requirements for 'steady, punctual, industrious and temperate' workers, and to reward favourite employees with cash gifts.

Gradually, the relationship between employers and employees evolved, which took various forms. In some instances, workers adopted a simple strategy for coping with the industrial order through obedience. This was, in large measure, a consequence of the personal and kindly dimensions of management's authority and the resulting loyalty and sense of indebtedness some workers came to feel toward their employers. In other instances, strikes emerged from a background of employees and employers struggling to establish the lines and limits of their relationship. Workers slowly acceded to the formal, bureaucratic structures of the regimen: time discipline. Together, all these institutions laid the foundation for business concerns that had no precedents in either size or complexity (Cochrane 1998).

Interaction between Human Capital, Social Capital, and Institutional Capital

Early eighteenth century manufacturing techniques in America were crude and there were few power tools. The colonists recognized they could not support life with imports from the mother country and so they began to manufacture almost immediately. The first products like glass and soap ashes were the joint result of local need and the necessity of providing a return to the English promoters of the colony. Diversification of effort appeared as men of many skills migrated to the new world. The manufacture of goods by skilled manual craftsmanship, both in workshops and in homes, became the most prevalent form of manufacture. Most of the finished articles for use and trade were manually fabricated. In this form of manufacture, great skill was achieved in the handling of material and hand tools. Most of the important mechanical inventions had English origins but were adapted to American conditions and improved by American ingenuity. By the 1790s many of the inventions were made in small shops. Entrepreneurs could find skilful native mechanics to assist them. Their training in the workshops and mills of colonial America ensured that native mechanics, after a short acquaintance with the machines, were able to reproduce and improve them without assistance. These working skills made the American IR possible and enabled a rapid transition to an industrial economy. The importation of key English inventions in the closing years of the eighteenth century acted as a catalyst, giving new direction to the existing native skills (Gibb 1946).

Continual migration produced a large group of consumers. A migrant to a new settlement crafted what was needed and often shifted readily from one occupation to another. Money or economic rationality, rather than land or family ties, was the common measuring rod of the society. Americans with skills were often lured away by new opportunities and there was a continuous change in partnerships. In many areas there was greater public concern with attracting scarce skilled labour from abroad. This constant shifting meant that many new firms started up. Continuous new startups set a trend of innovation in the economy (Cochrane 1998). The human capital that initiated the IR in America was the flexible supply of all-purpose artisans who knew how to use tools and could improve on old processes imported from elsewhere.

The creation of networks increases because of the necessity to counteract the individual disadvantage against missing institutions.

Manufacturers in the early nineteenth century attempted to construct an industrial base for the country. To succeed, they required assistance from the federal government in the form of protective tariffs, a national banking system, state-supported transportation improvements, and other public conveniences. The government was successful in providing relatively high protection against war, politics, or other non-market forces, and giving entrepreneurs legal security and freedom to act.

But American manufacturers were dependent on wealthy families for financial resources. Large scale ventures in the early industrial period involved the pooling of monies. Investors pooled their monies to establish banks for handling their projects. Likewise, despite initial government sponsorship, the spread of telegraphic communication remained a private industry accomplishment. State and local governments similarly made only minimal investments in public education. Entrepreneurs were a group bound by ties of economic rationality, money, religion, social approval, and joint labour in sharing tasks of creating an industrial base for the country. Their social capital facilitated them in negotiating with the state to create the necessary infrastructure for a smooth functioning of the economy.

Social capital directs attention to the relationships that shape the realization of human capital's potential for the individual and for the network.

The social capital brought by the settlers to the New World assisted them in combining labour and investment capital and thereby transformed their new settings. They could select whatever was most useful to their specific efforts at social reconstruction. In the process, they discarded much and, in the course of adjusting to the new situations, simplified or modified everything from economic practices and social organization. The human capital of individuals with specialized skills effectively translated into social capital (Greene 1999), as in the case of groups of entrepreneurs who established banks, constructed infrastructure (Wallace 1998).

Institutional emergence arises from a structured bargaining between actors who agree to a self-organizing governance system when they organize themselves into groups and networks.

The American IR began with the adoption of machine methods and factory organization in the production of cotton textiles in southern New England at the turn of the eighteenth century. The textile mills depended at the outset on the collection of mechanical inventions springing into activity in Britain. The interruption of trade between 1795 and 1815 forced the industry to depend on its own resources. In other industries, light machinery skills and techniques of plant organization already developed in New England were married to the heavy-equipment industries, such as the steel and rubber works, to create the prototypical American Industry (Parker 1996). What facilitated the growth of American industry were the industrial enclaves created by entrepreneurs who helped the early employers and employees teach themselves how to respond to one another. Employers and employees working in these enclaves were the earliest New World participants in factory labour. They created the rules of the game for being industrial employers and employees. Their complex relationship was an early instalment of an educational process for the initial generations of every American occupation affected by industrialization (Prude 1998). Flexible human capital and social capital built through religious ties and the rules of the game learnt in industrial enclaves enabled Americans to accomplish complex manufacturing (production broken down to a series of small, easily repeated operations on parts).

***

Beginning in the late eighteenth century, America was transformed from a predominately rural agrarian society to an industrial economy centred in large metropolitan cities. The history of American industrialization includes the expansion of market activity, the spread of wage labour, mechanization, the coming of the factory system, massive migration of peoples into and through the country, urbanization, occupational change, labour organization, the emergence of a distinct middle class, and ultimately the rise of the large scale corporation. The most commonly cited reasons for the rapid growth of the American IR are the abundance of mineral resources, technological innovation, the evolution of the American system of manufacturing, lowered costs of transportation, education and human resources, and the rise of the managerial firm.

At the time that America won its War of Independence against Britain in 1783, most of its manufactured goods were imported from Britain. Skills levels in America were usually lower, capital more scarce, labour more dear, distances enormously greater, and government weaker and more impoverished. These differences affected both the machines themselves and the manner in which they were put to use.

The migration of skilled craftsmen created the conditions for further industrial development and because of the ever-present need for new construction, there was an emphasis on practical or useful skills. 'Mechanicians' encouraged the transmission of technology by methods of demonstration and practice and by their travel abroad. Local adaptation accompanied the transfer of technology and stimulated invention and innovation in America. Entrepreneurs and their networks not only established new factories but also established industrial enclaves to build a community where employers and employees taught themselves the first lessons in industrial relationships. Entrepreneurs pooled their resources to develop the infrastructure in the country. Voluntary organizations also played their role in the promotion of industrialization. State and local governments exercised more direct efforts in favour of manufacturing along with efforts to provide guarantees to entrepreneurs keen on developing the infrastructure.

The accumulation of human and social capital led to the economic sphere, a greater specialization of production and lower production costs, better transportation and lower distribution costs, more efficient markets, tighter organization, and rising technical capacity. The proliferation of social and human capital was also observable in the social realm. The simultaneous interaction between human capital, social capital, and institutions during the early phase of the American IR set the stage for faster and further industrial development which started in the 1840s and propelled US to global prominence as an industrial power.

8 Japan's Growth Experience
Post–Second World War and Recent Times

The rapid growth of the Japanese economy has been one of the most remarkable economic phenomena of the post-War period. Although Japan was a latecomer to industrialization relative to nations in Western Europe and North America, it was the first non-Western nation that entered the epoch of modern economic growth. And since the early 1990s it has been the only developed country which has suffered a prolonged decline and has failed to show significant signs of economic dynamism after 20 years of weak performance.

The first phase in the development of Japan's modern industrial architecture began after the Meiji Restoration in 1868 and continued through the pre-War era. The half-century period, spanning from the late 1800s through the 1920s, witnessed considerable economic change and entrepreneurial initiative as thousands of new companies were founded and new industries created. During the second phase, between 1937 and 1945, the Japanese economy was a militarized economy but diverse and sophisticated in ways that facilitated conversion to peacetime activity. Many of the Japanese auto manufacturers came into existence during the war time. After the war, the economic system enabled Japan to emerge from the devastation and demoralization of defeat, when its per capita income fell to the lowest in Asia, to become the second largest economy in the world, with a per capita income among the highest worldwide. Japan successfully transformed itself technologically, economically and socially in a short span of time.

Between 1953 and 1971, the real GDP in Japan increased at an average annual rate of 10 per cent. By 1990, Japan was the world's second largest economy and GDP per capita was 20 per cent higher than that of the United States (Hill 1995).

As the first non-Western country to industrialize, Japan's organizational and industrial arrangements underpinnned its economic development. Between 1960 and 1975, the value added per employee in industries like steel, automobiles, electrical machines, and petrochemicals reached the same level as that of their counterparts in Europe and the US. The export and production ratio in major industries climbed significantly. For example, the passenger car export ratio was 4.2 per cent in 1960 but went up to 40 per cent by 1975. The export ratio for steel climbed from 11.4 per cent in 1960 to 30.3 per cent in 1975. In addition, there was a rapid increase in foreign investment by Japanese companies, from US$ 159 million in 1965 to US$ 3,280 in 1975.

As the growth of the manufacturing industry has been the core of industrialization, it accounted for 71 per cent of the increase in the GDP from 1955 to 1980. The growth rate of the manufacturing industry increased by 4.4 per cent from 1878 to 1900, by 5.4 per cent from 1901 to 1920, and by 6.5 per cent from 1921 to 1938. One of the reasons for this acceleration was the continued growth of the textile industry. After a sharp drop due to the Second World War, the manufacturing production index began to increase and in 1955 it surpassed its highest pre-War and War-time levels. Its rate of growth in the 1950s and 1960s was unprecedently high (14–16 per cent), and although it fell to 5 per cent in the 1970s, it was still high compared with the developed countries of the West.

Starting in the 1950s, the driving forces of Japan's economy were capital-intensive industries such as steel, chemicals, and automobiles. The changeover from light industry to heavy and chemical industries as the leading sector took place rapidly in Japan; before the growth of the former slowed down, the growth of the latter had already begun to accelerate. Gradually, Japanese manufacturing became known for technology-based industries. This was made possible by the integration of innovation and production, the establishment of new organizational environments to incubate new innovations, and the diffusion of technological innovations into manufacturing processes.

The role of government in supporting economic growth in the post-War period began in the form of a stringent direct control of energy and foreign exchange allotment in the early reconstruction period. This turned into indirect means such as protective tariffs, preferential tariffs, preferential allotment of government bank credits and interest subsidies, and advantageous scheduling of depreciation allowances to selected industries.

The post-War Japanese economic miracle can be best understood in terms of the actions of a centralized developmental state, private industry, and long-term credit banks; the nature of political and economic linkages; and the fundamental transformation and organization of the production system harnessing the human capital of engineers, R&D scientists, and managers. This chapter looks at the simultaneous interaction between human capital, social capital, and institutional capital and how that interaction contributed to Japan's industrial success in the post-War period.

By the second half of 1980s, growth in Japan was being sustained by increased bank lending, operating both directly and through a self-reinforcing cycle with increased land and stock prices. But once asset prices began to fall, undercapitalized banks restrained lending to maintain capital adequacy standards. Insufficiency of demand drove the downturn, as Japan entered a liquidity trap—with nominal interest rates unable to fall below zero, and real interest rates too high to stimulate economic activity. With the burst of the bubble economy of the 1980s, real economic growth in Japan slowed from an average 4.1 per cent in the 1980s to 1.5 per cent in the 1990s (OECD 2004). In 2003, stock prices were more than 80 per cent off from their 1989 highs, and the 2005 prices of residential land in Japan's six major cities stood some 65 per cent lower than what was at the peak in 1991 (Witt 2006). There was a sharp fall in productivity stemming from the increasing failure of the traditional Japanese economic model to adapt to the requirements of a more deregulated and competitive world economy, societal ageing and technological change. This chapter also looks at how institutional capital and social capital have impeded fundamental changes that could have positively affected the way things are done in business and in the economy.

Human Capital in Japan

Japan, being a latecomer to industrialization and modern economic growth, invested heavily in education, especially in its early development stage, in order to catch up with advanced economies in the West. The primary national goal of modern Japan after the Meiji Restoration of 1868 was to catch up with the economic strength of Western nations. This motivation has been reflected in its progress in education. Before 1868, education was fairly widely diffused in Japan, even among ordinary people below the warrior class. Their children commonly attended informal private schools to receive basic education. Accordingly, at the time of the Meiji Restoration, primary education attainment in Japan was around 20 per cent (Dore 1965). The old education system was modernized after the Meiji Restoration when the feudal state was replaced by a centralized nation state.

One of the main causes of the Meiji Restoration was the threat of invasion and colonization by Western colonial power; the aim thus was to industrialize the country by means of borrowing modern technologies from the West. Leaders in the Meiji government recognized that effective borrowing of Western technologies could not be achieved without developing a modern education system that was able to produce high quality manpower. As early as 1872, the government promulgated the School System Rule, which specified the design of a modern educational system. The Primary School Order of 1886 later introduced compulsory education and established two types of primary schools: ordinary primary schools and higher primary schools. The former provided four-year compulsory education. The latter provided an additional two to four years of schooling for those who completed compulsory education. The municipal authority in each district was mandated to support an ordinary primary school so that all children could attend it. Compulsory education was extended to six years in 1907 (Dore 1965).

Due to the policies of the Meiji government, total enrolment in Japan started increasing. By 1880, Japan had total enrolment in primary education of 42 per cent. By the start of the nineteenth century, about 40 per cent of Japanese boys and 10 per cent of girls were getting some form of formal elementary education outside their homes (Dore 1965). By 1940 the total enrolment had increased to 100 per cent. After the war, with the exception of a brief period in the 1940s during the American occupation when the education system was modified, total enrolment in primary education remained at around 100 per cent.

Total enrolment in secondary education also started to increase in the 1890s. An increase in vocational education, along with high level of primary enrolment, created a demand in the population for further education and contributed to a marked rise in secondary education. The developing Japanese technical industry and the Sino-Japanese War of 1894–5 increased the demand for technically trained people. Therefore, a vocational educational law was drafted and passed in 1894. Enrolment in vocational education was only 2.2 per cent of total enrolment at secondary level in 1890 which increased to 7.8 per cent by 1900 (Passin 1965). This increase in vocational enrolments was continued with The National School Ordinance Enforcement Regulations, followed by the National School Ordinance in 1941, which stipulated, among other things, that secondary education should deepen the knowledge and technical skills of the people. The strong intention of pre-War Japanese leaders to use school education as a means of economic catch-up is also reflected in a heavy emphasis on vocational education. The average number of years of vocational schooling increased more than three times, faster than the average of all schools before the Second World War. As a result, the share of vocational education in total schooling years at the post-primary (secondary and tertiary) level rose from only 3 per cent in 1900 to 45 per cent in 1940. This disproportionate growth in vocational education was the response to the high demand for middle level engineers, technicians, managers, and clerks in the process of technology borrowing from the West (Godo and Hayami 2000).

By 1930, there was already a substantial number of large firms in Japan that were comparable with big businesses in the US, and the number of white-collar workers increased in the 1920s and 1930s. The emergence of large firms generated a demand for white-collar workers with expertise in such areas as law, accounting, marketing, and human resource management. Direct recruitment of school graduates came to be the major means by which large firms recruited white-collar workers (Okazaki 2011).

Japan's pre-War higher education was divided into higher schools, universities, colleges, and higher normal schools (Miyazawa 2010).

During the post-War period, the Japanese education was reformed after the American model. It included the adoption of '6 years primary education, 3 years junior high school, 3 years senior high school, and 4 years of university' (Nishimoto 1956). Attending primary and lower secondary schools was made compulsory. These changes made access to secondary education much more egalitarian. The enrolment in secondary education increased from 70 per cent to 90 per cent. The total enrolment in higher education also increased significantly during 1950–70 (Nishimoto 1956).

Japan's education system has undergone various structural reforms since 1990 (Eades et al. 2005). Much of the effort seems to have gone into making the extant system more flexible and decentralized.

Japan's investment in developing human capital ensured that it had the capability to absorb new technologies and pave the way for the emergence of a modern economy. At the beginning of industrialization, Japanese industry relied heavily on the guidance of foreign engineers. These engineers were gradually replaced by Japanese engineers trained at factories and educational institutions in Japan and other countries. In addition, Japan's 'cultural receptivity' developed through its long history of introducing culture and technology from China, facilitated the introduction of Western technology.

With this human capital base, it was not difficult for Japanese firms to start R&D activities that took place before the actual application of modern technology.

Institutional Capital in Japan

The publication of the 1972 Report of the US Department of Commerce, 'Japan: The Government–Business Relationship', succinctly describes the Japanese industrial economy and its concomitant institutional capital. According to the report, 'Japan Incorporated is not a monolithic system in which government leads and business follows blindly', but there is cooperative interaction between government and business.

> What makes government–business interaction in Japan different from what takes place in other countries is the extent and the scale of such interaction and a qualitative difference, a style peculiar to the Japanese, derived from Japan's history and culture with its emphasis on the consensual approach, a tradition of government leadership in industrial

development, and a generally shared desire to advance the interest of the Japanese nation.

Japanese industrialization originated with the political transformation that took place in 1867—the Meiji Restoration. From the late 1860s, the new Japanese state undertook a self-conscious policy of industrialization. It was an industrialization sponsored and encouraged from the top by the state. After the initial state funding, shipyards, textile mills and steel works quickly passed into private ownership. The owners were large family businesses.

The requirements of Japan's War-time economy—a period beginning in the early 1930s and extending to Japan's defeat in 1945—brought important changes in the Japanese political economy. The relationship between state and industry was fundamentally altered, as Japanese policymakers found it increasingly necessary to manage an industrial production system for their rapidly expanding colonial empire. They created a stable core of enterprise groups that could be presumed to have both the broad capabilities necessary to make complex expansion projects work and the reliability and trustworthiness necessary to carry them out. They organized enterprises into horizontal and vertical networks that could be counted on to follow state production plans (Morck and Nakamura 2004).

Many changes were brought to reshape the nature of the Japanese corporation itself. Profit seeking was made subordinate to nationalist goals which shifted the conception of the firm from a specialized instrument for the creation of shareholder wealth to a social institution in which employees and the community were dominant stakeholders. This focus continued after the War but now included long-term employment guarantees, internal promotion, and enterprise-based unions (Shirai 1983). The internal labour markets in large firms prompted wide use of subcontractors to buffer the core workforce from fluctuations in labour and product market demand. They also required stable shareholders willing to overlook short-term performance shortfalls for the sake of long-term business growth.

The post-War period from the late 1940s witnessed institutionalization of what came to be known as the Japanese business system. After 1952, when government recovered full political autonomy, the Japanese government continued to find network structures useful in executing industrial production plans. What was then the Ministry of International

Trade and Industry (MITI) helped rebuild the trading companies, its powerful Industrial Rationalisation Council called for 'keiretsuization' of trading companies and manufacturers. MITI winnowed about 2,800 trading companies that existed after the Occupation, down to 20 big ones, each a bank keiretsu or a cartel of smaller producers (Johnson 1982). The Ministry of Finance and MITI were both involved in promoting stable cross-shareholdings within keiretsu networks, as War-time concerns over strategic control of resource mobilization were replaced in the post-War period by concerns over capital liberalization and foreign takeover of the Japanese industry (Lincoln and Gerlach 2004).

MITI went to great lengths to confer with industry and, with this feedback, it set guidelines to strengthen the growth posture of important industries. In Japan, with only a partially developed economy and a later start on the road to industrialization, the general consensus was to obtain economically advanced status as quickly as possible. To reach this goal, it was necessary for the government to take the lead in guidance and direction. The government acted as a mediator to placate firms in the private sector. It also provided supportive industrial measures for businesses with comparatively higher income elasticity and with relatively higher speed in technical progress (Shinohara 1976).

Vertical relationships between manufacturers and suppliers also tightened from the 1950s onwards, as Japan's rapidly growing economy led industrial producers to rely more heavily on subcontractors and secondary subcontractors to help meet demand. Internal labour markets, main banks, cross-shareholding, and vertical supply and distribution relationships evolved together, each a necessary component in making the others work: cross-shareholding freed managers to focus on company and employee interests, and helped reinforce ties with suppliers; internal labour markets ensured continuity in personal relationships underpinning ties to banks and other affiliates; subcontracting allowed the parent company to remain small enough that it could provide employment guarantees to its core workers (Lincoln and Gerlach 2004).

For many years following the War, government bureaucracy used the large commercial banks to funnel scarce capital to those industries it considered vital for rebuilding the Japanese economy (Nakamura and Odaka 2003).

MITI's post-War industrial policy was quite effective in nurturing infant industries. MITI adopted measures such as administrative guidance, import restriction, coordination of investment in plant and equipment, merger and other methods of production consolidation, approval of cartels, postponing of liberalization of direct investment from outside, tax incentives for leading industries, low interest loans and other measures (Shinohara 1976).[1] To deal with industrial crises when industries were saddled with over capacity as in the aftermath of the first oil crisis, the government enacted the law on Temporary Measures for the Stabilisation of Specified Structurally Depressed Industries in 1978. Through this law the government began to enforce a structural adjustment assistance policy towards several depressed industries (Uekusa 1987).

The government also encouraged companies to build consensus with the labour force helping companies to eschew confrontation with labour. During the period 1955-70, 'Japanese management developed a sophisticated labour management style which encouraged workers' loyalty to their supervisors and competition among the workers themselves' (Hideo 1983). 'The "success" of the Japanese management in the 1970s has very much depended on the full-scale cooperation of the enterprise unions' (Hideo 1983).

Japanese thus created a significant complementarity in their business institutional capital. Institutional complementarity worked well for Japan during its rapid industrialization phase but as the economy matured it reduced the rate of institutional change because of the increased complexity of change.

The 'industrial policy' included all measures by the government to promote the growth of industries—financial aid to important industries, protection of infant industry, preferential allocation of foreign currencies to important industry, a special accelerated depreciation system for imported machinery, encouragement to adopt foreign technology, financial and monetary means to guide and control private activities and administrative guidance. This system enabled the government to exercise direct influence over Japanese enterprises by giving certain information, advice, and instructions to them informally rather than taking legal action. Administrative guidance enabled the government to promote mergers, control production by forcing a reduction in operations, and mitigate excessive competition by controlling purchase limits in equipment.

Institutional change in Japan involved extensive societal coordination expressed in mutual consultation and information exchange about possible steps and their practical feasibility. This process served Japan well in the post-War period of rapid industrialization. But it counters restrictions when swift and major changes are required in the face of constantly changing conditions (Lincoln 2001).

Social Capital in Japan

Fukuyama (1995) claims that Japan is a country that enjoys a high level of trust, as evidenced by its low crime rate and by its business practices, which rely on informal understandings rather than documentation.

Japanese culture de-emphasizes the individual and places significance on the importance of conformity and the success of the group. This social ethic is called *giri* whose essence goes beyond simple social courtesy. It consists of maintaining a very intimate link and relationship of reciprocal confidence in personal, social, or business relationships. The link is always conditioned by the respect for superiors and the protection for inferiors. In obedience to giri, a person must be frank, sincere, and faithful in relation to the other, always seeking to fit in with the other's presumed intentions as if they were someone who was dear or close (Kitamura 2001). Japan is a society based on assurance of security (Yamagashi 1988). Japanese society and business are characterized by networks of stable relationships of commitment that provide insiders with assurances of mutual cooperation. It is the stable nature of the relations constraining people and organizations involved that provided assurance that partners will meet their commitments (Toshio 2003). In the upper levels of society, the *kone* (connections) multiply to form whole networks of special relationships. These may derive from one-time favours, school ties, or shared experiences, or they may involve intricate mutual back-scratching deals, which are called *jinmyaku* (*jin* meaning 'personal' and *myaku* meaning 'vein'; so that jinmyaku means a vein of personal connections running through the fabric of society) (van Wolferen 1989).

Given Japan's emphasis on collectivist principles, identification with the group or business system, accordingly, is rich in networks. Japanese networks in the business sector include the business groups or keiretsu, supplier networks, R&D consortia, and the nexus of state associations and firms (Witt 2006).

Business groups come in two types: former zaibatsu and 'bank-led' groups (Ito 1992). The zaibatsu type, comprising the Mitsubishi, Mitsui, and Sumitomo groups, has its origin in the pre-War and Wartime zaibatsu, which were holding companies that controlled vast conglomerates of firms in unrelated industries. On the other hand, the bank-led business groups—Fuyo, Ikkan, and Sanwa, as well as some smaller groups—coalesced around banks after the War, partially forced together by MITI (Johnson 1982).

Closely related to business groups is the second type of networks, supplier networks or vertical keiretsu. These networks come in three varieties. The first are the production keiretsu which are elaborate hierarchies of primary, secondary, and tertiary level subcontractors that supply through a series of stages to parent firms. The second are the distribution keiretsu. These are linear systems of distributors that operate under the name of a large scale manufacturer or a wholesaler. The third are the capital keiretsu, which are groupings based not on the flow of product materials and goods but on the flow of capital from a parent firm (Gerlach 1992). There is a continuous informal social networking that occurs among the actors active within the same industry.

The third type of networks is the R&D consortia, which owe their existence to specific, often state-sponsored research projects. These networks link large firms in the same industry together for the duration of a project, typically 5–10 years (Witt 2006). Until about 1980 their projects focused on catching up technologically with the Western competitors (Witt 2006).

The nexus of state associations and firms is another form of network in Japan. This nexus represents a conduit for coordination and information flow between the private sector and the state. The historical origin of the nexus lies mainly in government's efforts to increase coordination among industries as a response to the Great Depression. The network between the state and the firms is enforced through *amakudari* and the *genkyoku*. Amakudari involved an older, high-ranking government official leaving his post to become a senior manager in industry. This practice started in the immediate post-War period, when there was a serious shortage of talent due to the purging of senior executives who had cooperated with the military government. The genkyoku principle, involves specific ministries claiming exclusive regulatory power over specific industries (Morck and Nakamura 2004).

The nexus was instrumental in coordinating post-War industrial policy (Okimoto 1989). Industrial policy in Japan is not imposed by the bureaucracy in a top-down fashion but coordinated in a process of reciprocal consent (Samuels 1987). Industry associations aggregate individual company interests and opinions which act as conduits for information and requests from industry to government, which in turn uses the associations for administrative guidance and to distribute information and money to industry (Okimoto 1989; Schaede 2000). Firms and associations hire retired bureaucrats in order to reinforce their ties with the bureaucracy (Schaede 2000). The process of interaction between state-associations–firms is facilitated through personnel interlock, numerous meeting opportunities (Witt 2006), and 'administrative guidance' is provided through tailor-made, verbal, and ad hoc agreements.

Interaction between Human Capital, Social Capital, and Institutional Capital

From the 1950s till the 1970s, Japan grew rapidly. The dominant view in academic and policy circles was that Japan's distinctive economic institutional capital was a cultural anomaly. In the 1980s, Japan emerged as an equal, in business and technology spheres, while retaining its networks. Network ties, bank monitoring, stable shareholders, and active industrial policy were considered best practices for many emerging countries to emulate.

The creation of networks increases because of the necessity of networks to counteract individual disadvantage against under-developed institutions.

The Japanese economy is described as network-centric, where even the Japanese state is one more network actor. Enforcement of compliance with the existing institutional structure is facilitated by the extensive social networks. The role of the networks as conduits of information, norms, and values also makes them effective means of stabilizing established institutions by fostering compliance (Witt 2006). Japan's late-developing legal system contributed to the shaping of its business networks. Modern property and contract law was slow to emerge, so that recourse to the courts as a means of dispute resolution was not generally an option. Private ordering within clusters of enterprises served as a substitute mechanism for ensuring reliable performance by business partners.

Social capital directs attention to the relationships that shape the realisation of human capital's potential for the individual and for the network.

Japan's system of consultation between management and enterprise unions and long-term employment eliminated many of the organizational rigidities for workers to resist automation and work redesign, which encouraged greater flexibility. Consequently Japanese firms could experiment with flexible forms of manufacturing. There was little need for elaborate job classifications. Given this context, rotation and skill-sharing were used to upgrade skills and increased interaction among workers (Aoki 1988). Life-time employment also enabled large corporations to make sizable investments in human capital with little regard for employee turnover or exit. This enabled Japanese corporations more broadly to harness workers' knowledge as a source of value. Japanese manufacturing came to be characterized by high degrees of knowledge mobilization and learning by doing (Aoki 1988). Workers obtained a broad view of the production process, and were more completely integrated into industrial enterprise (Knudsden et al. 1994). Knowledge mobilization at a variety of levels gave the Japanese firm extraordinary problem solving capabilities. The R&D network and the general legacy of institutional flexibility resulted in new technologies being diffused rapidly. Over time, this pushed Japan's industry toward new technological frontiers (Kenney and Florida 1993). Thus, Japanese firms' advantages in organizational learning and networking allowed them to develop new technologies, turn them into products, and market them faster and more effectively than firms elsewhere (Chandler et al. 2001).

Institutional emergence arises from a structured bargaining between actors who agree to a self-organizing governance system when they organize themselves into groups and networks.

The network of state associations and firms ensured that investment in an industry was coordinated. Although ministerial policies were not specifically designed to buttress network structures, they often in practice had that effect. MITI also played the role of an arbitrator between different firms; the 'network state' acting as a mediator among competing firms.

The social capital embedded in network structures helped companies and ministries to work together and successfully implement industrial policies. MITI operated through an informal process of administrative guidance rather than through direct orders or explicit sanctions (Johnson 1982).

Japan maintained and regulated its network structure through its idiosyncratic devices and human capital. Human capital and informal institutions acted to prevent the Japanese network system from pursuing narrow interests.

Do Institutions Prevent Networks from Rent Seeking?

The economic policies, network structures, and institutions, which were responsible for the country's spectacular industrial rise in the 1950s and 1960s, have now come under criticism for producing rigidities that have undermined the economy. Policies that favoured large producers over smaller ones, and guided capital investment and labour to chosen sectors, are now seen to be barriers for further growth (Rowen and Toyoda 2002). The network structure and its rigidities are now overwhelming Japan's manufacturing strengths. In addition, the social norms and attitudes toward entrepreneurship are considered critical barriers in Japan. Although attitudes are slowly changing, 'the cost of failure for someone willing to swim against the current and join a venture company is high in Japan...failure is regarded not as a valuable learning experience but as a sign of ineptitude or moral turpitude' (Kneller 2000).

Keiretsu are considered to be rent seekers because of their size. Successful keiretsu were enthusiastic political rent seekers, raising the possibility that large corporate groups were better at influencing government than free-standing firms. Keiretsu managers lobbied for institutional weaknesses and blocked the entry of competitors. This rent seeking probably retarded financial development and created long-term economic problems (Morck and Nakamura 2004). It seems likely that keiretsu undermined the market for corporate control; and other corporate governance mechanisms, like proxy fights and institutional investor activism. The large banks and the keystone firms of the great horizontal keiretsu almost certainly lobbied for the suppression of the corporate bond market in the post-War Japan. Thus, weak institutional capital may well have been a consequence, as well as a cause, for business groups (Morck and Nakamura 2004).

The Keiretsu also altered the Japanese institutional capital to favour their continued importance. By participating enthusiastically in government's industrial policies, keiretsu nurtured relationships that generated both subsidies and political influence. Since civil servants in ministries were prime candidates for amakudari, the ministries rapidly became vocal advocates within government for the interests of their industries. This influence was often instrumental in keiretsu securing lasting advantages over competition. Entire ministries were captured by industrial groups through genkyoku and amakudari. Amakudari and genkyoku devolved into a system of regulatory capture (Stigler 1971). This undermined the state's ability to prudently regulate the economy and the financial system. This regulatory capture is now thought to be the root cause of Japan's current economic and governance problems.

Although keiretsu were created and encouraged by the state and its policies, their size and influence have now undermined the role of the state itself. The all-pervading network structure in the economy has created a policy gridlock because of its rigidity as well as embedded, entrenched, and vested interests. The bargaining power of large firms is now leveraged in hampering institutional changes and slowing the process of institutional adaptation.

Institutional adjustment has been slowed by a combination of highly coordinated and thus time-intensive adjustment processes because of the norms of extensive consultation and consensus building, paired with relatively limited adjustment pressure from the micro level.

***

There are two broad types of coordination in an economy, strategic coordination and market coordination. Market coordination draws on market forces, especially the price mechanism, to achieve order in an economy. In societal coordination, the organization of economic activity and the building of economic institutional capital occur through formal and informal non-market interaction and cooperation of actors. Social networks and the social capital underlying them play a key role in societal coordination. Post-War Japan adopted strategic coordination to create an industrial organization that was embedded in social relationships, norms which helped realign work organization, and technology to create a flexible production system and institutional space. This, in turn, generated and harnessed new sources of values and productivity improvement and turned them into reinforcing economic growth.

The essential elements of the Japanese business system were learning-by-doing, social capital that allowed information to be continually passed down, reciprocal relationships among stable business partners and civil servants, networks of various forms, and industrial policy. All these features point to rational responses to a variety of institutional failings. The Japanese business system and its network structures evolved to possess high efficiency, quality, reliability, flexibility, business environmental adaptability, low transaction costs, risk sharing, resource shifting, enhanced coordination and communication, access to stable financing, insulation from market pressures, monitoring benefits and reduction of information asymmetries, engendering a long-term perspective limiting opportunism, and mutual assistance. This system proved beneficial for the early post-War period and the ensuing high growth era in terms of filling the gaps in Japan's still-maturing economy.

As time progressed, the very same features of the Japanese business system became reasons for rent seeking, institutional inertia as change was blocked by vested interests, prolonged and engendered institutional weaknesses, misallocation of resources at the keiretsu level because of performance levelling, and group value maximization at the expense of outsiders and even individual group members. Institutional adjustment has been slow because of these reasons and there has been relatively limited adjustment pressure from the micro level.

Note

1. The industrial policies adopted by MITI in the mid-1950s were intended to make the heavy and chemical industries the leading sectors in economic growth. But MITI's industrial policy changed in the early 1970s. In 1971 MITI published a report called 'The Basic Direction of Trade and Industry', which emphasized on 'knowledge-intensive' industry in place of heavy and chemical industry. These new industries included R&D-intensive industries which employed very advanced manufacturing techniques, like fashion industries (Minami 1986).

9 China
The Manufacturing Sector

The root of China's recent success has been its export of manufactured consumer electronics goods. However, it is the increasing functionality (and value) of these products today that makes them useful. Value creation through 'software' makes the case of India, despite its much smaller economy, when compared to China. India is the first developing nation whose integration into the global economy is not through manufacturing, but rather through what can be termed as 'virtual' work. Chapters 9 and 10 look at the growth experience of these two countries in the recent past.

Both China and India have been star performers in aggregate GDP growth since the 1980s. China grew at an average rate of 8 per cent per year during 1980–2013, while India's GDP grew at an average rate close to 6.5 per cent during the same period. China began reforming its closed, centrally planned, non-market economy in 1978. In comparison, India always had a large private sector and poorly functioning markets that were subject to rigid state controls. It ushered in systemic and broader market reforms after experiencing a serious macroeconomic crisis in 1991. The political environments under which reforms were initiated and implemented in the two countries were very different. China was a willing and committed 'reformer'. India was a reluctant one; reformed half-heartedly to deal with a crisis. However, in both countries, the issue of future sustainability of current growth rates is important.

China's and India's per capita real incomes show that, starting from roughly equal levels in 1870, India forged ahead of China until the outbreak of the First World War (Maddison 2002). Though both experienced declines in their per capita incomes thereafter, by 1950, India's per capita income was about 40 per cent higher than China's. It took the next three decades for China to catch up. But since 1980, China has forged much farther ahead. India, on the other hand, during those three decades, grew at the 'Hindu rate of growth', an uncomplimentary phrase referring to India's inability to match its economic growth with its population growth. In the 1980s, India grew at an annual average of 5.7 per cent, but this growth was unsustainable as it was fuelled by a build-up of external debt which culminated in the crisis of 1991. The average growth rate from 1992–3 to 2001–2 was around 6 per cent. Since 2002, the average growth rate has been around 7 per cent. Despite these impressive growth rates in the last 20 plus years, India has still lagged behind China. But these statistics tell only the macroeconomic side of the story. At the micro level, in those segments of the economy in which markets and private firms dominate, India displays as much dynamism as China, which is supported by analyses (for example Goldman Sachs and others) that point to a significant re-alignment of the global economic order. Emerging economies, led by China and India, now account for a much larger share of global economic output. Measured at market exchange rates, Goldman Sachs projects that by 2050, the Indian and Chinese economies will respectively be around 80 per cent and 125 per cent of the size of the US economy.

Both countries offer different models of economic development; India relies primarily on organic growth, while China has chosen the FDI-driven approach. While China built up its economic strength by investing heavily in the manufacturing industry and facilitating foreign trade, the service sector has been the leading driver behind India's economic growth. China has used its vast resources of cheap labour and domestic savings to build infrastructure and has successfully attracted large amounts of FDI to spur the development of its manufacturing industry. India's strength, on the other hand, is based on its knowledge-based sectors such as IT and pharmaceuticals, more developed financial markets, and a more robust private sector. China has been successfully able to transfer its surplus labour from the rural areas to the manufacturing industry, and from low efficient State sectors to high-efficient commercial sectors. Without any particular training, Chinese rural workers have shown an ability to work in manufacturing industries, which has led to an increase of output. India, on the other hand, has used its abundant, English-speaking cheap labour to its advantage in the services sector.

China's manufacturing sector accounted for 45 per cent of GDP in 2012. The latest available figures show that manufactured goods were 90 per cent of exports or almost a quarter of the gross value of industrial output. China is a significant importer and exporter in manufacturing. In contrast, India's trade in manufacturing has not been all that remarkable to date, accounting for a far smaller share of its GDP—15.2 per cent in 2013 (Winters and Yusuf 2007). Along with being the world's largest trader with its share in global exports at 11 per cent in 2012, it is also the manufacturing hub in Asia. The country is now deeply involved in regional production and distribution networks in East and Southeast Asia (including ten ASEAN countries, plus Japan, China, and South Korea). On the other hand, India's services sector accounted for 57 per cent of real GDP in 2013–14. Despite the higher share of services in India's GDP and dominance of industry over services in China, in terms of absolute value of services GDP as well as growth in services, China is still ahead of India. However, IT-related services and the pharmaceutical industry will be key drivers of Indian's future trade growth. India's National Association of Software and Service Companies (NASSCOM) estimated that by 2020, India's share of the offshore market for engineering services—of a projected value of more than US$ 1 trillion—could be 25–30 per cent—up from the current 12 per cent, provided that the country's capacities, capabilities, infrastructure, and international reputation are in place (NASSCOM 2006).

The growth experience of both countries provides significant implications for future growth in other developing countries and how policy experts think about economic development generally. Chapters 9 and 10 explain how China and India gained their respective success in manufacturing ('factory of the world') and services sector (the 'world's back office') and the role played by human capital, social capital, and institutional capital in that success.

Human Capital in China

Since the late 1950s, China has made tremendous efforts to improve education, with the aim of promoting economic and social development. Starting in the 1960s, China began to expand its educational system rapidly and reached out to more people of all ages than in any previous period. The country has attempted to mobilize its entire population to achieve universal literacy over a relatively short period and has devised new ways to expand and deliver all levels of schooling to its citizenry. The most ambitious year for education in the country was 1986, with the passage of 16 education-related laws. Of these, the most far reaching was the Law of Compulsory Education, which mandated the gradual introduction of nine years of compulsory schooling throughout China. High school, which runs from grades 10 to12, is not compulsory and therefore does not have the full support of the government and is not free. After high school there are entrance exams to the next level of schooling. The National Higher Education Entrance Examination determines which college a student is allowed to attend, which, in turn, likely determines the quality of the student's job prospect post-graduation. Thus, there is great pressure to get into a good school so that one can receive a good enough education to pass these tests. The issue, however, is that the country's high quality schools tend to be located in the cities, while the majority of the population lives in the countryside (Chow 2006; Ke 2006).

The differences in population growth between the urban and rural areas, with much slower growth in rural areas, and vulnerability to poverty, correspond to much lower national investment in rural education, which has complicated the educational development of millions of people in rural China (Ke 2006). Per capita education expenditure provided by the government for urban residents was higher than for rural residents (Chow 2006). China's allocation for education budget was inadequate for rural communities (Tomasevski 2002). The government's under-funding of education in rural areas over the last decade has created serious and widespread problems, especially in rural areas where the bulk of the funding for schools' day-to-day operations often comes from fees charged to parents. The high cost and poor quality of the rural school system has led to increasing numbers of children dropping out of school early and going into work while still below the legal minimum employment age of 16.

Despite the government's attempt to improve education, there is a low level of public support for education in most provinces of China. Since schooling is mostly funded at the local level, rich provinces tend to produce more human capital per capita than do poor provinces. Resource constraints have created different levels of access to schooling in different parts of the country (Knight and Song 1999). The result of long-term neglect due to insufficient funding of education has left nearly one-fifth of the Chinese people illiterate.

The place of a person's birth is one of the most important determinants of that person's adult skill level (Knight and Song 1999). The created serious regional disparities has been a source of inequality in Chinese society across people contemporaneously and across generations. This inequality has been reinforced by the vestiges of *hukou* policy that charges additional fees from children of interregional immigrants for schooling that can amount to as much as 10 per cent of a family's total income (Xie 1999).

China has a literacy rate of 80 per cent compared to 60 per cent at the end of the Cultural Revolution. The mid-1980s policy to provide universal education for grades one through nine has helped the literacy rate among people between the ages of 12 and 40 to reach 96 per cent by 2005. Despite China achieving enough of the basics of education, Chinese planners worry that the system cannot accommodate the next stage of growth and want policy focus to shift to pedagogical quality.

Higher education was not open to ordinary people until the late nineteenth century, when the first modern Chinese higher institution was established during the Qing Dynasty (Constant et al. 2010). During 1912–49, Western university models began to gain in popularity and Chinese students were sent abroad to learn advanced technologies. By 1949, 205 universities had been founded in China (Brandenburg and Zhu 2007). The beginning of the People's Republic of China (PRC) in 1949 heralded an end to educational expansion. By 1953, the number of comprehensive universities had fallen from 49 to 13. Colleges specializing in applied subjects, such as medicine and agriculture, were spared (Ouyang 2004). Many universities were forced to close between 1966 and 1971. Shortly after, they were allowed to reopen, but the emphasis was on political studies rather than a standard college curriculum (Zhang et al. 2007). Deng Xiaoping's opening up in the late

1970s brought about many reforms in higher education. A two-way approach was implemented—that of learning from the West and that of attracting the West to China. In 1977 China resumed the National College Entrance Examination, granting more people the opportunity of higher education (Mullins 2005). The academic system was based on British and American models, with associate degrees offered by short-cycle colleges, and bachelor's, master's and doctoral degrees granted by standard institutions of higher education; a post-doctoral research system was also enacted (Constant et al. 2010).

Since 1978, the number of higher education institutions has increased from 600 to more than 2,000, accompanied by student enrolment of 20 million now (Constant et al. 2010). Since 1990, the Chinese government and the Ministry of Education have initiated, sponsored and carried through various programmes to encourage highly talented Chinese expatriates to return and contribute to the country's economic reform and human capital. Returning scholars have played a leading role in fostering new high-tech start-ups and upgrading educational institutions (Naughton 2007).

Vocational Training

Following progress in agriculture production during the 1980s, an increasing proportion of rural labourers were no longer needed to farm their traditional crops of wheat and corn. Around 1990, there was a surplus of 100 million rural labourers. Accordingly, production patterns and income sources needed to be expanded. In the context of this development, the Chinese government proposed a rural economic pattern late in the 1980s known as the 'integrated development of agriculture, science/technology and education'. It aimed to disseminate relevant scientific knowledge and technologies of production among rural community members, especially the youth, through both formal and non-formal methods of education. China has succeeded in providing basic learning to all people, through a massive literacy campaign and the universalization of the nine-year compulsory education. Among the active rural labourers, 60 per cent have completed their nine years of schooling and have received short-term vocational skill training. There are only 16 qualified technicians for every million farmers.

The government has introduced a number of measures, both at national and provincial level to try to overcome financial barriers and ensure that as many vocational students stay on in school—this includes a national scheme to offer an annual subsidy of CNY 1500 (Yuan renminbi) to students in VET (Vocational Education and Training) schools, largely covering their fees by making tuition free. China has strong arrangements to ensure that teachers in vocational schools remain abreast of the requirements of modern industry. Teachers in vocational schools are required to spend one month in industry each year, or two months every two years. In addition, many schools employ a significant number of part-time teachers who also work in industry (OECD 2010).

Workplace training is actively encouraged by government subsidies and current policy is that each student should spend one year on workplace training during their upper secondary programme. But cooperation with employers is variable. There are few quality standards for workplace training and few regional, sectoral, or national bodies to engage employers and to link them to the vocational training system (OECD 2010).

There are also clear minimum standards for vocational schools in terms of equipment, teachers and so on. While there are some national guidelines, they are only implemented where resources are available. (OECD 2010).

Social Capital in China: Guanxi

Social capital in China is synonymous with the concept of *guanxi*. The Chinese phrase 'guanxi' consists of two characters. The character *'guan'* means a gate or a hurdle, and *'xi'* refers to a tie, relationship, or a connection. Guanxi literally means 'pass the gate and get connected'. Guanxi refers to a social connection and includes special favours and obligations to the guanxi circle. Individual rights within the Chinese context are not universalistic, but guanxi-specific and particularistic, that is no ties, no obligations, and no rights. Guanxi substitutes for impersonal market transactions where such markets are restricted; thus guanxi refers to social relations involving the exchange of favours or a reliance on personal connections and networks of mutual dependence, in addition to obligation and indebtedness (Walder 1996; Yang 1994). In effect, guanxi involves the use of personal relationships, obligation, and reciprocity in relationships.

These informal connections are said to be essential in gaining approval for or access to just about everything in China. Such interpersonal relationships in China can be categorized into three groups; between family members; between familiar people, such as neighbours, friends, and colleagues; and between strangers or mere acquaintances. When Chinese people talk about guanxi, they often imply an interpersonal relationship outside the family, primarily with a familiar person, because the relationship between family members is that of an expressive tie, and obligations are dutifully assumed (Walder 1996; Yang 1994).

There are three components of guanxi: (1) *Ganqing* (emotions or effect)—Ganqing refers to human feelings and is related to enduring and emotional commitments found in long-term and intimate social bonds, such as those between parents and their children, close friends, and teachers and students. (2) *Renqing* (reciprocal favour)—Reciprocity in Chinese is called *bao* or *huibao* and reciprocal favour is called renqing. If a personal relationship partner gets into difficulties, the partner should help him or her and afterwards, the recipient of the favour should return it as soon as the opportunity arises. Reciprocal favour is a strong social norm and is morally binding for Chinese people; those who do not repay favours are considered to have 'no credibility', 'no conscience'; they lose face, reputation, and ultimately personal relationships and their peers' trust. (3) *Mianzi* (face preserving)—Face, in this context, refers to a person's claimed sense of positive image in a relational context. It is gained by performing one or more specific social roles which are well recognized by others. Face is lost when people, either through their actions or the actions of those closely related to them, fail to meet essential requirements placed on them by virtue of their social position. The Chinese idiom 'would rather make sacrifices than lose face' illustrates the importance of face. The norm of preserving face in Chinese society encourages people to play proper social roles, to meet the requirements of, and to be liked by peers of, the same affiliated group (Walder 1996; Yang 1994).

Guanxi is first and foremost about the cultivation of long-term personal relationships, but those relationships depend on trust; and therefore trust is the precondition for the establishment of successful and enduring guanxi (Tung and Worm 2001). Trust, in the Chinese context, is a two-dimensional construct that includes perceived credibility and benevolence. The first dimension focuses on the credibility of an exchange partner with the expectation that the partner's words or written statements are reliable. The second dimension, benevolence, is the extent to which a partner is genuinely interested in the other partner's welfare and is motivated to pursue joint gain. For in-group relationships, in which expressive ties are predominant, Chinese people pay more attention to attachment, harmony, and long-term relationships by going along with the group and avoiding rejection. For out-group relationships, in which instrumental ties are predominant, people distrust one another and treat each person like a guest, but guard against him/her like a thief. Trust is an important variable that greatly influences interpersonal and intergroup behaviour. It affects relational expectations regarding the resolution of conflicts of interests and the enhancement or diminution of solidarity (Wong 1998). Trust is creating and consolidating the triangularity of mianzi, renqing, and ganqing, which makes the informal, unofficial phenomenon of guanxi tangible and lasting. The production of guanxi simultaneously creates human feeling and material obligation; therefore, in guanxi feeling and instrumentality are a totality.

Because China is a transitional economy with many uncertainties, particularly of a legal nature, guanxi has become vital for securing continuity and relative stability. Guanxi networks have become a force for economic evolution in China, helping the country overcome the lack of institutional infrastructure. The existence of these networks has complemented the development of markets and institutional capital. Although, the phenomenon of guanxi is ubiquitous, widely known, and generally understood, its workings are hidden. Guanxi networks are like the hand inside the 'glove' represented by formal institutions (Parnell 2005).

For businesses, Guanxi possesses the capacity to reduce transaction costs associated with environmental uncertainties, such as communicating, negotiating, and coordinating transactions, as well as maladaptation and/or failure to adapt. The development of a guanxi network reduces costs associated with searching for partners (Standifird and Marshall 2000). As in other instances of initial capitalist accumulation, during China's first decades of reform, private firms faced government predation, ambiguous and fluid institutions, and barriers to markets. Therefore, the cultivation of long-term, reliable guanxi built the trust that was necessary to conduct business transactions and was essential for survival. Guanxi networks enabled firms to influence policymaking, gain timely information on policy changes, access bank credit, and create greater certainty in their business environments (Standifird and Marshall 2000).

The guanxi-based network has become arguably the most effective mechanism for turning the economic engine that has driven wealth creation and prosperity in the GSCS (Greater Southeastern China Sub-region). The phenomenon began with Hong Kong and Taiwanese residents returning to visit the villages and towns of their ancestral origins. These visits provided the occasion and opportunity for initiating business deals that included making philanthropic donations and setting up factories, sometimes using the former to realize the latter. Typically, factories in the region have connections with or are owned by the mainland relatives or close friends of the respective Hong Kong investors/contractors. The factories provided investment confidence and exchange reliability based on the mutual trust established by the kinship or close social relationships between Hong Kong investors and their mainland subcontractors. These networks contributed to the establishment of thousands of small and medium sized manufacturing enterprises that produce labour-intensive consumer goods for export. In addition, hometown connections led wealthy overseas Chinese to fund large scale infrastructure projects such as highways, power stations, hospitals, and universities in Guangdong and Fujian provinces (Wank 1998). At the firm level, these networks facilitated the recruitment and management of badly needed workers for labour-intensive manufacturing.

But there is a delicate balance between using trans-border social capital to generate economic benefits and not letting it induce undesirable behaviours and practices (Chen 2005). In southern China, hiring relatives and sticking with them even if they are not productive sustains a moral and social obligation, but the practice is economically inefficient (Smart 1993). By preferring to hire people from certain places, some employers tend to discriminate against using workers from other neighbouring provinces. Cross-border social capital does not always lead to business deals, which are often subject to arbitrary approvals by local officials. Local government officials are appeased through material or non-material gift exchanges (Smart and Smart 1991). This however has a tendency to slip into bribing and corruption. To minimize the downside of this type of social capital, however, such labour practices may and should be gradually replaced by formal administrative structures and impersonal market mechanisms with its form and functions modified or shifted as it evolves. Although this shift towards more formal institutions of law, market, and governance may weaken or deplete existing social capital, it eventually leads to a new type of social capital embedded in the economic system, rather than the other way around (Stiglitz 2000). Although the institutionalization of legal and economic rules is proceeding apace in China, guanxi networks have continued to penetrate business-industrial activities, lending China's emerging capitalism its unique characteristics (McNally et al. 2007).

Institutional Capital in China

Economic reform in China is a partial reform strategy, characterized by institutional innovations and regional experimentation. Reform began in the countryside with early successes in the Township and Village Enterprises (TVEs). The creation of TVEs in 1979 injected industry and market orientation into the rural economy, which, at the time, was characterized by abundant labour. Before TVEs, the Household Responsibility System (HRS) gave incentives to farmers so they could retain some return on their effort within a framework of communal ownership of land (see the section on HRS in the chapter). These reforms re-oriented national savings to households, created a profit motive in an economy that did not recognize private property, and re-allocated the essential factor of labour to more productive enterprises. Output grew rapidly in the early 1980s, leading to the observation that China's growth began in the countryside so when these rural measures were seen to be successful, China introduced reforms in urban areas in 1984. Managers in state-owned enterprises (SOEs) were granted more autonomy and allowed to retain a portion of profits (Xiao Zhou 1996).

In allowing enterprises to sell part of their output at market prices, the authorities were able to control the sale of goods to the administered part of the market in order to implement the partial liberalization strategy. At the same time, China sustained a degree of decentralization that permitted regional experimentation with marketization to take place. The final prong of China's reform approach was the 'open door' policy whereby China created Special Economic Zones (SEZs) initially in two southern provinces, which were essentially export-processing zones (EPZs) that were open to international trade and foreign investment. The introduction of market forces into SEZs allowed the government to experiment with a limited degree of opening. These measures began in 1979, but did not take off until 1992. Since then, China has created further forms of SEZs, such as Free Trade Zones (FTZs) and High-technology Development Zones (HTDZs), which are geared at attracting foreign investment in technology sectors and promoting research and development.

Following several amendments to the Constitution in 1988, 1993, and 1999, promoting private sector and implementing the basic principle of running the country according to the law has become the fundamental direction for China's transition. China has constantly strengthened the economic legistation required by the market economy; for example, Company Law (1993), the Partnership Enterprise Law (1997), the individual owned Enterprise Law (1999) and the Property Law (2007).

Despite these trends towards greater recognition of private property, insecure property rights, government discrimination, and legal and political uncertainty have fostered a culture of opaqueness, informality, and collusion in China's private sector. The politically questionable status of private firms in Chinese history has resulted in many private entrepreneurs employing hybrid forms of ownership and colluding with local government institutions and officials (IFC 2000). These arrangements have created manifold opportunities for rent seeking and corruption (IFC 2000).

Formal institutions, particularly those that are required to support contracting and reduce the risk of appropriation, are still considered weak in China. China has not had formal property rights conventionally defined and only in 2004 recognized the existence of private property when the notion was included in the constitution. But China has successfully established a system of contracted-for rights spanning its institutional innovations, such as those governing households, firms, and even local governments, as well as foreign enterprises. This system of legally defined but arguably informal property rights has stimulated

China's impressive economic growth during the reform period, despite the incomplete legal system.

The Chinese financial system is characterized by a large and dominant banking sector consisting of four large state-owned banks and several minor players that include policy banks. Lending to SOEs is considered a low-risk option by these banks, leaving companies in the private sector credit constrained. Given the state of China's banking system and capital markets, curb market finance (finance provided outside of general market regulations) has played a significant role in the Chinese economy by serving the needs of the private entrepreneurs who have been shut out of the formal banking system (Allen et al. 2006; Tsai 2002). In addition to informal associations, there were also private money houses and underground lending organizations that function like banks but charge very high interest rates (Farrell et al. 2006). While these were technically illegal since they charged interest rates above the state-mandated interest rate ceilings, most forms of informal finance that private entrepreneurs used fell into the realm of quasi-legality because while they were not sanctioned by the People's Bank of China, but were legally registered by another government agency (Tsai 2002).

China lacks some of the key institutional foundations of a market economy, which 'makes it impossible to efficiently carry out other important changes in the economic structure through the decentralized processes of the market. Instead decisions have to be pushed up to higher level government bureaucrats in the ministries or elsewhere' (Perkins 2005: 31).

China's remarkable economic growth in recent decades despite poorly defined property rights, a relatively weak legal system, and a biased financial system presents a puzzle to the general literature of law, finance, and economic evolution.

In developing and transition countries, a lack of well-defined formal property rights and a legal system is the norm rather than the exception. When formal institutions are lacking, societies may attempt to evolve along the path of existing institutional capital to protect their economic activities (Dixit 2004). In developing countries, social arrangements become equally important as the state institutions, and that small institutional changes specific to the context makes a big difference to growth (Rodrik 2003).

China's Growth Phases

China's growth experience is divided into three phases and each phase focuses on the simultaneous interaction between human capital, social capital, and institutional capital and its role in explaining the growth pattern during that time period.

China's reform-driven growth experience saw three distinct phases. The first phase involved market-oriented economic reform, which was launched in 1978 when the Third Plenary Session of the 11th Communist Party of China (CPC) Central Committee adopted a set of policies whose objective was to reform the domestic economy and open it to the outside world. These reforms dissolved the communes and replaced them with the rural household responsibility system. Under this system, farmers were given the right to use the land and considerable management autonomy, resulting in rapidly increased farm productivity. By 1984, 99 per cent of Chinese rural population became part of the rural household responsibility system. The second phase, which began in 1984, was the growth of rural enterprises which forced urban reforms, in which SOEs were restructured. This restructuring emphasized reforming management practices, providing incentives to workers, developing a dual pricing system, and introducing contract labour practices to improve labour productivity and efficiency. Many inefficient SOEs were gradually replaced by collective entities and private firms. The third phase was the growth of private enterprises, which began in 1992. Special economic zones were introduced in China's coastal cities, followed by ownership reforms of many large SOEs. Chinese financial firms, such as large state banks, were restructured to get them prepared to be listed in overseas and domestic stock markets. Huge injections of foreign capital followed, drastically increasing the contribution of MNCs in China's economic growth. China's acceptance into the World Trade Organization (WTO) in 2001 further accelerated the pace of economic growth and speeded up China's integration into the world economy. These reforms made it possible for China to sustain average economic growth rates of about 9 per cent per annum in the past decade.

Household Responsibility System

This section looks at how the combination of human capital, social capital and institutional capital made the first growth phase in China a success and how this phase laid the foundation for later reforms that were carried out in urban areas. Economic growth was extremely volatile in the pre-reform period (1954–77), with the rate of growth ranging from 21.3 per cent in 1958 to −27.3 per cent in 1961 (Chow 2006; Dernberger 1980; Lin et al. 1996; Rawski 1994). Starting in 1978, several factors, such as development of the rural non-farming sector, massive inflow of foreign capital, structural transformation, reform-induced efficiency improvement, and promotion of trade, played an important role in China's transformation into an increasingly dominant player in the global economy. A large part of China's success in raising rural incomes originated from a series of reforms in agriculture in the late 1970s and early 1980s. During this period, China's policy for rural areas evolved toward a more market-based approach and involved a relaxation of agricultural controls and a less centralized production system called the household responsibility system (HRS). In addition, other policy changes were introduced, which included market and planning reforms designed to reduce excessive production quotas and promote the functioning of local free markets, and pricing reforms in which the government dramatically raised agricultural prices that had been suppressed for almost three decades under central planning (Yang and Li 2008). These reforms contributed to a stronger diversification of economic activities and to a more autonomous rural governance system.

The traditional farming institution in rural China, prior to the founding of the PRC, was the independent family farm. Farmers were given the land in the late 1940s and early 1950s in recognition of their support for the Communist Party. But they never received titles and, by 1958, all their productive property and all the land had been socialized, without any compensation. During the famine period, there were a number of reform efforts to overcome the worst incentive drawbacks of the commune system, including lending land to the farmers and giving discretion to the brigades. But those experiments lasted only a few years. Under the commune system, a mixture of egalitarianism, state interference in collective decisions and poorly designed payment methods meant that there was very little relation between labour productivity and reward. Total factor productivity in the collective system was about 20 to 30 per cent lower than in the household system. Farmers, especially the very poor, made several efforts to break away from the rigidity of the communes.

Institutional emergence and change arise from a structured bargaining between actors who agree to a self-organizing governance system when they organize themselves into groups and networks.

After Mao's death in 1976, a number of experiments that assigned land to individual households or small groups of households began. Some of those experiments were individual, with cadres being bribed to permit a family to farm a plot of land. Much of the experimentation occurred in Sichuan and Anhui Provinces, with encouragement from the provincial leaders. The experiments sanctioned the assignment of land to small groups of households, but not to individual households. To some degree the early support for the more modest reforms was a plan designed to prevent the spread of assigning land to individual households—what later became the HRS.

The HRS started in early 1979 when 20 villagers of Xiaogang Village in Fengyang County, Anhui Province, illegally signed a secret contract with the village cadre. This contract not only gave them the right to use and gain from the land, but it also obliged them to submit the specified amount of grain to the government. Later their contract idea was used in other rural areas and was promoted by the federal government. The production responsibility system was regarded as federal government policy in two kinds of circumstances: (1) in poor and backward areas, where the population had 'lost faith in the collective', and (2) where household contracting had already been carried out and was found satisfactory (Xiao Zhou 1996).

In late 1981, when full official approval of the household system in agriculture was eventually given, 45 per cent of the collectives in China had already been torn down, and by the end of 1983, 98 per cent of the collectives had adopted the household system. As a result of this swift decollectivization, agricultural performance dramatically improved, with output value growing around 9 per cent per year between 1978 and 1984. However, only about half of this growth was attributable to the institutional change of adopting the HRS. The other half was the result of price and market reforms because higher prices and market opportunities induced farmers to raise their cropping intensity and to use more productive inputs such as fertilizers and machinery (Lin 1992). In 1984, the federal government announced a new decision to extend the state lease of land use by farmers. To encourage rural households to invest in the land, the federal government promised that the lease period would be at least 15 years. This fortified farmers' confidence in the government and drove another wave of economic growth (Qiu 2008).

The reform of the communes and their eventual abolition was due to a bottom-up process. In effect, what began as a social capital experiment, started 'illegally' by farmers and cadres, quickly developed into a country-wide movement of farmers seeking family gains. As a group they had the bargaining power to negotiate with the village cadres. The strength of this farmer movement was that it was not an organized resistance. The leadership did not support assigning land to households in the beginning but was forced to recognize the system as legal and to promote it when HRS improved agricultural production and reduced poverty. The success of HRS convinced Chinese leaders to undertake urban reform. A social capital–generated movement led to ground-breaking changes at the institutional level. The government recognized and accepted the autonomous efforts of farmers as legal and encouraged HRS, which challenged the government's earlier focus on urban industrial development and its view of the agricultural sector primarily as a source of subsidized food for urban Chinese. This breakthrough has been crucial for China's current modernization. An experiment with the attributes of social capital and human capital successfully led to changes in institutional capital.

A society well-endowed in human capital is highly interconnected, sharing information and strengthening knowledge through a never-ending web of connections.

Under HRS, land was distributed almost equally to every household. Each farming household acquired small plots of land dispersed over a large area. Households negotiated to work a particular plot in exchange for a portion of their crops which were used to pay for collective expenses. Any surplus output over the quotas needed to pay collective expenses could be kept and sold by the farmer, thus farmers' earnings were directly linked to their productive output. Additionally, farmers gained control over some capital assets such as draft animals, smaller implements and machinery, and houses (Ng et al. 1998). Driven by personal interests and market mechanism, farmers made decisions with the objective of obtaining optimal returns. As a result, there was an **unprecedented period of increased motivation in improving productivity.** Farmers used better technology, fertilizers, and varieties of seeds leading to a rapid increase in productivity per hectare and per worker. Farm families made effective use of the land around their houses and gardens to produce for the markets. Farmers were motivated to produce more suitable, more diverse, and more profitable crops from medicinal herbs to fruits, vegetables, and other specialty items. These farmers were increasingly motivated to use seeds from outside their locality to experiment with hybrid seeds. The striking aspect of the rapid increase in productivity in China was its long duration (1978–92) and diversity of agricultural products affected (Xiao Zhou 1996). Farmers visited their friends and relatives in different villages to learn about and procure the best seeds, with each new kind of hybrid seed bringing new technology. Farmers either studied about the new technology or learnt from other farm households that were using scientific knowledge (Xiao Zhou 1996).

The accumulation of scientific knowledge saw an increase in the demand of new inputs as well as the diversifying of agricultural investments, which put pressure on the need for more highly educated farmers. Education played an increasingly dominant role in the agricultural economy as agriculture evolved and technology was more extensively used. The country's basic education (reading, writing, counting, and the ability to absorb scientific knowledge) and technological education (advanced skills, for example, the adoption of improved variety of seeds, the scientific application of fertilizer, water efficiency, irrigation to aid farmers' technical efficiency, and knowledge about information and management) helped farmers to understand market information and operate accordingly, make decisions on what products should be produced, which would improve their net income and the farm yield per capita (Jing-zhi 2002).

Social capital and informal institutions direct attention to relationships that shape the realization of human capital's potential for the individual and for the network.

The state, however, was unprepared to deal with the increased farm production; its commercial organizations were not equipped to deal with 200 million farmer households. The government lacked storage facilities for the increased farm produce. Farmers also successfully manipulated the state procurement system so much so, raising the state's financial burden to an extent that the state was forced to abandon its procurement system by 1985. The state was equally unable to meet the new consumption needs of farmers. After HRS, increases in productivity enabled the farmers to have more cash to buy desired farm inputs and consumer goods. The government's inability to deal with rural abundance sparked initiatives from farmers, including independent marketing of their own produce (Xiao Zhou 1996).

Farmers used their social capital to coerce village cadres to enter into secret contracts to till the land and gain from it. Human capital accumulated through formal and informal education and personal motivation helped farmers to produce higher output from which profits were generated. These profits helped farmers to gain leverage with village cadres. Bribery and guanxi allowed farmers to continue with their surreptitious economic activities and to undermine, avoid, and evade government control, forcing the state to initiate further reforms. In this case, the combination of human capital and social capital successfully forced institutions to change and adapt (Xiao Zhou 1996).

The creation and strengthening of networks increase due to the necessity of networks to counteract individual disadvantage against under-developed or entirely missing institutions.

While farmers tried to co-opt village cadres through bribes at the beginning of the reforms, as farmers' economic power slowly increased, they used their social capital and established informal institutions which either functioned as marketing or finance channels. The HRS itself emerged in a community of acquaintance. At the beginning, HRS was only regulated by guanxi without being recognized by policies or laws. Farmers sought mutual aid by setting up neighbourhood or kinship associations such as *hui*—associations in which several households from the same locality or relatives pooled their money to help someone in need. The hui was a way of starting up private farm businesses, functioning as a network for capital formation. Farmers also established the *xiehui* (mutual assistance association), which were first organized among farmer households that specialized in commodity products. The chief purpose of xiehui was to provide farmers with information about production and marketing. Their primary motto was self-reliance and self-help. Another focus of xiehui was the farm produce itself. For example, chicken producers organized themselves into a chicken xiehui and cotton growers into a cotton xiehui. They exchanged information on market, new technologies, and state policies. These associations greatly altered dependency relations in the countryside and reduced cadres' control over information and the market. Xiehui often extended over many provinces, providing mechanisms for members to evade local intervention, effectively becoming marketing organizations for farmers (Xiao Zhou 1996). Networks of farmers came together this way by pooling together their human capital and social capital to counteract underdeveloped and missing institutions (Xiao Zhou 1996).

The HRS brought many changes to the Chinese countryside and resulted in introducing dynamism to the rural economy. The most rapid growth in the agricultural sector occurred in the first half of the 1980s, but then it subsequently slowed.

The slowdown in agricultural growth is attributed to the considerable level of uncertainty and insecurity in terms of land tenure rights, land use and transfer rights, and village policies regarding land management. As the power of cadres was undermined by the increase in the farmers' income, the cadres were determined to reverse that trend. Local cadres wielded considerable power to set land regulations and policies. The practice of readjusting village landholdings to reflect household population changes, redistributing land rents to favoured groups, moving land to higher valued uses,[1] and taking land away from households that did not meet tax obligations presented the greatest obstacle to farmers' long-term tenure security under the HRS. Given the almost universal adoption of the HRS form of agricultural management within China, and despite the fact that the Chinese federal government consistently supported improved land-tenure security and land-transfer rights for agricultural households in its policy statements, land rights in China varied significantly from county to county and even from village to village (OECD 2000).

The land tenure system has been unable to raise agriculture productivity further. Frequent land readjustments and unclear land tenure rules and their arbitrary implementation and enforcement by local officials have led to conflict situations between farmers and local governments (OECD 2000).

Despite the unfair land tenure system, HRS successfully breathed life and brought dynamism into the rural economy by realigning the relationship between village cadres and farmers. The HRS increased the agricultural output by more than 61 per cent and agricultural productivity by 78 per cent in that period (McMillan et al. 1989). As a result of the agriculture reform's success, the commune system was officially abandoned in 1984. Consequently, commune governments were converted into township governments, whose major function was transformed from agriculture to managing or setting up TVEs.

Township-Village Enterprises

Township-village enterprises were a major component of China's rapid industrialization since the 1980s. TVEs played a key role in fostering entrepreneurship and served as a stepping-stone for institutional changes when legal protections of private property rights were not in place as SOEs were slow to react to changing market demand. A basic feature of TVEs was the deep involvement of local governments, particularly the township governments (Xu 2008).

As productivity increased in the farming sector because of HRS, farmers experienced an unprecedented increase in their income. Also, rural savings expanded and surplus rural labour emerged rapidly in the early 1980s. This increase in income meant that demand for many daily consumer products rose. At the same time, rural residents were prohibited from migrating to the cities due to the stringent household registration system. As a result, farmers developed their own industrial sector, the so-called TVEs.

The growth and development of TVEs in China is distinct in the world and was directly the result of rural–urban segregation and of disallowing farmers from changing their occupations and dwelling places under the hukou. China's rural industrialization was characterized by the principle of 'leaving the farm but not the community'. The TVE sector was the most dynamic sector and essentially became the main driving force for China's economic growth in the 1980s. In terms of employment, the TVE sector overtook the state sector in 1990. By 2001, its size was more than twice as great as the state sector. Though individual TVEs vary in scale, some of them have become multinational corporations (MNCs), such as Haier (Naughton 1995; Peng 2001; Rawski 1994; Wong 1988).

Officially, TVEs were collectively-owned enterprises located in townships or villages. All the people in the township or village that set up the TVE owned the firm collectively. A township government was regarded as the representative of the people in the community, and thus it was the de facto executive owner of the TVE. Typically the control rights of TVEs were partly delegated to managers through a contract (the management responsibility contract). It was common for employees of a TVE to collectively sign a contract with the executive owner—the township government (Weitzman and Xu 1994). As the de facto executive owners of the TVEs, local governments had a strong incentive to promote TVEs in their communities. But their method of involvement was not necessarily the same across regions, as the following three models demonstrate. First, the 'Sunan' model, which refers to the governance mode of TVEs located in the southern Jiangsu province. In the Sunan model, local/community government officials were the leading entrepreneurs. They set up the TVEs, took business risks, were in charge of the TVEs' daily operations, helped obtain credit from state banks, secured land to build factories, won access to raw materials, and built marketing channels, sometimes through their connections with SOEs. Second, the 'Guangdong' model refers to the features of TVEs in the Pearl River delta area. The Guangdong model was characterized by the local government's presence with heavy FDI involvement, which also brought in technology, management know-how, and marketing channels in the international market. Third, in the Wenzhou model, more institutional innovations were made to promote private ownership and cluster-based[2] production. In Wenzhou, most businesses were driven by private entrepreneurs. The critical role of local government was to provide a favourable business environment, particularly protection. Although development of private business is the central feature of the Wenzhou model, the constitution of China did not protect private property rights until 2004. To avoid direct conflicts with the legal system and with political resistance, many private enterprises resorted to cover-up practices such as attaching themselves to state agents (what is referred to as TVEs wearing as red hats[3]). With the 'red hat', the enterprises not only managed to legalize their private enterprises but also gained access to formal financing. In 1985, top national leaders visited Wenzhou and gave a nod to the practice of private firms' wearing a 'red hat'. In 1987, the State Council officially approved Wenzhou as one of the national rural pilot reforms with a focus on TVE institutional building (Zhu 2007). The so-called pilot reform was centred on developing regulatory remedies to allow private business to develop in the absence of constitutional protection of private property rights. In the same year, a regulation was officially issued in Wenzhou that gave private businesses legal identity and status (Xu and Zhang 2009).

Local governments had a strong incentive to promote TVEs, so they assisted TVEs in securing reliable access to resources they needed, especially those in short supply. They also oversaw local labour markets and appointed managers of TVEs, served as intermediaries in critical negotiations with banks for access to credit, fixed local prices on select number of commodities, and approved and coordinated investment of extra budgetary funds under their control for projects proposed by TVEs. In short, local governments provided the backing and resources needed by entrepreneurs to compete effectively. The network between rural entrepreneurs and local governments was one of the key factors that contributed to the success of TVEs as it worked as a bargaining tool for the rural entrepreneurs in their negotiations with banks, SOEs, state commercial bureaus, and the government-run department stores.

The TVE performance was spectacular. Between 1981 and 1990, the total industrial output of TVEs grew at an average annual rate of 28.1 per cent, which was double the national average and more than triple that of the state sector. With the rapid growth of TVEs, the status of the TVE sector changed from a subsidiary subsector of agriculture to the second largest sector in the national economy. In the non-state sector, about 80 per cent of the output was produced by TVEs. The TVE sector outcompeted the state sector in both growth rate and productivity (Qian and Xu 1993). The growth rate of total factor productivity of TVEs was about 10 times that of state enterprises (Weitzman and Xu 1994).

The development of TVEs peaked in the mid-1990s. In 1995, employment in the TVE sector reached 61 million and TVEs' share of GDP hit 37.5 per cent, up from 14.3 per cent in 1980. Despite many disadvantages, like access to raw materials and less educated personnel, rural industries survived because their budget constraints forced them to make good products, respond to customer desires, and operate efficiently (Xiao Zhou, 1996). The success of the TVEs rose from their internal institutional form, which facilitated cooperation through implicit contracts among community members (Weitzman and Xu 1993). TVEs relied more on personal ties than on legal contracts to provide assurances that the terms of a transaction would be met by both parties (Carroll et al. 1988). At the early stage of these enterprises, village institutional capital played a very active role, and guanxi helped to reduce the cost of market operation. The demographic stability of

China's rural communities promoted the emergence of 'invisible institutional capital' to provide a 'moral framework for rights' or a 'cooperative culture' (Byrd and Lin 1990). As TVE employees and managers and a substantial number of township-village officials had lived in the same community for generations, close long-term interactions among community members fostered social norms within the community and implicit contractual relationships between community governments and TVEs, between TVE employees, and between TVEs themselves (Weitzman and Xu 1994).

While the market was underdeveloped, guanxi enabled budding entrepreneurs to develop themselves through long-term interpersonal interaction in the community (relations based on blood, marriage, friendship, and locality) and build the trust of villagers, which significantly reduced the cost of cooperation. Guanxi also helped to overcome the problem of collective ownership. Informal ties between local governments and TVEs encouraged the former to promote local industry because of the importance of TVE profits in local government budgets and the close links between local economic performance and the status, income, and career prospects of local officials. Local government officials also provided protection from some of the excesses of the Chinese business environment, including predation from SOEs and other favoured market players (Luo et al. 1998). Region-specific local social norms and trust were two of the important factors that facilitated TVEs.

The managers and employees of TVEs had only recently stopped working on the land and in fact some still worked part time as employees and part time as farmers. Peasant entrepreneurs compared favourably in almost all aspects except education—they were market-oriented, motivated by achieving business success, enjoyed autonomy, and took high initiative. But most peasant entrepreneurs had only limited formal education; the competitive marketplace rendered their existing knowledge and skills inadequate. They urgently needed to learn about modern production and management techniques in order to remain competitive. Enterprise management was far from professional and proficient. Managers were also from the local community and had a poor educational background. They had strong incentives to develop their business but lacked skills to deal with market competition and to improve internal efficiency. The shortage of competent engineers and technicians also undermined the improvement of TVE technological management.

To circumvent employees' low level of technical education,[4] TVEs relied on hiring or contracting with urban technicians and experienced workers to improve their human capital. In the 1970s, when TVEs just started, these firms relied on young urban technicians who were previously sent out to the countryside to be 're-educated' by peasants. At the beginning of the 1980s, when these young technicians returned to the cities, TVEs began contracting with retired urban technicians and experienced workers from SOEs by paying attractive salaries. Almost every TVE in the Yangtze River delta hired retired workers from Shanghai in their early stage of development. They brought information and expertise to the firms and contributed tremendously to the early development of the TVEs in that area. By the mid-1980s, their attention shifted to scientists and technicians working in research institutes and SOEs. By the 1990s, TVEs competed with large and medium sized SOEs for talented staff and attracting foreign experts (Harvie 1999; Wang and Yao 2003). By developing joint ventures and sub-contracts with foreign firms, TVEs—especially in coastal areas—gradually upgraded their technology and many of them were involved in joint ventures with foreign companies. By employing technocrats from urban areas, the rural enterprises not only circumvented their lack of human capital but also developed inroads into the urban economy. By importing human capital and combining with the existing social capital, TVEs could successfully compete with SOEs forcing them to change and adapt.

The other constraint for TVEs was the lack of access to raw materials. Rural entrepreneurs rewarded anyone in the rural enterprise who, through personal connections, arranged to get raw materials or to expand the sales of rural products (Xiao Zhou 1996).

In the absence of institutionalized mechanisms, the strategic factor for success in China was not choosing the industrial sector but choosing the right people—inside and outside the firm. Chinese rural entrepreneurship did not only depend on an individual's faculty for identifying opportunities for profit, but also on 'the ability to form an alliance' with those who possessed or controlled financial or physical resources, or the human capital necessary for entering a market.

Thus, TVEs played a key role in fostering entrepreneurship and in creating economic conditions for private business and served as a major stepping-stone for institutional changes when legal protections of private property rights were not in place (Che and Qian 1998; Mukherjee and Zhang 2007; Weitzman and Xu 1994). TVEs adapted to the weak legal environment and local comparative advantages in China's transition from a planned to a market economy. In the early 1990s, policies were issued to protect the autonomy of TVEs. In 1996, the Township and Village Enterprise Law was enacted which required that formal contracts be established between TVEs and local governments. However, it was only during the period from 1978 to 1996 in which TVEs showed spectacular performance. TVEs, after reaching their peak in the mid-1990s, phased out quickly.

The post-1996 period was one of retrenchment. The rural industrialization that propelled the Chinese economy in the 1980s took a different turn in the 1990s. TVEs failed because the national environment became inhospitable towards rural entrepreneurship when the federal government tended to perceive TVEs as a threat because TVEs turned out to be a strong competitor for resources and markets, weakening the position of SOEs.

Concurrent with the decline of TVEs was the rise of private entrepreneurship firms, which were formally recognized by the Chinese constitution in 2004.

Private Entrepreneurship

Since the late 1990s, China's entrepreneurs have been the key drivers of growth. They created the de novo firms that formed the dynamic and innovative private sector—an essential force in any developing country (Wu 2002; Zhang et al. 2006). Since the start of the reform era in 1978, the private sector has grown at an annual rate of 20 per cent, far above the economy's 9 per cent average growth for the same period. More than 30 million private businesses have been established, which has contributed to a significant share of tax revenue to the government and employed millions of people laid-off from failed SOEs. The non-state sector in China accounts for two-thirds of total productivity and GDP. The dramatic growth in the share of self-employed entrepreneurs in the Chinese workforce has been most apparent in the rural areas where there were no recorded private enterprises until 1994. Overall, the increase in entrepreneurship in China has bode well for its sustained economic growth.

China's private sector development can be divided into three phases. During the first phase, from 1978 to 1984, private enterprises were restricted to small-scale private firms with no more than eight employees. During the second phase from 1984 to 1992, private enterprises grew in size and actual private firms were sanctioned in 1988. In 1987, the communist party reconfirmed that cooperative, collective, and private economies were important supplements to the socialist economy and encouraged their development. This change in policy saw a surge toward the private sector. The number of private enterprises grew 93 per cent in 1987 alone. But private firms continued to face political uncertainty, discrimination, and heavy restrictions, some of which were reinforced after the Tiananmen Square incident (student-led demonstrations over the direction of economic and political reforms) in 1989. Private entrepreneurs had to deal with hostility and social prejudice on the part of cadres and people in general who regarded them as dubious, ignoble, or even despicable.

During the third phase that ushered in after Deng Xiaoping's 1992 southern tour, new reforms generated a more tolerant environment for the private sector. One important legal move came with the promulgation of the Chinese company law in 1993. The implementation of this law generated the conditions for convergence among the governance structures of private and state-owned firms. Private firms switched from corporate structures with murky ownership to limited liability corporations. In 1997, the 15th party congress changed the position of the private economy from the previous 'supplement to the SOE' to an 'important component of the socialist market economy'. Recognition of China's private sector gathered further steam as China faced the prospect of increased competitive pressures from abroad after its entry into the WTO. In 2004, an amendment to Article 13 was passed at the National People's Congress which expanded protection of production, and the term 'ownership rights' was changed to 'property rights' to make the concept of 'rights' clearer and broader. This constitutional change triggered the promulgation of the Property Law in 2007, which codified earlier constitutional changes and afforded equal protection to state and private property. This gradual institutionalization of the external environment of private firms encouraged many aspiring entrepreneurs. Peasants, industrial workers, or urban youth 'sent down' to villages and towns during the Cultural Revolution formed the first business enterprises. Small-scale private enterprises emerged early in the manufacturing, construction, and transportation industries, followed by the professional services sector (Unger 1996; Zhou 2000). In urban areas, the lifetime employment system in SOEs strongly discouraged urban workers from venturing into private businesses. Not until the dismantling of the employment system and the massive layoffs accompanying the restructuring of SOEs in the mid-1990s did private Chinese firms begin to flourish (Knight and Yueh 2004). Thus the restructuring of the Chinese economy loosened fetters on business ventures.

Despite several economic, legal, and political measures that allowed private firms to clarify their ownership structures, Chinese government's policy has been volatile. Property rights are insecure and rule of law is still in its infancy; businesses remain subject to unpublished regulations and the caprices of courts. Entrepreneurs have to deal with local, provincial, and federal governments, which often have different and sometimes conflicting agendas and demands. In addition, entrepreneurs have limited access to credit. Aspiring entrepreneurs have also faced a shortage of key assets, such as land or property.

The adverse economic environment, institutional ambiguity, and the discrimination suffered by the private sector ultimately led to private entrepreneurs finding new ways to make their operation easier. Many private firms during the 1980s and 1990s chose murky ownership structures and relied on collusive practices with local governments. Guanxi networks with government officials and economic actors emerged as a necessary ingredient for protecting private ownership and gaining access to commercial opportunities. Thus, Guanxi, murky ownership structures, and interpersonal harmony became tools to hedge against an unpredictable environment. Interpersonal harmony and guanxi were important tools, not only for reducing risk, but also in dealing with intense market competition.

In the early stages, the private economy in China comprised family-based industrial plants, which produced small merchandise while simultaneously engaging in agricultural and industrial operations. With the help of local government-provided political and economic infrastructure, small entrepreneurial firms grew extremely rapidly, not only in numbers but also in efficiency. An important efficiency-enhancing trend was that many family-based plants in one village or a town came together to form an industrial cluster. People relied on family relationships and friends to establish mutual trust and cooperative relations to reduce uncertainties instead of signing business contracts. This was an important factor that enhanced the centralized structure of specialized production clusters for industrial division because it was based on the mode of one family, one product. These small firms were linked together by networks of sub-contracts, where each final product was produced by a collection of many specialized firms. With concentrations of a vast number of small specialized firms, townships in different provinces became national or international centres of certain products. For example, Datang township produces one-third of the world's socks, 40 per cent of the world's neckties are made in Shengzhou township (Xu and Zhang 2009), and Songxia township produces 350 million umbrellas per year (Hessler 2007). Industrial clusters also helped entrepreneurs to transform their informal inter-personal networks into informal and formal inter-organizational ties for information sharing and input–output transactions, which partly facilitated internationalization. Social networks provided knowledge of foreign market opportunities, advice and experiential learning, and referral trust and solidarity (Zhou et al. 2007).

In the urban areas, however, educated Chinese professionals mainly started their business ventures through organizational, career-based, and collegial networks (Salaff et al. 2006). The Chinese educational system had produced well-trained technicians and professionals, but prior to 1978, these workers were assigned to state-sector jobs where they finished their apprenticeships, became certified, and moved up the organizational ladder. In the years during which private enterprises were launched, many professionals and skilled workers left state firms, agencies, or joint ventures to start businesses of their own (Pearson 1997). They retained close ties, and got licenses, orders, materials, and funding through these organizational and political networks (Wank 1998). Often they mobilized colleagues to share the financing risks since it was hard to raise loans from state banks. They hired those with whom they had once worked, and got accounts from former clients as well. Having worked in the field, they knew about shortages of many commodities and services, and they bridged the structural holes to provide those commodities and services.

Thus, the development of the private sector in China was driven mainly by the growth of social capital–based agglomerative economies which created the knowledge necessary to exploit economies of scale and China built its place in exporting manufactured goods to the rest of the world again through its networks of overseas Chinese trading businesses.

* * *

The conventional mechanisms of growth in a typical market economy, such as private ownership, property rights security, financial liberalization, and reforms of political institutions were not central components of China's growth story. There exist two Chinas: an entrepreneurial rural China and a state-controlled urban China. The impressive growth story of China was set in motion in the rural areas where farmers were the driving force behind the social change that has taken place in the country since the early 1980s. Farmers took advantage of a small political opening and restored family autonomy in farming, created new markets, established rural industries, and migrated to cities despite rigid government controls. As a result, farmers have not only changed themselves but the urban Chinese and the institutional capital of the state. Their spontaneous yet effective movement was based on a mix of two intangible types of capital against an impassive state-run institutional setup.

TVEs fostered entrepreneurship in the 1980s and in early 1990s when market-based institutions, such as the legal protection of private property rights, were not in place. TVEs adapted well to the weak legal environment and local comparative advantages, that is, community social capital and a network between entrepreneurs and local officials, and flourished until the mid-1990s. But as underlying economic conditions changed, TVEs lost ground to large domestic firms because they did not represent an enduring organizational form. TVEs were also unable to survive the credit constraints imposed by the state when TVEs' performance threatened SOEs.

Private-sector growth in China also took place in an environment that was openly hostile to entrepreneurs and private businesses. Since 1978, several laws were enacted to encourage private enterprises, but

China 161

private firms continued to face political uncertainty, discrimination, and heavy restrictions. Guanxi, murky ownership structures, and interpersonal harmony thus became tools to hedge for an ever-changing environment. Under an unpredictable environment, the Chinese have learned to look after their own interests and to escape reliance on political systems so they display a high level of entrepreneurship.

An important trend that enhanced efficiency in the development of China's private sector was that family-based plants in one village or a town came together and formed an industrial cluster. Social capital embedded in industrial clusters helped entrepreneurs to form interorganizational ties. Social networks provided knowledge of foreign market opportunities, advice, referral, trust, and solidarity.

The three distinct growth phases in China show that the simultaneous interplay between human capital, social capital, and institutional capital has helped China deal with its complicated economic transition. The spontaneous economic experiments in rural China, based on social capital, influenced and changed state-run institutions, making China a unique bottom-up entrepreneurial economy.

Notes

1. Arable land under contract to village households was subsequently re-contracted by the village collective to non-villagers for cultivation. The motivation behind re-contracting was profit for the collective cadres, who could not legally impose contracting fees on the land if it was contracted directly to households, but could impose such fees on the third party contractor (Li Ping 2003).

2. Clustering is said to help stimulate knowledge flows through the formation of up-stream and down-stream linkages between firms (Porter 1995), raise local know-how through labour pooling and product specialization, allow the circulation of ideas and know-how through local labour mobility (Breschi and Malerba 2001; Glaeser 1998), and generate knowledge spillovers in the local industrial atmosphere (Marshall 1920) associated with product specialization. 'Social learning processes work smoothly between entrepreneurs in a cluster compared to the outside world, because of an abundance of strong and weak ties...facilitated by the geographical proximity of local entrepreneurs. Proximity promotes face-to-face interactions along with monitoring, and, hence, shared experiences and points of reference' (Lorenzen and Foss 2002).

3. In the early 1990s, many private businesses chose the strategy of 'wearing a red hat'—registering themselves as 'collective enterprises' (Che and Qian

1998; Gore 1998; Pearson 1997). The disguise of 'collective ownership' not only made these firms ideologically acceptable, it also won them material advantages, such as favorable tax treatment, and better access to credit and other resources (Naughton 1995; Nee 1992). The term 'red hat' meant that the firm could obtain a collective or state license for production and operations by paying certain administrative fees to the state, collective unit, or local government organization. Normally the fee was about 1–2 per cent of the firm's output value or 5–10 per cent of its turnover. After paying these fees, the private owner was able to evade government prohibitions on private firms and ideological harassment. According to a survey conducted in 1984, such firms made up 19 per cent of all collectives in Hebei, 30 per cent in Tianjin, 40 per cent in Liaoning and 50 per cent in Ningxia. Since the loosening of ideological and political constraints in the 1990s, many of these private entrepreneurs have sought a new and even more powerful 'red hat' by choosing to actively participate in politics (Li et al. 2008).

4. In the early 1990s, only about 200,000 employees in TVEs had a degree or higher education, and only 420,000 held a medium-level technical qualification. These two figures equalled to less than 1 per cent of their employees.

10 India
The Services Sector

This chapter focuses on the contribution of India's services sector to the country's recent economic expansion. The chapter specifically looks at the contribution of human capital, social capital, and institutional capital to the growth in the services sector in India. India's recent growth has been led by the dynamism of its services sector, particularly high-end, knowledge-intensive services exports. Services now occupy about 57 per cent of India's GDP, making the sector the most productive in India. The upward trend in services' share of Indian GDP has accelerated since the major economic reforms initiated in 1991. In 1970–1, services stood at just 39 per cent of GDP, but by 1990–1, they accounted 48 per cent, and by 2013, services' share of GDP had risen to 57 per cent. Deregulation, liberalization of foreign investment, greater private sector participation since 1991, increased industry outsourcing, and high income elasticity of demand for services have been the key factors driving the high growth in India's service sector (Gordon and Gupta 2004). The overall growth in services has grown at a faster pace than the economy since 1991. Certain services stand out in terms of their role in driving economic growth like the Information Technology–Information Technology-enabled Services (IT–ITeS) sector. Building on India's large pool of engineering talent and its rapidly expanding telecommunications sector, IT–ITeS have in recent years been the key catalyst of growth. Their success has come largely through rapid expansion of exports tapping into the increasing worldwide demand, as rapid advancements in telecommunications infrastructure enabled an increasing array of activities to be performed remotely.

The unique characteristic of services industry, such as its low dependence on large-scale investments, has helped it to escape the unwieldy investment related regulatory hurdles. Compared with the manufacturing sector, gross product in service sectors (outside of community, social, and personal services) is more concentrated in the largely unregulated 'unorganized' sector. Transport infrastructure shortcomings also tend to have less of a bearing on most service sectors. The government's light-handed approach to regulation in the sector, combined with a supportive policy environment, played a particularly important role in facilitating its growth. The expansion of IT–ITeS was helped by a number of other features, including India's large pool of qualified professionals, its widespread use of English, its rapidly increasing stable of world-class companies, and cost advantage over other locations. The rapid expansion of IT–ITeS had a significant impact on the broader Indian economy by generating substantial export earnings and tax revenue, creating significant numbers of high-quality jobs, and precipitating productivity-enhancing technology diffusion to other industries and the public sector. The industry consisted of more than 3,000 firms and exported US$ 47 billion of ITeS in 2008 (NASSCOM 2009).

India's IT industry took off in the late 1990s when the global IT industry was unable to meet the exponential growth in demand for IT services precipitated by Y2K compliance concerns. It has since benefited from rapid reductions in the cost of digitizing, transmitting, and processing information (Friedman 2005). In addition to being the largest exporter of ITeS–business process outsourcing (ITeS–BPO) services, India is a major exporter of IT services and software, which accounted for nearly two-thirds of total IT–ITeS exports. IT service and software exports contributed 3.3 per cent of the GDP in 2013. The ITeS-BPO segment was initially dominated by call centres and the undertaking of 'back-office' functions, but gradually there has been a shift towards the provision of higher value knowledge and analytic-based processes as capabilities improved. India has emerged as a prominent player in a number of these segments, and has helped to redefine which service components are tradable. India has gained strength in legal services (legal research, drafting contracts); engineering R&D; medical services (diagnostic services, telemedicine); education and training (tutorial services using Voice over Internet Protocol, curriculum design); software product development; market research; and data analytics (PricewaterhouseCoopers 2005). The outlook for India's IT–ITeS sector has remained buoyant. Observers anticipate a continuing trend over the coming years in trade in ITeS-BPO services, whether by outsourcing to third parties or by captive units (UNCTAD 2004).

Human Capital in India

Since the opening of the economy in the early 1990s and the subsequent evolution of India into a knowledge-based economy, the demand for higher levels of specific skills has been constantly increasing. Availability of skilled manpower is a critical success factor for driving the service sector, which in turn fuelled the development of a knowledge economy. Software, perhaps more than any other high-tech industry, relied more intensively upon human capital. Software services, the engine of the Indian software sector, was arguably even more human capital intensive than software products. According to National Association of Software and Service Companies (NASSCOM), to keep up its 30 per cent annual growth in IT services, India requires more than 65,000 newly graduated engineers a year.

According to the Indian constitution, higher education, particularly technical education, is the joint responsibility of the federal and provincial governments. The federal government is solely responsible for determining standards for teaching and research. The provincial governments are supposed to establish universities and colleges that meet these standards, allow private colleges to affiliate with universities, and the universities' funding and management. Prior to 1991, the federal government took the view that all higher education should be state provided. The division of responsibilities between the federal and state governments blurred when India's first Prime Minister ordered the federal ministry of education to establish universities directly controlled by the federal government. This was because the Prime Minister was keen to speed up the quality of technical education in order to realize his vision of the country as an industrial superpower. The Indian Institutes of Technology (IITs) were the outcome of that vision. There are 18 federally run universities out of a total of more than 300 universities that offer a higher quality of education than state universities for several reasons, including superior funding. Ministries of education at the federal and state level, departments of education, and various organizations like National Council of Educational Research and Training (NCERT), University Grants Commission (UGC), and All India Council of Technical Education (AICTE) regulate the education sector (Bagde 2008).

In 1981, the vast majority of engineering colleges were in the public sector, that is, funded by the federal or provincial governments and bound by their rules regarding admissions, salary, promotion, and tenure. Tuition fees were very low and the vast bulk of the expenses were met from the budgets of the respective provincial governments, with the exception of a few institutes and colleges directly supported by the federal government. Budget-constrained provincial governments faced severe limits on increasing capacity. Therefore capacity expansion in the public sector was infrequent, and mostly limited to accommodating new disciplines such as computer science in the 1990s and information technology in the early 2000s. Capacity expansion at existing institutions required approval of All India Council for Technical Education (AICTE). Access to engineering education was rationed for several years because expanding engineering education capacity was not a high priority for provincial and federal governments, due to the slow economic growth in the 1970s and 1980s when the social return to such investments was considered low. The private return, however, was high, especially for those engineers who went to work overseas. The effect of regulation on capacity expansion combined with states' constraints in adding capacity meant that new private colleges had to fulfil the gap in tertiary education and a key policy innovation was to allow privately-funded colleges to satisfy this latent demand (Bagde 2008).

A few states in southern India supported non-profit private tertiary education providers through subsidies. Private provision subsequently dramatically affected supply in these states. In spite of a negligible presence up till 1990, private providers account for half of the total undergraduate enrolment and more than 75 per cent of the number of degree-awarding institutions. In consequence of the past decade, India has seen a large increase in the number of enrolments. The states that were quick to permit private engineering colleges benefited when the demand for software engineers boomed in the early 1990s. Software exports took hold in the states where engineering graduates were plentiful, owing to the more number of private engineering colleges in these states (Arora and Bagde 2006).

The number of institutions offering undergraduate degree in engineering has increased over the years, as has the total intake capacity of these institutions, there has been a marked decline in engineering PhD graduates. This decline in PhD graduates suggests that while there are strong private incentives to invest in engineering undergraduate studies, these do not extend to investing in research degrees.

As tertiary education is a fundamental requirement for any economy that aspires to be competitive in the global economy, National Knowledge Commission has accordingly recognized that improving the quality of higher education was a key to improved performance. This is particularly the case among the undergraduate colleges where quality is variable—even among the one-third that are assessed by the University Grants Commission, one-quarter were found to be of low quality and most of the two-thirds not assessed are presumably of low quality (Thorat 2006), forcing employers to spend further on training new graduates. Indian engineering courses are skewed toward basic science and technical courses, which account for 88 per cent of the course load, but the skewed load does not necessarily mean that Indian students are more technically advanced.

Private schools have introduced several initiatives to improve the quality of their graduates by establishing innovation and incubation centres, introducing play-and-learn approaches where classes are divided in part lecture and part hands-on training, and collaborating with IT companies to provide course material and train lecturers on developments in areas such as chip design, radio frequency identification, and network management (Thorat 2006).

Yet, at the macro level, India's gross enrolment ratio in tertiary education is only 12 per cent of the eligible population compared to the 35 per cent who completed secondary school. Historically, the government has spent about 3–4 per cent of the GDP on education, which has accounted for 13 per cent of public spending (Hiromi 2006). These numbers are comparable to many other developing countries such as China. On a per capita enrolment basis, however, the amount spent on tertiary education is three times that spent on primary and secondary education combined. By contrast, in China, about two-thirds of the amount is spent on primary and secondary education on a per capita enrolment basis.

Social Capital in India

India is an enormously diverse country with broad linguistic, religious, geographic, and political variations across its territory. It is not surprising then with a heterogeneous society and a large population that people have a wide array of identities available to them. These identities are grounded in caste, religion (including loyalties to sects within larger religious groups), language, class, region (urban/rural, national, regional, sub-regional, and local identities), plus varying types of 'tribes'. But Indians generally do not fix on any one of these identities fiercely and permanently (Manor 1996). Instead, they tend to shift from one identity to another and then another in response to the changing circumstances. Consequently, solidarity among people is undermined when these identities run up against the heterogeneity of the Indian society and the tendency of most people to shift from one identity to another frequently and with great fluidity. Due to these two realities, social tensions do not become concentrated along a single fault-line and do not produce prolonged and intractable conflict (Manor 1996). But these multiple identities have become impediments for forging solidarity between different groups. In effect, there is ample bonding social capital but a lack of bridging social capital in the country.

In terms of religious identity, the single largest religion in India is not focused upon a single sacred text and a single god or historical figure. Hindu Vedas, or sacred texts, are numerous and varied and Hindus worship a great variety of gods. Many village temples are devoted to one of the more prominent deities, but many also focus on divine figures known only locally. Following the migration of upper class Muslims to Pakistan in 1947 (Engineer 2001), the Muslim community in India consisted disproportionately of the urban self-employed. Muslims account for about 12 per cent of the Indian population. Social distance between Hindus and Muslims is vast, exacerbated by political posturing of Hindu nationalist political parties. Christians, Jains, and Sikhs account for about 4 per cent of the Indian population, and while there is considerable overlap between Jains, Sikhs and Hindus in day-to-day lives, Christians tend to be outside this circle. Thus, it is not surprising that the social networks and social contacts in India are shaped by caste and religion (Srinivas and Bèteille 1964).

In terms of linguistic identity, Hindi is spoken by a large minority of the population but efforts to make it a national language have not succeeded. India does not have a common written language like China, which enables most Chinese linguistic groups to communicate on paper. Rather, Indian languages have phonetic scripts, many of which differ radically.

In terms of regional variation across states, India is one of the most heterogeneous countries in the world (Sinha 2005). Even before the conquest and colonization by the British, the Indian states were extremely diverse. Some areas in India were directly governed by the British Empire with residents located in some major cities. Other areas were governed through civil service by local landlords, and some were ruled as princely states with a variety of local rulers. These diverse structures resulted in a variety of local governance mechanisms which continued in a modified form following Independence in 1947.

Post 1947, a new level of complexity was added to the Indian political structure. In India, there is a clearly articulated division of responsibilities between federal, provincial, and local governments. However, even with respect to the activities that lie in the purview of the federal government, provincial-level bureaucracy is charged with its implementation resulting in tremendous differences. In some areas, villages are small with considerable distance between each (such as the Himachal Pradesh); in others, villages are very large—more than 10,000 individuals—and located close to urban agglomerations (such as in Western Uttar Pradesh). Certain states (such as Maharashtra) have well-developed road and rail networks; in other states (such as Bihar), transportation networks are very sparse. All these regional differences have a strong impact on the development of various organizations and institutions. They are also reflected in many dimensions of social life (Desai 1994; Desai and Sreedhar 1999).

Of all the social identities in India, caste has remained the most enduring feature. Two images of caste are central to the understanding of the Indian society: caste as a community and caste as marker of dominance and hierarchy laid down at birth. Many caste groups in India embody a lot of social capital or interpersonal trust and networks, as Srinivasan (2005) has noted: '[T]he important feature of social mobility in modern India is the manner in which the successful members of the backward castes work consistently for improving the economic and social condition of their caste-fellows. This is due to the sense of identification with one's own caste, and also a realisation that caste mobility is essential for individual or familial mobility.' As regards caste as a maker of hierarchy, Gupta (2000) suggests that 'there are probably as many hierarchies as there are castes in India. To believe that there is a single caste order to which every caste, from Brahman to untouchable, acquiesces ideologically, is a gross misreading of facts on the ground.'

In India caste identities, and the existence of castes as independent units, are continually reinforced. Caste associations are widespread and create a strong feeling of intra-caste solidarity, accompanied by stiff competition and often conflict between different castes. Rivalry among different castes has strengthened community solidarity within individual castes. The consolidation of caste identity has come about due to the affirmative action programme of the Indian state through the reservation of a certain percentage of government jobs and places in government-aided educational institutions. The caste consolidation also has further been intensified due to the rise of Hindu nationalist parties and caste-based parties in the 1980s and 1990s (Gupta 2000). Internal solidarity in a community helps the caste to negotiate effectively with outside governmental and non-governmental agencies and social groups. Intra-caste solidarity has allowed the caste system to engage with the market successfully to reinvent itself, becoming a great source of entrepreneurship. Studies show that the caste-based industrial clusters lead the nation's industrial development. A UNIDO study (1999) shows that out of the 370 small-scale industrial clusters and 2,600 artisan-based clusters—which generated 70 per cent of India's industrial output, 66 per cent of exports, and 40 per cent of employment—only 13 were government-sponsored. The rest evolved out of the caste/community-based networks. The World Development Report 2002 found that the social networking within the Goundar caste and the circulation of capital by trust enabled Tirupur's rise as a global knitwear hub. Entrepreneurs belonging to the Goundar caste in Tamil Nadu owned the largest fleet of lorry, tanker, and transport vehicles in

India. A study of 25 caste-based industrial clusters conducted by the Tamil Nadu Swadeshi Academic Council found that many of these caste groups rose as competent entrepreneurs mostly by leveraging on their kinship-based social capital. Most of them have had very little education; but their community acted as the knowledge provider through kinship and social network.

Though these social identities are important forces in India, knowledge and practical application of knowledge have become essential measures of social status. Education, knowledge, networking, and access to material resources are all important elements that contribute to one's position in the social hierarchy. Traditionally, access to knowledge and information was confined largely to the higher castes, while values, attitudes, and beliefs were formed almost entirely within the matrix of the caste system. The introduction of mass media and education has significantly undermined the traditional caste system in India. The success of the IT industry shows that the Non-resident Indian (NRI) networks which mentored, supported, and promoted the Indian IT industry were not centred around family or any of the social identities.

Due to the existence of multiple social identities and a paucity of bridging social capital, attempts have been made by the government, non-governmental organizations (NGOs), and the private sector to forge bonds across communities. These attempts to create and sustain inter-group solidarity include cooperative societies, self-help groups, and other voluntary organizations.

Most of these networks focused on stakeholders' participation during their early phase of existence. As these networks became large and grew into formal institutions, government patronage, intervention, and subsidies often led to their politicization. The networks became subordinate to other state-run institutions and unions and became subservient to the interests of political aspirants. Elections of the office bearers and other administrative procedures took precedence over stakeholders' interests, and as a consequence, these institutions came to be dominated by a few. When resources of an institution become concentrated in the hands of a few, they structured the institutions to benefit only those few, resulting in poorly run and operated institutional capital (Second Administrative Reforms Commission 2008).

Institutional Capital in India

Determinants of economic development, such as institutional capital, change and evolve slowly, or hardly at all. Yet countries like China and India have gone through remarkable transformations in the last two decades in their economic performance, while many others have experienced sharp deterioration. India's pace of change was moderate in country-specific circumstances (policies and institutional arrangements), but when the country interacted with the external environment, change in economic performance was significant.

The popular perception in India is that public institutions are declining. Academic debate on this subject is much more circumspect, partly because India's size and heterogeneity do not allow for an easy generalization. Although an observer of contemporary India may be tempted to conclude that India's public institutional capital is severely stressed and weakening, in reality their performance has varied both across institutions and over time (Kapur and Mehta 2005). It is true that not all signs point to institutional decline. Certain referee institutional capital, especially the Supreme Court, the Election Commission, and the Presidency have witnessed rejuvenation (Kapur and Mehta 2005). The Election Commission, especially since the late 1980s, has fiercely safeguarded its independence, and presided over many difficult elections. In a country where everything is so politicized, it is remarkable that election results are never contested. The other referee institution, the Supreme Court, has moved beyond the politicized appointments of the late 1970s that did not give India an independent judiciary (Kapur and Mehta 2005). Through public interest litigation, it has moved aggressively, behaving more like the executive than the judiciary, in resolving long-standing public policy issues. As a result, the Supreme Court has gained popular legitimacy (Mehta 2005).

Some of the new institutions such as the Telecommunications Regulatory Authority of India (TRAI), Securities and Exchange Board of India (SEBI), and Insurance Development Regulation Act (IDRA) have performed very respectably. Greater decentralization and transparency have been introduced through the Panchayati Raj initiatives and the Right to Information (RTI) Act. Hitherto disadvantaged groups, having acquired a voice through the political process, are finally asserting themselves and demanding that public institutions serve their interests too, threatening the exclusive hold of the elites (Mehta 2005).

If the verdict on the quality of institutional capital in India is mixed, what explains India's growth experience since 1991? India's growth since 1991 has been achieved through the growth of private enterprises, the large influx of foreign direct investment (FDI), and the increased volume of foreign trade. This growth owes to the policy reforms that began in the 1980s that reined in over-regulation in the economy. Prior to the 1980s, a policy regime that was unfavourable to the private sector was holding India back. In the early 1980s, there was a significant attitudinal change towards the private sector on the part of the government. The government went from being hostile to private business to mildly supportive, and eventually quite supportive. These small shifts elicited a large productivity response because India was far from its income possibility frontier (Rodrik and Subramaniam 2004). In addition, there was a growing decentralization of policy facilitated by the gradual dismantling of the industrial licensing system. Greater economic decentralization meant states could differentiate themselves by their ability to attract private sector investment. Policy reforms of the 1980s therefore changed the economic landscape of the country. But this is not a sufficient explanation. Like India, many countries in Latin America and sub-Saharan Africa have also implemented policy reforms, sometimes broader and deeper than those in India. Yet the growth response in those countries did not match that of India's. This contrast can partly be explained by India's institutional capital, which was built up through decades preceding Independence and created the conditions for the rapid growth. Even a small trigger—relatively modest reforms—was sufficient to engender a large growth response because of the considerable under-exploited potential provided by the quality of its institutional capital. India's legacy was so good as to provide it with considerable institutional slack (Rodrik and Subramaniam 2004).

What was the institutional legacy that India inherited at Independence? The British government established a kind of institutional capital in India which was based on private property rights and an English-type judicial system for the native population. In a land where property rights were informal, complex, overlapping, and locally defined by tradition and village leaders, the British attempted to introduce an impersonal, bureaucratic, modern form of property rights. The British introduced a system of private property rights in India. After Independence, India's founding fathers bequeathed a strong set of institutions, much stronger than that for the average country (Rodrik and Subramanian 2004).

While the changes in the 1980s were undoubtedly small in relation to those in the 1990s, they were quite significant when compared with the regime prevailing until the 1970s. The modest economic reforms in the 1980s accelerated India's robust and stable growth post 1991. Yet many scholars have argued that India's performance is surprisingly low when compared to the quality of its institutional capital. Rodrik and Subramanian (2004), for instance, using geography, openness, economic, and political institutional capital as fundamental determinants of growth, conclude;

> India's level of income was about a quarter of what it should be given the strength of its economic institutional capital. On the other hand, if political institutional capital is the true long-run determinant of income, India's income is about 15 per cent of what it should be. India has thus been a significant under-achiever in the sense that it has not exploited the potential created by having done the really hard work of building institutional capital.

Surprisingly, India's growth experience of the past two decades has not improved the country's political and economic institutional capital. When people become richer, they demand more from their public institutions—better public services, more security and law and order, and greater political participation. But in India, average incomes have risen fourfold, yet institutional capital has not improved. Economic growth has not contributed enough towards the emergence of public institutions characterized by robustness, reliability, resilience, flexibility, and affordability. The competitive strengths achieved by India in IT and in macroeconomic management have been eclipsed by the weaknesses that pervade its public institutions and infrastructure. What is surprising is that in the last two decades, India has witnessed a number of developments that should have improved its institutional capital: greater transparency with the explosion in the quality and quantity of the media; the progressive dismantling of the license–quota–permit raj which fostered corruption and patronage; the rise of civil society striving to hold public institutions and officials accountable; and the unleashing of the dynamic of competition between states, allowing citizens in lagging states to question why they cannot expect the same standards of public institutions and public service delivery as in the more progressive states (Mehta 2005).

In India, reforms to enlarge markets with private capital, property rights, and free trade have not kept pace with building requisite institutional capital. The consequence is that growth in India is unequal, which has had subtler effects on institutional capital. If growth is more concentrated at the upper ends of the income spectrum, there is the distinct possibility of what Albert Hirschman called 'exit': the rich opt out of the public system, turning to the private sector to get essential services. The normal pressures for improving the provision of public goods get attenuated. The second major factor contributing to the decline of public institutions has been its increasing inability to attract talent.

The institutional capital that India inherited from the British and India's founding fathers have played a key role in the turnaround of India's economic performance. But India's institutional capital has not kept pace with its fast evolving economy and as a result the growth in the country has been unequal.

Evolution of the Indian IT industry

1970s

The era of the 1970s was marked by an unfavourable regulatory framework, paucity of relevant human capital, and a non-existent social capital to aid the Indian IT sector or its growth. Not surprisingly, the sector made a hesitant start and faced an uncertain existence.

Though the first electronic computer arrived in India in 1955, the first computer policy was created in 1963 when the Committee on Electronics was established. Since electronics was considered to have a strategic role in national development and security, the committee recommended ways to strengthen the country's technological base in electronics. In its report submitted in 1966, the committee argued that computers played an increasingly important social and scientific role and constituted a Working Group on computers. The Working Group, in its 1968 report, called for a national effort to attain self-sufficiency within 10 years in small and medium computers. In calling for the development of across-the-board design and manufacturing capabilities, the report argued:

> A computer system is only as versatile as the software that is made available with it... Software is business. Software is strategic. Thus it would

be very foolhardy if a programme for the manufacture of the computer systems...does not have built into it a scheme for the development of appropriate software... Software development can be farmed out to other organizations...this is also a labour intensive activity except that it requires intellectually skilled manpower... Software development would seem to have very high employment potential in a country like India... the export potential, as well as the value added in the case of software, is very large.

Initially, policy-making was in the hands of Electronics Committee of India. When the US cut off the supply of electronic equipment during the war with Pakistan in 1965, the committee came to be dominated by the Defense Ministry's Department of Defense Supplies. The defense establishment was keen on ensuring access to electronics and computers. Thus, in the 1960s, it allowed International Business Machines (IBM) and International Computers Limited (ICL) to operate in India, though IBM's Indian operations were mostly limited to reconditioning and leasing obsolete computers (Rubin 1985).

This development in electronics was hampered by the macroeconomic policy regime of the time that not only isolated the Indian economy from the world and stifled entrepreneurship and innovation, but also hindered the growth of the electronic computer industry. Thus, until the early 1980s, the overall policy framework constrained the development of computing in India. Consequently in the 1970s, there was no separate software industry. Multinationals such as IBM and ICL were the largest providers of hardware bundled with operating systems and a few basic packages that were written in FORTRAN and COBOL languages (Rubin 1985).

Larger enterprises (including the Indian defense and public organizations) that needed customized applications employed in-house teams that did everything from installing systems to writing software. When specific software applications became popular, standalone boxes were made for them. But to export software, Indian companies had to design it for hardware systems that were the standard worldwide, which in the 1970s were the IBM mainframe computers. However, Indian import duties on hardware were extremely high (almost 300 per cent); hence, during the late 1960s and early 1970s, Indian companies relied on old, refurbished, and antiquated IBM machines as they were the only machines that Indian companies could afford. Although the

Indian government lowered import duties on all IT equipment a few years later, there was a precondition that the exporters would have to recover twice the value of the foreign exchange spent on importing computers within five years—a clause that was modified only in the 1980s. As software was not considered an 'industry', exporters were ineligible for bank finance (Sridharan 1996).

Institutions are powerful external forces that help determine how people make sense of their world and act in it.

The Indian policy in the 1970s has been described as statist and protectionist (Rubin 1985). In IT, the state was the main producer of products and services. Its strategy was to create 'national champions' (Sridharan 1996). A key protectionist policy was the Foreign Exchange Regulation Act of 1973 (FERA 1973). FERA 1973 forced all multinationals to reduce their equity share in their Indian subsidiaries to less than 50 per cent. Many foreign firms closed their Indian operations, including firms as diverse as Coca-Cola and IBM, citing concerns about the protection of intellectual property. FERA 1973 thus closed the door on software development in India by Transnational Corporations (TNCs) (Rubin 1985).

Overall, the regulatory or institutional scenario was not favourable for software exporters and this constituted the nebulous beginning of the Indian software industry. But the Indian state's much maligned trade and industrial policies had inadvertent positive effects for the IT sector. The departure of IBM and the protection of India's hardware sector led to the development of software skills in the form of induced innovation. The very limitations and technological cost of hardware in India meant that developing software skills was necessary. Most of these new systems used the UNIX operating language and as it gained popularity worldwide, Indian programmers had an early advantage. The Monopolies and Restrictive Trade Practices (MRTP) Act, which limited the entry of existing large industrial houses in new sectors, meant that new firms began to enter the sector in the early 1980s. Due to IBM's exit from India, the Indian companies relied less on mainframe computers, which paved the way for the introduction of minicomputers and microcomputers. Many who had imported hardware either evaded their software export obligations or stopped exporting once they had fulfilled their obligations. Instead, they established service bureaus to lease out computer time in the domestic market. The establishment of service bureaus not only reflected unmet demand in the country, but also marked the beginning of a software industry in the private sector. Many of IBM's former employees were involved in establishing those service bureaus before they moved to software development (Subramanian 1992).

As early as in September 1970, the Department of Electronics (DoE) issued newspaper advertisements inviting proposals for developing software, especially for export. But the response was poor. In 1973, the government established the Santa Cruz Electronics Export Processing Zone (SEEPZ) in Bombay (now Mumbai). Guidelines issued in 1974 stated that computer time for exports would be guaranteed on a non-profit basis at the government's Regional Computer Centres (Subramanian 1992). The first software exporting company from India was Tata Consultancy Services (TCS) that started operations in 1968. After a few local orders, TCS bagged its first big export assignment in 1973–4 when it was asked to provide an inventory-control software solution for an electricity generation unit in Iran. During this period, TCS also developed a hospital information system in the UK along with Burroughs Corporation and became a role model for other Indian IT companies to follow in the 1980s (Ramadorai 2002).

Since TNCs could not develop software in India, they, along with domestic companies, discovered an innovative solution: Indian programmers were sent to developed countries instead. This strategy began in 1974 when mainframe manufacturer, Burroughs, asked its India sales agent, Tata Consultancy Services, to export programmers for installing system software for a US client (Ramadorai 2002). Initially, the exported programmers worked for global IT firms. Later in the decade, as IBM grew in market share, end-users, such as banks, used Indian firms to convert existing applications software into IBM-compatible versions. By 1980, there were 21 firms with annual exports of US$ 4 million. Although the private sector discovered a way out, the solution forced on domestic firms was to choose the lowest end of the business, one that reduced opportunities for learning.

While protection led to labour exports, it slowed the inflow of new skills into India. The industry learned global skills primarily through programmers returning from overseas assignments (Ramadorai 2002), but many chose to remain overseas, further slowing the inflow of new skills. The high employee turnover only reinforced the tendency of Indian firms to compete on the basis of low costs rather than on a repository of technical and managerial expertise acquired from previous projects. It also led to an under-utilization of Indian engineering talent (Parthasarathy 2004). An important, though a thin resource, was the return of US-educated engineers, who provided advanced project management and engineering skills.

In July 1976 the government announced a programme to encourage NRIs to invest in India. Under the programme, software firms could be established with imported computers with an export commitment equal to 100 per cent of the value of the computer. Custom duties on hardware imports were also reduced in 1976 from more than 100 per cent to 40 per cent. While duties were reduced, guidelines for the import of computers costing more than Rs 5,00,000 (US$ 56,000) were elaborate (Parthasarathy 2004). The cumbersome guidelines led to delays and took between 6 to 64 months to procure the computer after the initial application was made. Despite the tedium of the procedure, 441 computers of various makes were imported between 1976–7 and 1980–1 in contrast to the 35 computers that were approved for imports between 1970 and 1975. But exports did not grow because of difficulties in importing computers and software tools, a lack of relevant human capital, and problems with obtaining foreign exchange for overseas marketing and business expenses.

The Minicomputer Policy of 1978 allowed the setting up of systems engineering companies to design and assemble computers. The permission was not without restrictions: no foreign financial or technical collaboration was allowed, annual production was limited to Rs 20 million (US$ 254,000), no more than five different types of systems could be produced, and none could cost more than Rs 300,000 (US$ 38,000). Despite the restrictions, four firms quickly established themselves to produce microcomputers (Parthasarathy 2004).

The non-resident Indians (NRIs) played a very important role in the late 1980s and 1990s in making the Indian IT industry a global industry. Their participation in the 1970s was, however, limited to being tolerant mentors of early Indian software development companies. Indian engineers in the US were quickly recognized as excellent technologists, but during the 1970s and 1980s they had to fight a strong perception—in some cases a self-perception—that they did not have a front office or general management capabilities. As a partial reaction, many engineers made a conscious decision to not emphasize their ethnicity and there was remarkably little ethnic collaboration (of Indians) within the US. In fact, their emphasis was on their careers within American companies and they were rarely aware of the progress being made by Indians in other organizations. Not only did the Indian engineers and IT professionals in the US not collaborate with each other, they also invested very little in the Indian IT industry (Pandey et al. 2004). The few attempts and investments made by NRIs in the 1970s were quickly abandoned because of bureaucratic obstacles and the limited capabilities of Indian partners.

1980s

During the 1980s, the institutional framework was slowly becoming conducive to IT companies, initial steps were taken to create IT specific human capital and overseas Indians as a network and a group were more willing to help Indian IT sector stand on its feet. This nascent combination of institutional policies, human capital, and social capital helped the Indian IT sector to make a mark in the overseas markets.

Despite the tough policy with respect to imports, by the early 1980s, India was the only developing nation to have any significant software exports at US$ 12 million, a substantial increase from US$ 4.4 million in 1979; 30 companies had begun exporting software. As the ineffectiveness of autarkic policies became apparent by the late 1970s, a few reform-minded bureaucrats redefined the role of the Department of Electronics (DoE) and its policies to support the growth of the computer industry in the private sector (Parthasarathy 2004).

As a result, the Indian IT industry witnessed the Indian government's policies becoming more favourable in the 1980s with the New Computer Policy 1984 (NCP 1984) that consisted of a package of reduced import tariffs on hardware and software (reduced to 60 per cent), recognition of software exports as a 'delicensed industry', that is, eligible for bank finance and not subject to the intrusive licensing regime (Heeks 1996), and permission for foreign firms to set up wholly-owned companies. In 1985, all export revenue (including software exports and income from the provision of services at customers' sites overseas, including bodyshopping) was exempted from income tax and software export over satellite data links were permitted. The DoE established Software Development Promotion Agency to promote development efforts both for the local and export markets, and also set up a research, design, and development facility. The state's investment in R&D labs and tertiary education was also important in creating human capital clusters. The state's much maligned over-investment in tertiary education, especially in engineering, was critical in laying the human capital foundation for this sector. The six key IT clusters in India—Bangalore, Chennai, Hyderabad, Mumbai, New Delhi, Pune—had the highest concentration of public sector R&D establishments as well as publicly-funded science and engineering educational institutions. Several government initiatives in the 1980s nurtured capabilities. The new policy also encouraged access to overseas technological developments by allowing easy imports of the latest software and software tools.

But policy confusion and bureaucratic hurdles continued to afflict the software industry partly because of a limited understanding of the industry. Despite the industry being permitted to export with satellite data links, establishing an earth station was a time-consuming procedure requiring permission from various government departments. It also required breaking 25 government rules before Texas Instruments (TI) could set up the first earth station in Bangalore with a direct satellite link to the US (Parthasarathy 2004). In 1989, an Indian government telecom company (VSNL, or Videsh Sanchar Nigam Limited) commissioned a direct 64-kbps satellite link to the US, thereby offering software exporters a completely new way of functioning. But these facilities were still not affordable for many IT companies.

The main competitive advantage of Indian companies was the cost and the ability to communicate using the English language. The total cost for a software developer in India varied between US$ 32,000 and US$ 42,000 annually. Comparing this to the total cost of a US software developer (US$ 60,000 to US$ 95,000 yearly) in 1980, the savings were clearly quite significant (Pandey et al. 2004).

Despite the cost advantages and a relatively good proficiency in English, the Indian software industry continued to face a lack of availability of hardware and a shortfall in trained manpower. Import of hardware, especially mainframe computers, was very tedious and expensive. The advent of personal computers (PCs) in the 1980s reduced the cost of importing hardware substantially (Parthasarathy 2004).

The relocation of work to India, though gradual, was led by TNCs and domestic firms and experimentation with different activities. Some TNCs did R&D and wrote product software using cross-country teams (such as Texas Instruments and Hewlett Packard); others wrote custom software for in-house use (such as ANZ Bank and Citigroup) and for clients. Domestic firms, such as TCS, shifted from exporting programmers to outsourced custom software while others started product development (such as Wipro). The number of software firms went up from 35 in 1984 to 700 in 1990 (Parthasarathy 2004).

Although the education system was producing substantial number of engineers who were talented, few colleges offered any computer training or IT courses. Realizing that the Indian college system was unable to provide any computer training or IT courses, a few Indian entrepreneurs took it upon themselves to provide tutorials and training classes in IT. Their early days were often marked with one person driving a scooter or a motorcycle and the other riding behind with a PC in his lap so they could impart training in rented college and school spaces in the evenings (Pandey et al. 2004). The training institute (NIIT) started by them is today a US$ 2 billion company and continues to provide IT courses and training.

In the pre-1984 period, a handful of firms competed for thin financial and entrepreneurial resources and had limited access to domain skills. Post 1984, software projects were developed within India. There was considerable experimentation on the type of work done and many new entrants, leading to an overall rise in selective capabilities and organizational and functional skills in the country. The location of campuses in Bangalore and proximity to TNCs in such cities facilitated learning on how to manage software projects remotely. Despite this progress, a large number of software-exporting companies relied exclusively on on-site services, as they had few other options. In the absence of easily available and affordable data communication facilities, firms could not shift to offshore services. As reputation mattered in software contracting, on-site services in the 1980s provided ample opportunity to gain the confidence of Western customers. While Indian engineers had the necessary technical skills, on-site services provided exposure to not just new technologies but also management processes, market trends, and socially specific communication protocols with customers (Parthasarathy 2004).

In the early 1980s, several small Indian companies went to Silicon Valley in search of low-end contract software-development work. Several NRI executives were willing to help but most found the Indian companies' work to be unsatisfactory, with many of these companies also suffering from deficient development tools and computers. This is partly because even until 1985-6, the Indian government was promoting Russian computers over American computers and Indian companies had just started working with PCs; hence, the companies' professionals could not meet, or sometimes even understand, US standards for quality and timeliness. To mitigate this problem, the Diaspora executives sometimes created programs within their US companies whereby Indian programmers could work in the US with US technology (at Indian wages plus travel-related costs). Further, they coached and guided the Indian companies to help them improve their quality and performance standards (Pandey et al. 2004).

In 1988, the industry formed its own trade body, NASSCOM, to promote its interests. When it was formed, NASSCOM had 38 members who accounted for 65 per cent of the industry's revenues. A decade later, it had 464 members, accounting for 95 per cent of industry revenues. NASSCOM created platforms for the dissemination of knowledge and research in the industry through its surveys and conferences and acted as an 'advisor, consultant and coordinating body' for the ITeS/BPO industry and liaison between the government and the industry (Pandey et al. 2004).

During the 1980s, the government removed many of the hurdles faced by IT companies in India, the private sector set up specialized schools to impart IT training, and the Indian Diaspora in the US began to play a crucial role in guiding Indian IT companies. In all, the 1980s saw the state policy become more favourable to the IT industry, despite tightening trade and import policies, IT-specific human capital being developed by the private sector, and social capital being built by Indian Diaspora. The 1980s built the foundation on which IT companies could leverage in the 1990s for their significant growth.

1990s and beyond

In the 1990s, the Indian state, both at the centre and the sub-national levels, had at least relative to other sectors of the economy, played a facilitative role in responding to the needs of the IT sector. The economic reforms of 1991, while helpful to all sectors of the economy, were particularly important for the software sector. Software firms, which had found it difficult to raise financing through debt because they lacked collateral, could now raise resources easily through equity. With domestic firms able to import hardware and uplink easily, they were in a better position to compete off-site and reduce their on-site work abroad. The government granted the sector preferentially low-tax policies. In the early 1990s, the government set up a chain of software parks to promote software exports from India using data communication facilities. In addition, Software Technology Parks (STPs) provided infrastructure such as core computer facilities, reliable power, and ready-to-use office space (Parthasarathy 2004).

Consequently, the Indian software industry underwent significant changes. There was a shift away from on-site to offshore projects following the commissioning of the STPs (Parthasarathy 2004). Offshore development offered the advantage of having most employees under one roof allowing them to interact with one another and learn from each other and different projects. It also helped firms to build a repository of knowledge that helped in competing for subsequent projects. With the availability of data communications facilities, offshore software factories emerged complete with the infrastructure, technology, training programmes, and quality processes.

Social capital and informal institutions direct attention to the relationships that shape the realization of human capital's potential for the individual and for the network.

Even as the Indian firms were establishing their reputation in the global market with quality assurances, many Indians who had migrated to the US were distinguishing themselves professionally. Many Indian engineers who had migrated to the US in the 1960s had by the 1990s either become entrepreneurs or venture capitalists or high-level executives in large- and medium-sized companies. Indians were running 9 per cent of Silicon Valley start-ups from the period 1995–8, 70 per cent of which were in the software sector (Saxenian 1999). These absent Indians retained their connections and cultivated relationships with people and businesses back home. These professionals came together especially because many had graduated from the same engineering schools in India and most of them also knew their counterparts in India. Some of them started their own IT companies in India, whereas others invested in nascent IT and Dot.com companies in India. Some started IT research and development laboratories in India, whereas others moved to supervise US investments, outsource contracts, and to train and manage

Indian professionals to US efficiency and standards. Their knowledge of the needs and capabilities of both US- and India-based firms made them potentially useful intermediaries in the search and matching process. Their ongoing relationships with both US and Indian firms made them well situated to use their reputations to support complex transactions. Their success as technologists, managers, and entrepreneurs in Silicon Valley changed the perception of the Indian technology businesses in general. This aggregate human capital was waiting to be interconnected through a never-ending web of connections in order to share information and strengthen knowledge and their social capital quickly matured into networks.

Institutional emergence and change arise from a structured bargaining between actors who agree to a self-organizing governance system when they organize themselves into groups and networks.

Diaspora professionals quickly matured in forming non-profit associations such as TiE (The IndUS Entrepreneur) and SIPA (Silicon Indian Professional Association). TiE is a group of Indian IT entrepreneurs and network professionals founded in 1992. While most of their wealth was directed at funding US companies, they also funnelled funds into a new generation of start-ups in India, as well as hybrid companies that operated in both India and the US. Members of the group have played an important role in advising and pressurizing the Indian government to change the regulatory framework for venture capital in India and put in place a more attractive context for returning entrepreneurship (Kapur 2001). Collective action on behalf of the private sector was much stronger. NASSCOM managed to work in tandem with the Indian state to jointly promote the sector's interests. The combination of social capital and human capital through networks successfully changed the relevant institutional framework.

Then came the Y2K problem, the Internet Telecom boom, and the Dot.com boom. All these forced companies in the US, the UK, and Canada to hire numerous computer programmers. Since the US, the UK, and Canada faced a shortage of IT professionals during 1996–9, many in the Indian Diaspora convinced their companies to hire Indian IT professionals. The US government had to increase its H-1 visa quota from 65,000 in 1998 to 130,000 in 1999 and then to 195,000 soon thereafter (Pandey et al. 2004). The so-called Y2K problem galvanized the developed world's IT industry, as it sought to debug a problem created in the 1980s by the high costs of computer disk drive memory. Indian companies played an important role in resolving the problem. Though debugging was a simple activity, Y2K brought India to the forefront of the world's IT industry. Working on Y2K contracts helped Indian firms enter new markets and build trust with their client enterprises. These capabilities assured their continuing significance in ITeS (Pandey et al. 2004).

India continues to be a significant player in offshore ITeS, accounting for 49 per cent of IT services and 36 per cent of BPO services. In this respect, India is well ahead of its global peers. But the proportion of such services that are offshore is small—10 per cent of IT services and 30 per cent of BPO services; this ratio has remained the same since 2000. Moreover, IT outsourcing to India has stabilized at the low-end over the past decade with limited potential for change (Dossani 2010). Project management and technical skills are considered to be inadequate in India to be able to move up the value-chain.

***

The emergence of a strong Indian IT industry happened partly by design and partly by accident. In the late 1970s, policymakers believed that if India were to realize its software ambitions of becoming to software in the 1990s what Taiwan and South Korea were to hardware, it would have to begin with high-volume, low value-added exports and then moved up the value chain. But the statist and protectionist policies of the period, instead of being constraints for the development of computing in India, helped the industry unintentionally. The departure of IBM and the protection of India's hardware sector led to the development of software skills in the form of induced innovation. The 1980s saw the advent of private engineering schools and training institutes which built a strong human capital base that was helpful in the late 1990s when the Y2K problem galvanized the developed world's IT industry. The period also saw government policies becoming more favourable in improving communication infrastructure.

Initially, software exports consisted of sending software developers to work at the client site in the US on short term assignments. Later, teams of software developers were sent overseas, and only by the mid-1990s, was there significant software activity taking place locally. The key to growth were contacts with potential clients in the US and Western Europe, and access to high-quality engineers; the Indian Diaspora played an important role in facilitating such contacts. The relationships between Diaspora professionals quickly matured into institutionalized networks.

India's success in software is principally the result of domestic entrepreneurs, domestic capabilities, Diaspora social capital, and bureaucratic hurdles that were based on a limited understanding of the industry which actually helped the industry through induced innovation.

The Indian IT industry made a modest beginning during the 1970s, as it faced limited human capital and social capital. In the face of unfavourable government policies, the industry along with its international peers discovered an innovative solution of sending Indian programmers abroad to develop and install software and paved the way for India's remarkable success in software exports in the later decades.

III
Micro Analysis

This part of the book deals with the study of the behaviour of the economic unit of the firm. From the analyses of the functioning of the economy as a whole in the previous chapters, the following chapter moves to the analyses of the market behaviour of firms in an attempt to understand the decision-making process of firms. It looks at the existing theories of the firm and introduces the link between human capital, social capital, and institutional capital to the questions related to the existence of the firm and its boundaries.

11 Theory of the Firm

In line with the evolutionary economic process as outlined earlier, this chapter develops an integrated theory of the firm. By using the three analytical domains—micro, meso, and macro—this chapter establishes the evolution of the firm as a growth of knowledge process. The link established between human capital, social capital, and institutional capital in Chapter 5 is used as the basis for explaining how a firm can be defined and why firms differ. The firm is an appropriate unit of analysis to articulate micro–meso–macro linkages because it affects and is affected by macro-level processes and social actions at the meso level. The macro and meso links are important because without understanding the intricate and routine day-to-day organizational processes, it is hard to comprehend how firms attempt to control individual behaviour and orient that behaviour towards some ultimate end.

The theory of the firm has been one of the most exciting fields of economic research over the last 30 years. Theories of contracts, transaction costs, and entrepreneurship vie with each other and form the foundation for a comprehensive theory of the firm. Each of these theories has its own idea of what the key issue is, and each naturally claims that it alone addresses this particular issue head on. The theory of the firm deals with the nature and the boundaries of the firm as an economic institution, the internal structure of the firm, and the relationship between the firm and the market.

The theory of the firm can be located within the broader analysis of economic organization, which attempts to explain the observed diversity of institutional arrangements in the economy. For instance, why do some transactions occur in markets, others in firms, and still others in structures such as franchises, joint ventures, and strategic alliances? The study of economic organization seeks to understand the conditions that create this diversity. Ronald Coase's (1937) observation that 'firms exist because there are costs to using the market' has been the touchstone for the study of organizations by economists. Attempts to identify the costs of using the market have led to developments in economics like the transaction cost economics (Williamson 1975, 1985), incomplete contracts theory (Hart 1995), property rights and measurement costs (Barzel 1989; Cheung 1983), and agency theory (Alchian and Demsetz 1972). Since the 1990s, there has been increasing interest in the theory of the firm among strategy scholars (Foss 1998). Several theories of the firm have been proposed from a strategic perspective, using a variety of (related) theoretical lenses, such as resources (Barney 1996; Rumelt 1984), knowledge (Conner and Prahalad 1996; Grant 1996), competencies (Foss and Knudsen 1996; Penrose 1959), capabilities (Langlois 1992), and real options (Barney and Lee 1998; Sanchez 1998).

Before these theories came into existence, the neoclassical theory of the firm formed the basis of the competitive general equilibrium, in which a 'firm' was a production function or production possibility set, a 'black box' that transformed inputs into outputs. The firm was modelled as a single actor which faced a series of decisions portrayed as uncomplicated: what level of output to produce, how much of each factor to hire, etc. These 'decisions' were mathematical calculations, implicit in the underlying data. In the long run, the firm may choose an optimal size and output mix, but even these were determined by the characteristics of the production function (economies of scale, scope, and sequence). In short, the firm was a set of cost curves and the 'theory of the firm' a calculus problem.

Coase (1937) asked why there is a firm as an organization. For Coase, the origins of the firm lay in the response of individuals to the costs of transacting business. He saw the boundaries of the firm as being determined by the simple application of the marginal rule, with the producer continuing to internalize activities up to the point at which the cost of management equalled the cost of transacting in the market place. Arrow (1969) defined the generalized concept of transaction cost as the cost of using a resource allocation mechanism for achieving Pareto optimality of its social outcome.[1] In the 1940s and 1950s, neoclassical economists became more concerned with whether firms maximized profits or not. Dissatisfied with the theory of the firm and its central postulate of profit maximization, a number of scholars led by March and Simon began to investigate behaviour in organizations. The concept of the firm as a collective action was introduced, with attention paid to the ways in which conflicting objectives were resolved and transformed into goals. They also explored how efforts were made to push back the cognitive limits of the individual by the introduction of systems, structures, and rules so that it was possible to assimilate and act on the large amounts of information necessary for the firm to meet goals and adapt to changing circumstances.

Since the beginning of the 1970s, subsequent development of thought on the *raison d'etre* of the firm took place by revitalizing the Coasian analysis (Alchian and Demsetz 1972; Williamson 1975). This work included (a) making precise the contents of the transaction cost associated with any organization,[2] the imperfect market system, or another form of organization, (b) clarifying the specific mode of the firm as an organization, (c) comparing firms with different specific modes, and (d) studying the workings of these resource allocation mechanisms by specifying the behavioural principle and conflicting motives of the members of an organization.

Most modern theories that have taken their leads from the early seminal contributions of Alchian and Demsetz and Williamson are considered post-Coasian in the sense that they view the firm as an efficient contract between different parties; efficient in the sense that it best facilitates exchange, given the existing resource scarcities in terms of information and rationality. Despite the common Coasian origin, the contemporary theory of the firm is not monolithic (Holmström and Tirole 1989); in their attempts to operationalize, make more precise, and understand the original Coasian insights, modern theories have provided a multitude of answers. But these partial theories have proved difficult to synthesize into a comprehensive theory (Casson 2005).

Why do Firms Exist?

One of the most intensively studied topics in the modern theory of the firm is the make-or-buy decision. This is the firm's decision either to acquire some intermediate input by having an employee make it under the employer's direction, using the employer's tools, and usually being paid a fixed wage, or instead to hire an independent contractor who chooses his or her own tools and methods and is paid proportionally to the quantity supplied. Most analyses of the make-or-buy decision have focused on just one of the differences that tend to distinguish employment from independent contracting (Holmström 1999). For example, Coase (1937) and Simon (1959) emphasize the discretion that the employer has to direct the employee's activities; Klein et al. (1978), Williamson (1985), and Grossman and Hart (1986) focus on the firm's ownership of assets; the principal–agent literature (for example, Alchian and Demsetz 1972; Holmström 1982) stresses monitoring and compensation issues, and Penrose emphasizes different capabilities.

Accordingly, theories of the firm can be classified into three categories:

1. Incomplete contracting models, founded on the assumption that it is costly to write elaborate contracts and therefore there is a need for *ex post* governance. The works of Williamson, Grossman-Hart-Moore, Coase, and Simon, as well as implicit contract-theories, belong to this category.
2. Principal–agent models, which allow agents to write elaborate contracts characterized by *ex ante* incentive alignment under the constraints imposed by the presence of asymmetric information. The works of Alchian and Demsetz, Holmström, and Milgrom belong to this category.
3. Knowledge-based models, which suggest that actions taken by firms are based on routines and capabilities that represent where a firm's distinguishing competencies reside. This includes the works of Nelson and Winter, and Edith Penrose.

Incomplete Contracting Theories

The Firm as an Employment Relation

Coase argued that in the world of neoclassical price theory, firms have no reason to exist. Since we observe firms, he reasoned, there must be a 'cost to using the price mechanism' (Coase 1937). Market exchange entails certain costs: discovering the relevant prices, negotiating and enforcing contracts, and so on. Within the firm, the entrepreneur may be able to reduce these 'transaction costs' by coordinating these activities himself. However, internal organization brings other kinds of transaction costs, namely problems of information flow, incentives, monitoring, and performance evaluation. Coase (1937) attributed the formation of firms to market failure. He contended that the firm is created in order to reduce these specific costs as the firm internalizes the cost of obtaining information on the available labour and replaces a succession of short-term complete contracts by a single long-term incomplete contract, thereby avoiding the costs of bargaining. The central thesis of Coase (1937) was that a firm is a superior alternative to the market mechanism. The central drawback of Coase was that he did not analyse the internal organization of the firm.

Simon defined the employment relationship through a contract written between two autonomous actors. The contract specified the action to be performed in the future and its price, a range of acceptable orders, and established the right of the employer and the duty of the employee to accept orders within this range. The advantage of the employment relationship was in its flexibility. The action of the employee could be adapted to whatever state of nature occurred. Intuitively, the benefit of flexibility was greater the greater the uncertainty. On the other hand, Simon stressed that the employment relationship is to some extent reliant upon the employer's reputation for not abusing his authority (Foss and Foss 2005).

The Firm as a Governance Mechanism

Due to coordination problems that may arise in the market, the firm may be viewed as a way to access coordination mechanisms superior to those available in the market. This is the view taken by the transaction cost theory. Williamson improved the Coasian analysis when he defined the nature and sources of transaction costs. The difference he made between the environmental factors (uncertainty,[3] small numbers trading,[4] and asset specificity[5]), as well as behavioural ones (bounded rationality[6] and opportunism[7]), enabled him to distinguish why market, hierarchy, and eventually hybrid forms were selected. Transaction costs rose for ex ante reasons (drafting, negotiating, and safeguarding agreements between the parties to a transaction) and ex post reasons (maladaption, haggling, establishment, operational, and bonding costs). The Transaction Cost Economics (TCE) began with the assumption that market transactions were plagued by incomplete contracts and the development of lock-in among trading partners. Lock-in led the value of the relationship to exceed the value of the trading partners outside alternatives creating what Klein et al. (1978) called 'quasi-rents'. Contractual incompleteness gave contracting parties the ability to engage in opportunistic behaviour to increase their share of these quasi-rents, leading to efficiency losses in market transactions. Parties to a transaction often made investments that have greater value in their intended use than in their alternative uses. Specific investments gave a degree of monopoly or monopsony power to each party to a relationship. But investment in such assets exposed agents to a potential hazard: Once investments were made and contracts are signed, unanticipated changes in circumstances could give rise to costly renegotiation. One party could threaten to pull out of the arrangement—reducing the value of the specific assets—unless that party was allocated a greater share of the quasi-rents of joint production. The fear of being 'held up' in this way distorted ex ante investment levels, reducing the joint surplus produced by the relationship. When specific assets were involved, parties can write long-term contacts to protect themselves and their assets. But real-world contracts are normally incomplete. In that context, specific investments generated quasi-rents, and each of the parties to a contract had incentives to endeavour to capture those rents. This means they are likely to haggle with one another, thereby increasing the costs of writing and administering the contract, as well as attempt to renegotiate the contract or, more generally, engage in opportunistic behaviour ex post. These possibilities, which are the essence of the lock-in problem, clearly pose problems for long-term contracting, and those problems are exacerbated with uncertainty.

Bringing a transaction from the market into the firm under common ownership mitigated the hazards that accrue to opportunistic behaviour and improved investment incentives. The reason is that hierarchical forms of governance brought parties to an exchange under the direct control of a third party. This authoritative party would be able to monitor the behaviour of all involved parties. The firm was a coordination mechanism in which low-powered incentives, extensive administrative controls, and its own dispute settlement machinery were present. The main idea developed in the transaction cost economics was that the firm, with its distinctive capabilities, was able to govern transactions of particular kinds for which markets were not suitable by reducing or controlling more strongly opportunistic behaviours and transaction costs that may arise as soon as economic actors were in a dependency relationship (Joskow 2005). The task of economic organization, in Williamson's terms (1985), was to 'organize transactions so as to economize on bounded rationality while simultaneously safeguarding them against the hazards of opportunism.'[8]

By focusing on transactions as the basis unit of analysis, transaction cost economics regards economic exchange decisions as primary. The production function of firms was assumed to be more or less identical, which allowed scholars to focus on the allocation and exchange of goods and services. This neglected the ability of a firm to foster innovations, learning, and knowledge-creating processes for new products.

In TCE, the motivational assumptions were assumed to be *exogeneously* given and it focused on opportunistic or *extrinsic* motivation.[9] *Extrinsic* motivation was obtained when employees were able to satisfy their needs indirectly, most importantly, through monetary compensation. Extrinsically-motivated coordination in firms was achieved by linking employees' monetary motives to the goals of the firm (the ideal incentive system is pay-for-performance). Opportunism is a strong form of extrinsic motivation when individuals are not constrained by any rules. The existence of extrinsic and intrinsic motivation has important consequences concerning the incentives to invest in common pool resources.[10] From the common pool resources' perspective, the advantage of hierarchies over markets derives from obtaining joint benefits if firm members were motivated to invest in common pool resources, although the property rights were unassigned. TCE ignores issues related to common pool resources, that is, whether firm members choose to pursue their own interest or contribute to a cooperative solution.

Property Rights Analysis—The Firm as an Ownership Unit

Property rights theories, which are more recent and more formal than transaction costs arguments, were developed by Grossman and Hart

(1986), Hart and Moore (1990), Hart (1995), and others. These theories emphasized how asset ownership could change investment incentives. More specifically, they demonstrated how the allocation of property rights, which confer the rights to make decisions concerning the use of an asset when contingencies arise that were not foreseen or not specified in a contract. Grossman and Hart (1986) defined the firm with an explicit reference to the distribution of ownership of the assets, while Hart and Moore (1990) gave a perfect formal presentation of a property rights-based theory of the firm. There are two different property rights theories: Alchian and Demsetz (1972), and Barzel (1989) developed the first one, which is usually called 'old property rights theory' (OPRT) and Grossman, Hart (1986), and Hart and Moore (1990) developed the second 'new property rights theory' (NPRT).

Alchian and Demsetz (1972) considered that one of the main 'function[s] of property rights is that of guiding incentives to achieve a greater internalization of externalities'. He developed the idea that private ownership internalized many of the external costs that collective ownership induces. As an example, private ownership reduced negotiation costs because the owner negotiated directly with those who wanted to use his/her property, whereas all members of the community negotiated together the use of collective property in the presence of collective ownership. In Grossman and Hart (1986) and Hart and Moore (1990) the problem of the nature of the firm was based on a precise and specific definition of property rights. According to them, 'property rights approach takes the point of view that the possession of control rights is crucial for the integration decision' (Hart and Moore 1990). The rights possessed by the owner of an asset are only due to his/her ability to exclude others from using this asset. The theory defined ownership as the possession of residual rights of control, that is, rights to control the uses of assets under contingencies not specified in the contract. As a result, the allocation of formal ownership rights affected behaviour and resource allocation. For example, agents will be less inclined to invest in specific assets if they do not own these and relevant complementary assets. Defining the firm as a collection of assets that it owns, the theory focused on ownership as the purchase of the residual rights of control that existed as soon as incomplete contracting was considered. Owning an asset was important if one undertakes a non-contractible investment which is specific to the asset; if one does not own the asset, one is subject to the hold-up threat by the owner. Accordingly, the person who makes the most important asset-specific investment should own the asset (Foss et al. 1998).

A common strand uniting these theories was the role of incentives in aligning the interests of cooperating parties in a world of transaction costs and incomplete contracts. For both approaches, the design of incentive systems and ownership patterns that supported these incentives were the levers that allowed for efficient production through increasing specialization of assets. Both approaches were concerned with efficient production and extracting the best use of highly complementary assets, but there was little attempt to deal with how the productive knowledge, necessary for efficient production, affected governance modes (Araujo et al. 2003).

Implicit Contracts

When it is difficult to write complete state-contingent contracts, people often rely on 'unwritten codes of conduct', that is, implicit contracts. These may be self-enforcing, in the sense that each party lives up to the other party's reasonable expectations out of a fear of retaliation and breakdown of cooperation. The basic idea in the implicit-contract theory of the firm is that implicit contracts may function differently within firms than between firms; a person is hired as an employee rather than as an independent contractor when coordinating with him requires an implicit contract that is easier to implement within the firm than in the market place. The strength of the threat to leave the relationship determines the implementability of implicit contracts. The implicit contracts theory is linked to Williamson's idea that dispute resolution is easier to carry out within a firm than between firms (Foss et al. 1998).

The Firm as a Communication-Hierarchy

The theory of communication in hierarchies is based on the idea that one important function of the firm is to adapt to and process new information. In this approach while incentive conflicts are disregarded, coordination and communication are highlighted. The theory views the firm as a communication network designed to minimize both the costs of processing new information and the costs of communicating this information among agents. Communication is costly because it takes time for agents to absorb new information sent by others, but this time is reduced by specializing the processing of particular types of information. Each agent handles a particular type of information, and the different types of information are aggregated through the communication network. When the benefits to specializing outweigh the costs of communication, firm-like organizations arise (Bolton and Dewatripont 2005).

Principal–Agent Theories

The Nexus of Contracts View

Alchian and Demsetz (1972) argued that it is essentially misguided to draw a hard line between firms and markets. According to them, a firm is a nexus of contracts, backed up by special legal status and characterized by continuity of association among input owners. In their formulation, the authority relation associated with the employment relationship is not the defining characteristic of the firm.

The Firm as a Solution to Moral Hazard in Teams

Alchian and Demsetz (1972) emphasize that the firm is characterized by the technology of team-production, that is, the services of several specialists were required to produce an end product. While they viewed the coordination of production as relatively unproblematic, they felt it was very difficult to monitor the effort of individual workers in a team. Individual team members had an incentive to shirk by reducing their effort. Shirking reduced the surplus of everyone in the team prompting the hiring of a monitor to measure effort. But this created a new problem—monitoring the monitor. The solution was to award the residual income of the firm to the monitor (now called the owner). The incentive to earn an uncapped income would motivate the monitor to keep a close check on the team. A firm was therefore defined as team production in the service of a monitor holding residual income rights.

The Firm as an Incentive System

The connection between ownership and employment is in viewing the firm as 'a system', specifically as a coherent set of complementary contractual arrangements that mitigate incentive conflicts (Holmström and Milgrom 1994). In their opinion, the firm is characterized by the employee not owning the assets but by the employee being subject to a low-powered incentive scheme and to the authority of the employer.

Knowledge-based Explanations of the Firm

These theories have in common behavioural assumptions and a belief that knowledge and capabilities represent the firm's critical and distinctive resources. The evolutionary theory and resource-based view of the firm are knowledge-based explanations of the firm. The firm is conceived as an institution where competences are actively and consciously built, shaped, maintained, and protected. First, because knowledge of complex production processes is distributed (Hayek 1945) and cannot be fully grasped and controlled by a single individual, a primary role of the organization becomes that of coordinating this dispersed knowledge. Second, coordination in this case generally involves the creation of commonly shared bodies of knowledge: sets of facts, notions, 'models of the world', rules, and procedures that are—at least partly—known to all the members of the organization involved in a given interaction.

Resource-based View

Following Penrose (1959), the existence of the firm is explained as a heterogeneous bundle of productive resources under administrative direction. Those firms with hard to imitate resources earn rents and gain a sustained competitive advantage that other firms find too costly to imitate. Resources are 'all assets, capabilities, organisational processes, firm attributes, information, knowledge, etc., controlled by a firm that enable the firm to conceive of and implement strategies that improve its efficiency and effectiveness' (Barney 1991). Examples of resources include patents, capital equipment, and skilled human resources. A capability (or competency) is the ability to perform a task or activity that involves complex patterns of coordination and cooperation between people and other resources (Grant 1991; Schulze 1994). Capabilities include research and development, excellent customer service, and high-quality manufacturing. Emphasis is placed on the firm's internal processes and arrangements of production. Differences (heterogeneity) in firm resources and their degree of immobility determine firm trajectories. Resource heterogeneity is long lasting and therefore produces a sustainable advantage since these resources may not be perfectly mobile across firms. But resource-based theory cannot easily explain the existence of the firm, why firms are defined by their ownership of physical assets, when capabilities are important for an economic organization and when they are not, and causes of success (Foss 1998).

Evolutionary Theory

The evolutionary approach to the firm considers it as a 'processor of knowledge' (Fransman 1994). The firm is considered as the 'locus' of setting up, of construction, of selection, of usage, and of development of knowledge. In contrast, in the traditional case, the behaviour of the firm can be understood as an optimal reaction to environmental signals which are detected by the firm. The governance of the firm is therefore focused on the coordination and the development of new knowledge. Alfred Marshall's (1920) assertion that 'capital consists in great part knowledge and organization' is especially notable in his recognition of the importance of the knowledge that each business gains through its organization. The superiority of firms over markets in building knowledge comes from actions taken by firms that are based on routines and capabilities that represent where the firm's distinguishing competences reside. Whether the firm is better suited to develop knowledge is based on three arguments. First, knowledge is the result of learning and experience. Second, since knowledge is the result of learning, it is context and path-dependent. Finally, knowledge is partly tacit, and the organization is partly unaware of its existence because it is embedded in organizational routines and individual skills (Nelson and Winter 1982). For this reason, knowledge can be transferred only to a third party who has some absorptive capacity, that is, someone who has already accumulated the required knowledge to understand and integrate the transferred knowledge. If it did not have this absorptive capacity, the transfer would be too costly to implement. Firms are therefore viewed as a governance structure that possesses advantages in generating firm-specific language and routines that yield valuable capabilities.

Members of a firm are constantly engaged in repeated interactions among themselves. Each of these interactions involves idiosyncrasies that are related to the preferences of the individuals involved and the knowledge they hold, the environmental conditions, and the payoffs. In a world where agents differ in their perceptions of the environment and where communication, acquisition of information, and computation are limited and costly, coordination can only be achieved by means of the definition of a common set of rules, codes, and languages that are well understood and shared by all members of the firm involved in a certain interaction. Firms, therefore, exist because 'they provide a social community of voluntaristic action structured by organizing principles that are not reducible to individuals' (Kogut and Zander 1992: 384).

The evolutionary approach is criticized for its assumption that all individuals have a natural tendency to cooperate. It assumes that the firm identity improves the way coordination, communication, and learning takes place. As the firm is defined by its routine, the issue of incentives is not taken into account by the evolutionary theory and it does not throw light on why firm members should be willing to share and integrate their knowledge.

Firm as a Source of Leverage from Composite Resources

The foregoing discussion demonstrated that the different approaches to the firm are more complementary than contrary. The firm is an organization that simultaneously allocates, creates resources, and manages competences and transactions.

The origins of the firm lay in the purposive (and collective) action of an individual(s) who initiates the 'make' decision or specialized production, that is, producing for others rather than for his own household.[11] The decision by an individual or a group of individuals to start an enterprise implicitly reflects the belief that he/she can 'beat the market' and produce more effectively through a firm than via a set of market contracts.

The 'make' decision is not a matter of calculation, but a function of judgment, which includes both an estimate of comparative costs and levels of risk involved. What is required for action under these circumstances is an entrepreneur prepared to bear risk under conditions of uncertainty and to devise innovative solutions when opportunities arise. An entrepreneur perceives a market demand for a product, identifies a bundle of specialist inputs and human resources capable of meeting the perceived market demand, assembles the inputs and human resources, and ensures all parts are capable of productively working together to form the final product. The entrepreneur also determines the best form of economic organization for each input to maximize its collective performance. In addition, an entrepreneur has sufficient leadership skills, in particular a capacity to successfully implement and enforce her/his business conception and is able to induce employees to actually comply with the entrepreneur's business conception so that it guides their decision making in the firm (Witt 1999).

Entrepreneurs must also be able to exchange their output with others in the economy. Gains from production are only realized after an exchange has occurred. Exchange involves the acts of negotiating, executing, and enforcing an exchange, costs of discovering prices, searching and concluding contracts. A firm therefore needs all the technical, managerial, and commercial knowledge and skills required not only to develop and produce, but also to sell its products and services.

A firm initially focuses on creating and building a core collection of productive firm-specific[12] resources (human capital assets) and financial resources.[13] While many of the ideas of the entrepreneur/s may be achieved through market transactions, but through the coalition of individuals, that is, managers, workers, and stockholders, an entrepreneur realizes complex ideas, which he/she is unable to realize by herself/himself exclusively (Rathe and Witt 2001). Individuals are equipped with specific knowledge, skills, experience, external ties, and motivation in an inter-personal comparison. By pooling their inputs in a firm, they overcome certain constraints (like cognitive limits of human actors) that they cannot overcome on their own. A collection of resources is also important because of uncertainty, the different types of assets needed to support exchange, the need to adapt to new environments, and the mores and values of society.[14]

A coalition of individuals inevitably means that the firm consists of people having diverse and conflicting interests, yet each person gains from interacting with others, in particular through their coordinated activities. Learning at the firm level is for the greater part dependent on patterns of interaction. Through learning by doing at the firm, individuals accumulate relationship-specific human capital that makes it possible for them to produce goods and services more efficiently. Such human capital is of particular value to suppliers and customers who benefit from it. A firm also helps to improve the quality of decisions because the firm has information at its disposal that other people lack. The firm provides a specific organizational environment that fosters asset-refinement processes leading to the development of competences.

A wide collection of resources in a firm embodied in various forms of capital (financial, human, social) implies a wide range of competences[15] underpinning it from generic and multipurpose to counterpart-specific and idiosyncratic. It is such unique capabilities of firms that allow them a basis for profit, which, in turn, provides incentives to invest.

Due to its possession of these unique and valuable resources, assets, and competences, the firm as a party to a contract or agreement has the ability to influence the terms and conditions of that contract or subsequent contracts in its own favour and hence the future payoff from investing in the relationship. As a result, the firm develops an enhanced bargaining position and reaps the many implicit and explicit returns that accrue through its control over critical resources and competences. Upholding the leverage derived from the utilization of resources is important to maintain the firm as a going concern when the entrepreneur reassigns tasks between employees and resources between tasks accordingly as new contingencies arise.

If different agents owning different resources pooled their capital into a single enterprise in whose profits they jointly shared, such organizations would benefit from: accumulation of relationship-specific human capital, improved decision making, concerted problem solving, choice of a more productive specialized technology, an opportunity to create novel combinations of resources, superior ability to create value, the facility to eschew the quasi-rents associated with opportunistic behaviour, and the ability to act as a wedge against existing market power in upstream and downstream markets. In addition, they would win out in the competitive struggle against the contractual alternative. These wide-ranging reasons explain the existence of the firm and each has been analysed individually in the numerous theories of the firm, but the common thread binding these different issues is the bargaining power an entrepreneur builds and protects through the structure of the firm. In short, the decision to 'make' or 'buy' is related to the bargaining levers over outsiders and the derived efficiency of the firm in a particular part of the value chain.

However, the accumulation of exceptionally talented and productive resources is not enough for the firm. There must be a desire on the part of the individuals to invest their skills and expertise in the firm to maintain that leverage.[16] In other words, individuals must commit or engage with the firm if effective utilization of their human capital is to happen. Therefore, for human capital to effective, there must also exist social capital and institutional capital (Stiles and Kulvisaechana 2003). It is precisely such a combination that Penrose (1959, 1995: 149) employs in defining the firm as 'a pool of resources the utilisation of which is organised in an administrative framework'. Accordingly, a firm needs to coordinate interactions among its constituent parts and of the firm itself with its environment. Through qualitative coordination, firms help cooperating parties to align not only their incentives but their knowledge and expectations. Firms achieve coordination by designing appropriate incentive schemes, monitoring, supervising, creating routines,[17] and identifying a common set of rules and standards,[18] and relational contracts[19] (social capital) in order to direct self-interested individual action towards the common organizational goal. The firm, in other words, is essentially a structure designed to harness the advantages of an assembly of resources and competences (accumulation of specialized interdependent knowledge) and harmonize the decision-making efforts of this group of people focused on a single issue or set of related issues.

Boundaries of the Firm

Managers are increasingly challenged to navigate in a 'new competitive landscape' characterized by decreasing transaction costs, diverse technology and knowledge, and intense competition due to deregulation and rapid technological change and diffusion. Firms have responded to these challenges with increasing corporate disaggregation and a higher incidence of outsourcing. At the same time, the exceptional levels of mergers and acquisitions in the past three decades are a strong indication that economically significant forces determine firm boundaries. The activities of acquisitions and divestitures are constantly drawing and redrawing the boundaries of firms. Boundaries provide buffering[20] as well as bridging functions;[21] they separate as well as join the firm to its environment. More recently, the space between market and hierarchies has been looked upon as hybrid territory. Different types of hybrid structures mix in varying proportions elements of the two pure coordination instruments, price, and authority.

The study of firm boundaries originated with Coase (1937); for him the existence of the firm is due to the existence of transaction costs. Markets pre-exist firms and firms emerge as a result of friction in the use of the price mechanism. Once constituted as entities, firms are differentiated from markets by boundaries determined by the application of a marginal rule with firms internalizing activities up to the point where internal costs of management equal the costs of transacting in markets. There are three economic perspectives on firm boundaries: modern property right theory, modern transaction cost theory, and evolutionary theory. The first explains firm boundaries by the optimal allocation of residual decision rights to physical assets, while the second is premised on the idea that transaction attributes determine comparative advantages of make or buy decisions. In the evolutionary theory, the boundaries of the firm are determined by the capabilities or resources available to a particular enterprise.

The conventional approach to firm boundaries is based on the role of ownership in the provision of investment incentives and the resolution of hold-up problems (Holmström and Roberts 1998). Answers to question about appropriate firm boundaries revolve around their efficiency implications. The two main sources of efficiency are incentives and capabilities. But in reality, large lock-in problems have not deterred firms from experimenting with several disintegration mechanisms.

Transaction Cost Economics (TCE) showed that, under certain conditions, the costs of using the market would be such that the firm would decide to internalize a transaction through producing in-house.

A firm's decision about its boundaries became synonymous with deciding whether to integrate a particular transaction within its own governance structure. An assortment of conditions that limit firm size—costs of bureaucracy, the weakening of individual incentives, the hazards of internal politicking—suggested by Williamson and others are not easy to measure and accordingly have not played much of a role in empirical work.

Lock-in problems do not get resolved solely by the integration of buyer and seller into a single party—a firm. Disintegration, outsourcing, contracting out, and dealing through the market have used ingenious solutions to the lock-in problems. For example, long-term, close relations with a limited number of independent suppliers,[22] a shared understanding with the chosen supplier that he/she will have the business until a certain model is redesigned, mutual dependence between buyer and supplier, better incentives for the supplier through improved accountability, and the sizable future rents that can be reaped by continued good behaviour are significant incentives. Langlois and Robertson (1995) argued that over time, most sources of transaction costs will tend to disappear as once idiosyncratic capabilities are replicated by others and become widely available. The boundaries of the firm will shift as activities that were carried out internally are outsourced from the market.

In the property rights approach, the firm is regarded as a set of assets under common ownership and control and is equated with ownership. This view provided an unequivocal answer to where the boundaries of the firm should lie, since the boundaries coincided with decisions about physical asset ownership.

In the evolutionary approach, production requires access to an appropriate bundle of capabilities if a firm is to operate competitively, with the scope for expansion circumscribed by the nature of those capabilities and the extent to which they are utilized. The boundaries of the firm are determined by the capabilities necessary to undertake productive activities as well as by the capabilities the firm requires to interact with its customers, suppliers, and other external actors.[23]

Theories of the firm have traditionally hypothesized that firms determine their boundaries by selecting sourcing modes for individual goods and services, choosing whether to make or buy a particular component or participate in networks to supply inputs or outputs.

But these theoretically sharp distinctions between firm and market arrangements do not correspond to reality as firms have opened their boundaries and have disaggregated vertically resulting in blurred boundaries. Firms have used both the market and firm arrangements to the same ends including in-house production (using internal suppliers and transferring to internal buyers), tapered vertical integration (using internal and external suppliers for internal customers only), market procurement (using external suppliers and selling to external buyers), outsourcing (using external suppliers and transferring to internal buyers), out-streaming (using internal suppliers and transferring downstream as well as selling to external buyers on the intermediate market), brokering (using both internal and external suppliers and transferring downstream as well as selling to external buyers), and trading (doing pure 'matching' rather than being involved in several stages of the value chain, a firm operates on a very small part of the value chain) (Jacobides and Billinger 2006).

This way a firm can effectively use its resources and capacities and leverage its heterogeneous capabilities along the value chain. One of the benefits of using external suppliers, in addition to internal production, is that it counters cycles and swings in downstream demand. Likewise, in using external customers a firm can ensure that its upstream production is not subject to uneven downstream demand.

Firms seeking to set their boundaries jointly analyse asset specificity, firm specificity, and their resource endowments.[24] Every firm connects with the market, to both purchase the necessary inputs and sell the goods or services it produces. A firm connects with both final and intermediate markets. So, in setting their boundaries, firms have to take into account their own particular conditions and circumstances (Madhok 2002), that is, the type of activities a firm carries out, how these activities fit with others, and the capabilities underpinning them.

Given that resources at hand give firms bargaining power, firms should focus on their core strengths and pursue relevant activities in-house only when they have a greater relative bargaining (capabilities, experience, or skills) than potential suppliers. The boundaries of the firm are partly determined by the differential between the bargaining power they hold in relation to potential supplies, and the transaction and governance costs of generating capabilities internally against accessing them via non-hierarchical means (Argyres 1996). Accordingly, firms draw their boundaries through specialization in activities for which their resources offer some comparative advantage.

In order to interact with others, a firm needs capabilities which allow it to negotiate its relationship with the competitive environment. The drawing of boundaries is an interactive and negotiated process mediating a variety of internal and external relationships. A firm has to continually revisit the make-or-buy decision[25] depending on its changing relative bargaining power.

The decision of where to draw the firm's boundaries thus depends crucially on the relative bargaining power of the firm vis-à-vis external parties, the availability of complementary and distinctive capabilities of external parties, and the ways to access those capabilities and understand how they are organized in establishing, maintaining, developing, or terminating connections with external parties and networks.

Notes

1. Arrow (1969) classified the possible causes for Pareto non-optimality of social outcome into (a) purely technological conditions (such as increasing returns to scale) and (b) specific modes of economic organization (such as market failure).

2. Williamson (1975, 1985) was the most prominent in identifying various types of transaction costs and their influence on firms. Williamson introduced three dimensions for transaction cost: (a) asset specificity (b) uncertainty and (c) frequency. Other types of transaction costs arising out of behavioural patterns are bounded rationality and opportunism.

3. Uncertainty exacerbates the problems that arise because of bounded rationality and opportunism.

4. If only a small number of players exist in a market place, a party to a transaction may have difficulty disciplining the other parties to the transaction via the possibility of withdrawal and use of alternative players in the marketplace.

5. The value of an asset may be attached to a particular transaction that it supports. The party who has invested in the asset will incur a loss if the party who has not invested withdraws from the transaction. The possibility (threat) of this party acting opportunistically leads to the so-called 'hold-up' problem.

6. Human beings are unlikely to have the abilities or resources to consider every state-contingent outcome associated with a transaction that might arise.

7. Human beings will act to further their own self-interests.

8. Williamson (1985) argues that three dimensions of a transaction affect the type of governance structure chosen for the transaction: asset specificity, uncertainty, and frequency. As asset specificity and uncertainty increase, the risk of opportunism increases. Thus, decision makers are more likely to choose a hierarchical (firm-based) governance structure.

9. Motivation is intrinsic if an activity is undertaken for one's immediate need satisfaction. Intrinsic motivation 'is valued for its own sake and appears to be self-sustained.' The ideal incentive system consists of the work content itself which must be satisfactory and fulfilling for the employees.

10. Within firms, examples for tangible common pool resources are mainframe computer systems, intranet solutions, the department for human resources, and the commission for equal opportunity. Examples for *intangible* common pool resources are corporate culture, mutual commitment, common organizational rules and routines, and accumulated firm specific knowledge or absorptive capacity (for example, Grant 1996, Kogut and Zander 1996, Nonaka and Takeuchi 1995, Spender 1996; Teece and Pisano 1994; Winter 1995).

11. 'For each firm that is set up, there is a motive, that is the firm founder(s) must have some imaginings of what business to pursue and how. Such a business conception, no matter how elaborate, always rests on subjective conjectures about future events like the response of the markets, feasibility of inputs, price developments, actions of competitors, achievements of the firm members, etc. Some or all of these conjectures may turn out to be wrong, may challenge the underlying conceptions, and/or may demand modifications and learning' (Witt 1999).

12. Firm specificity refers to resources that lose in value when deployed in the same activity within another firm, but could be deployed in multiple activities within the firm (Zott and Amit 2006). Firm-specific assets are 'human assets, physical assets and company-specific routines and knowledge that are not deployable to alternative uses' (Williamson 1985). The greater the degree of a resource's specificity to a firm, the greater that resource's rent potential to the firm (Conner 1991).

13. Although market-making requires offices, shops and warehouses, all these forms of fixed capital can be easily rented or leased; they are not, therefore, specific irreversible investments. Few entrepreneurs will invest in owning buildings at an early stage of a firm's growth, when financial resources are limited. Only when a firm is mature, and cash flow is strong, will the typical entrepreneur consider property investments of this kind. There is, however, one form of investment which is almost mandatory for a market-making entrepreneur at the start-up phase. This is investment in working capital, such as finished stocks and work in progress. Financial resources are required to fund inventory.

14. Even if two firms were given identical bundles of resources, they would tend to use them in different ways. Over time a firm's stock of tradable and non-tradable assets and its performance will diverge from its competitors.

15. Competences are interpersonal patterns of action which rest upon the division of work and which support a goal-oriented social interaction of persons in a non-random manner.

16. To induce the firm members to work for the entrepreneur's business conception, it has to be conveyed somehow. In this case, cognitive processes are at work and the particularities, and the constraints they impose, can be expected to cause some regularities in spite of all subjective variance that prevails otherwise. These regularities are cognitive frameworks. The way in which these cognitive frames emerge and change over time is influenced by communication processes with the social environment which endow people with tacit knowledge, socially shared interpretation patterns, and social models of behaviour. Cognitive frames thus become an important source of commonalities that may limit the subjective variance in the perception of choices (Witt 1999).

17. Routines allow the predictability of individual behaviour indispensable for collective action: routines guide behaviours (Cohendet and Llerena 1999).

18. The organizational structure defines the rules of the games that individuals within an organization and parts (departments, units, services, and so on) of it repeatedly play. The structure of an organization 'designates for each person in the organization what decisions the person makes, and the influences to which he is subject in making each of these decisions' (Simon 1976).

19. Firms are riddled with relational contracts: informal agreements and unwritten codes of conduct that powerfully affect the behaviours of individuals within firms. There are often informal quid pro quos between co-workers, as well as unwritten understandings between bosses and subordinates about task-assignment, promotion, and termination decisions. Relational contracts within and between firms help circumvent difficulties in formal contracting.

20. The buffering function of the boundaries involves providing a space for the development of stable clusters of connections amongst capabilities within the firm (Potts 2001).

21. Boundaries provide a bridge to access capabilities outside the control of the firm, this function is provided by different types of indirect capabilities.

22. Having a small number of suppliers reduces the costs of monitoring and increases the frequency of transacting, both of which strengthen the force of reputation. The rents that are generated in the production process do not have to be shared too widely, providing a source for significant future rewards (Holmström and Roberts 1998).

23. The first set of capabilities is usually termed direct or core capabilities and the second type of capabilities have been labelled indirect or ancillary

capabilities (Langlois and Robertson 1995). The notion of indirect capabilities can be regarded as: capabilities required to organize access to complementary and dissimilar capabilities held by third parties, capabilities to design and test externally procured inputs, capabilities to coordinate and integrate internally and externally generated inputs into effective products and production systems, and capabilities to use the market effectively and to make good use of the capabilities of others (Granstrand et al. 1997; Loasby 1999).

24. The circumstances that render resources difficult to imitate also create the conditions for asset specificity. Resources are often viewed as an antecedent of transaction costs, which in turn affect the choice of governance form.

25. Firms consist of acquired pools of resources that come in lumpy bundles. In order to take advantage of excess capacity in some of the lumps, the firm may expand or diversify into areas in which that capacity is useful. This is in turn may lead the firm to acquire other complementary capabilities which will lead to further excess capacity (Penrose 1959).

IV
Conclusion

12 Concluding Comments

Human capital, social capital, and institutional capital are relevant to a range of policy areas vital to a nation's future. These concepts refer to different aspects of a society's human resources—individual assets, human collectivities, and systems of meaning that define the context within which agents operate, interact, and behave. The challenge is to transform situations where a community's social capital substitutes for weak, hostile, or indifferent formal institutions into ones in which both realms complement one another.

The emphasis on human capital as a factor in policymaking began four decades ago in recognition of the 'East Asian Miracle', when it was acknowledged that East Asian countries had sustained unprecedented levels of public and private investment in human capital over long periods of time. The notion of social capital gained importance in the 1990s, both at the academic and the policymaking levels, in the context of the shift in theoretical attention from the economic to the human/social face of adjustment (Fine 2003). Institutional capital has been recognized as critical factor in economic development since the early 1980s through overwhelming evidence accumulated from crises and failed transition experiments. Such evidence suggested that even the most basic determinants of economic performance are incapable of providing desired living standards in the absence of well-functioning institutions to support, enable, and apply economic incentives.

For modern economics, the rationality of human behaviour is assumed to successfully describe much of the economic world. But important areas of economic behaviour remain non-rational in origin. In the last two decades of the twentieth century, however, cultural explanations of economic behaviour, if not fully established within the mainstream of the discipline of economics, have found a more secure niche in the social sciences. The idea that shared cultural values and embedded social relationships could have a significant impact on economic development and growth has been most intensively discussed since the 1990s under the rubric of social capital. The concept of social capital remains controversial among economists, perhaps understandably in light of the fact that there is still no generally agreed upon definition as to what it is and particularly how it is to be measured. Most would not deny, however, that institutions and human capital were critical for economic growth, and that the cooperative norms that characterize social capital are also important. Human capital contributes to economic efficiency, provides the labour resources on which growth depends. Institutions are processes, behaviour rules that enable societies to function. Property rights, appropriate regulatory structures, the quality and independence of the judiciary, and bureaucratic capacity are of utmost importance in initiating and sustaining economic growth. Social capital, in turn, is created when the relations among persons change in ways that facilitate action especially in the knowledge economy, where it serves by cutting expenses and reducing time needed for knowledge exchange between individuals. In this case, social capital becomes the essential complement to human capital.

It is now established that technological knowledge and innovation are drivers for sustainable economic growth. Consequently, the world accepts that countries need to depend increasingly for their wealth, economic health and survival on the expansion of knowledge-driven activities. This has been the natural result of recent advancements in information technologies and the dominance of the service economy, in which competence is synonymous with productivity and knowledge (Barnow and Smith 2005). Now the main production factors are labour, with knowledge and information, intellectual property, education, R&D, etc. To build the knowledge economy, there needs to be a shift in our dependence from the more traditional forms of capital to intangible capitals like human capital, social capital and institutional capital. Throughout the world, social and economic policy is being shaped with the explicit goal of promoting the intangible capital and the knowledge economy. In other words, the acquisition of new knowledge—through education and learning—is now seen as the key to a dynamic economy. The nature of highly complex or technical knowledge usually requires an equally complex form of organization in order to flourish. Intricate social infrastructure and clusters endowed in social capital have become an essential feature of the knowledge economy. As knowledge is an unevenly distributed resource, some groups perform better because they can access this production factor thanks to their social capital. Social capital facilitates and speeds up economic actors' acquisition of information and knowledge. It promotes production and the exchange of knowledge and knowledge transfers (Westlund 2005).

Knowledge creation and diffusion processes depend on appropriate institutional performance. The institutional framework is crucial for gaining an adequate flow of knowledge between scientific research and technological applications as well as for good information between knowledge users and researchers. But institutions are not enough to support the type of complex transactions that often occur in knowledge-related activities. Norms and values aimed at cooperation may be a feasible alternative to support cooperation, in particular with complex transactions governed by implicit contracts. Members of a network with social capital will more easily share knowledge and build up knowledge together. In the absence of a sufficient degree of trust, knowledge increasingly becomes a factor that group members may use to their personal advantage. Then knowledge becomes power and sharing power is far from self-evident. In the case of societies as well, this is true. Societies can be rich in social capital within social groups and yet experience debilitating poverty, corruption, and conflict (Narayan 2002).

A society well-endowed in human capital is highly interconnected, sharing information and strengthening knowledge through a never-ending web of connections. The book postulates that although human capital may facilitate social networks, there are certain values and behaviours that characterize and bind a network. Those values and behaviours give networks a sense of identity and common purpose, help direct attention to the relationships that shape the realization of human capital's potential for the individual and for the network. Creation and strengthening of networks could increase because of the necessity to counteract the individual disadvantage against weak, ineffective, under-developed, entirely missing institutions (institutional voids) or institutions which fail to adapt to the needs of changing conditions. Social capital in this way is responsible for institutional emergence and change through structured bargaining between actors when they organize themselves into groups and networks. But strong unbiased institutions are required to reconcile conflicts among major social groups as well as among individuals or smaller and narrowly focused interest groups. Institutions can influence social capital either positively or negatively by affecting the trust of the citizens. When there is lack of trust, socioeconomic heterogeneity leads to a lobbying process either direct or indirect, to influence the decision making. The effectiveness of groups in appropriating resources through lobbying at the detriment of others is dependent on how organized the group is, relative to others, its relationships and networks with other groups, and its internal resources. Institutions therefore, need to be powerful external forces that not only help determine how people make sense of their world and act in it, but also prevent networks from rent seeking and the pursuit of narrow interests.

As economies evolve, institutional capital slowly but not completely replaces social capital as the guardian of social, business, and personal contracts. When that fails to occur, excessive claims on network members manifests itself through conformity pressures where opting out is relatively rare even when the existing system is no longer adapted to their needs. It is then that (taking Schumpeter's expression) a 'creative destruction' is necessary of obsolete social capital in order to facilitate the creation of new social capital. The transformation from industrial society to knowledge society is a large scale example of this economic restructuring and the needs of new economic and social networks to emerge.

The case studies show that those countries, which safeguard the expression of new ideas, and build and adapt institutions based on them, are most creative and progressive. Countries appear to remain vigorous only so long as they are organized to receive and assimilate novel ideas and thoughts. They also show that social capital plays a greater role in the developing stages, in which communities are relatively closed to outsiders, but that human capital makes a more critical contribution at all stages. Both the China and India examples show that pro-knowledge and pro-competitive institutional re-orientation, both hierarchical and horizontal, is the fundamental driver for the rapid growth witnessed in the sectors analysed by the case studies. There were unique country-specific features, yet behind the trajectories of the institutional reforms, the logic is broadly consistent with existing economic theories. The case studies on Industrial Revolution in Britain and America show that the interaction between the three intangible capitals led to the emergence of an unbroken chain of inventions or rather several chains of much wider impact leading to significant increases in productivity as well as the creation of new products but also, introduced a mechanism contriving continuous, unending irreversible improvements.

Appendix A.1

Measurement Issues in Human Capital

Initially, two predominant methods were used to estimate the 'value' of human beings: the costs of production and capitalized earnings over a lifetime. The former consisted of estimating the real costs incurred in 'producing' a human being, while the latter relied on estimating the present value of an individual's future income stream. One of the first attempts to estimate the monetary value of a human being was made around 1691 by Sir William Petty. Labour to him was the 'father of wealth'. The first truly scientific attempt at finding the capital or monetary value of a human being was devised in 1853 by William Farr. His approach was to calculate the present value of an individual's net future earnings as future earnings minus personal living expenses.

In economics literature, the concepts of human capital and education have not always received focused, continuous attention. The 1960s and early 1970s were marked, in the Western world mostly, by an enthusiasm for the issue of education and its presumed positive impact on economic growth. This enthusiasm led to various attempts at measuring both human capital and the rate of return on investment in education. Expenditure on education was treated as an investment rather than as consumption. Many contributions during that time were centred on the issue of the rate of return to schooling. Johnson (1970) developed a model that predicted life-time earnings based on several types of investments in human capital. Beyond the many attempts to measure the costs and benefits of education, the dominant hypothesis was that education affects economic growth positively since it increases the level of cognitive skills possessed by the labour force and consequently its marginal productivity.

However, after the early 1970s, the general enthusiasm about the beneficial impact of education seemed to diminish. As unemployment among school graduates became widespread during a quasi-generalized economic recession, caution and skepticism about the beneficial economic impact of education, grew commensurately (Benavot 1989). At the time, the dominant discourse in Europe was centred around the notion of 'technology lag', as R&D policy and innovativeness in some key sectors (electronics) were seen as the sources of comparative advantage in industrialized economies. Eventually, the debate among economists shifted during the 1980s to the impact of technology—combined with knowledge and skills—on economic growth. As a response to the criticisms voiced by development economists, and as a desire to catchup with the thinking in other disciplines (such as history and sociology) developed, it became obvious that technical change could not be seen independently from human capital; technology could not be seen separately from the human inputs that created technology or utilized it.

At the micro level, the methods for estimating the stock of human capital can be divided into two main categories: the income-based approach and the cost-based approach. The cost-based approach takes all costs of forming human capital into account retrospectively. Since this means that almost every aspect of human capital has to be calculated separately, this method is often far less broad than the prospective method. Engel (1883) was the first to apply the cost-based method when he estimated human capital from the costs of rearing a child. He argued that since it is difficult to anticipate future earnings, the production costs of human capital were better sources of the estimation. The retrospective method remained very popular up to the 1930s. This method excluded social costs and the depreciation of the human capital investments. In the 1960s, Schultz (1961) extended Engle's approach. They calculated human capital so that 'the depreciated value of the dollar amount spent on those items as investments in human capital is equal to the stock of human capital' (Le et al. 2003). The second method is the income-based approach calculated future earnings. The idea behind the income-based approach is that human capital embodied in individuals is valued as the total income that might be generated in the labour market over a lifetime (Le et al. 2003). Both income- and cost-based approaches have their advantages and disadvantages. Therefore, some authors have tried to integrate these two approaches. An important example of the combined method is Dagum and Slottje (2000). They equate the 'monetary value of a person's human capital with the average lifetime earnings of the population, weighted by the level of human capital with the average life earnings of the population' (Le et al. 2003). Although the new growth models created the possibility to theoretically distinguish between human capital and technology as the main source of growth, the empirical distinction has remained difficult. The new growth models use human capital as a factor of production and as a facilitator of technology. The available human capital data are unsuited to distinguish between the two theories and the lack of country-specific studies make it difficult to interpret the empirical results.

At the macro level, human capital accumulation includes a broad combination of formal education, on-the-job training, basic scientific research, learning-by-doing, process innovations, product innovations, and industrial innovations. But there are enormous measurement and definitional difficulties involved in assessing accumulation. There are as many kinds of education and training as there are kinds of machines. Some education and training is effective and has a direct effect on industry and growth, while much is not. A lot of education and training is informal, so not part of schooling. It is difficult to guess how fast skills and aptitudes depreciate or whether they develop further with use. The current indicators can be used to gain only a crude idea of the size of the stock of human capital and help detect differences in the stock of human capital across time and space. For example, 'average years of schooling of the population' and literacy rates, hours of schooling and formal training at different levels, wage differentials give some idea of the market valuation of different kinds and amounts of training and education. The educational stock approach has remained the most popular method to proxy the human capital stock.

The OECD considers three approaches in measuring human capital stock in the population. The first is educational attainment—the highest level of education completed by each adult, measured either by duration (number of years of schooling) or qualification (the proportion successfully completing different levels of formal education).

The second approach is to look directly at skills (by relying on the International Literacy Survey) and the third approach is to use earnings as a proxy, estimating earnings differentials associated with education.

There are also three distinct ways of defining 'returns to education': (a) the private return, (b) the social return, and (c) the labour productivity return. The first of these is made up of the costs and benefits to the individual and is clearly net of transfers from the state and taxes paid. The second definition highlights externalities or spill-over effects and includes transfers and taxes. The final definition relates to the gross increase in labour productivity (or growth) (Blundell et al. 2001).

Despite the interconnectivity between human capital and growth, most empirical studies have employed reduced-form equations that do not capture feedback effects and have found conflicting results. The literature often focuses either on the analysis of the growth effects in improving education or health indicators, or on the impact of public spending on these indicators. Furthermore, research has concentrated essentially on education, often focusing on the impact of the initial stock of education on growth. Among these studies (Barro 1996; Barro and Sala-i-Martin 1995; Levine and Renelt 1992; Mankiw et al. 1992; Sala-i-Martin 1997) find a positive relationship between enrolment and/or schooling and growth. Using a more refined measure of skills, Coulombe and Tremblay (2004) and others find that a country with literacy scores 1 per cent higher than the average experiences an increase in per capita GDP growth of 1.5 percentage points. Benhabib and Spiegel (1994) and Pritchett and Summers (1996) however find that some macroeconomic evidence conflicts with the findings at the microeconomic level on the returns to education and conclude that the positive link from education attainment to output growth is, at best, weak.

In all, ascertaining the causal impact of education is extremely difficult because education is a process in which there are many inputs, some of which reflect choices of individuals, families, and communities. There is an additional problem of reverse causality or the fact that both education and other outcomes of interest respond to innate determinants like unobserved prices, tastes, abilities, motivations, and other endowments. The existing knowledge on metrics, measurement, and valuation of human capital is still away from units of comparison or measurement 'technologies' in capturing 'human capital' in understandable and quantitative form, that is, measuring the level of human capital embedded in a doctor, lawyer, economist, etc., discerning what types, mixes and combinations of human capital are needed at particular stages of development.

Measurement and Conceptual Issues in Social Capital

The idea of social capital sits awkwardly in contemporary economic thinking. Even though it has a powerful, intuitive explanatory appeal, it has been proven hard to track as an economic attribute. Among other things, it is difficult to measure, although, at first brush, social capital may seem like a natural complement to the concepts of physical and human capital. However, this extension is far from neat and throws up serious conceptual inconsistencies. To Solow (2000), 'it is an attempt to gain conviction from a bad analogy'. And Arrow (1999) calls for an outright abandonment of the capital metaphor and the term social capital. To him, capital has three important characteristics: capital has a time dimension, capital requires deliberate sacrifice of the present for future benefit, and capital is 'alienable', that is, its ownership can be transferred from one person to another. According to Arrow, social capital may have a time dimension similar to physical capital, for example, reputation or trust takes time to develop hence it satisfies his first characteristic. However, social capital does not necessarily entail any material sacrifice, and, hence, does not generally satisfy his second characteristic. And finally, in most cases, as with human capital, it is difficult to change the ownership of social capital, and, hence, it does not satisfy Arrow's third characteristic. But it is possible to partially change the ownership of social capital by 'sharing' social capital. In addition, capital can be used, renewed and replenished and is an indispensable ingredient for future output and social capital possesses these attributes.

Solow (2000) raises some additional measurement problems. While physical and human capital can be measured and their rates of return calculated (very imperfectly as in the case of human capital), such rigorous measurements are much more problematic in the case of social capital, which is precisely what accounts for the ability of societies to accumulate capital and to mobilize skilled labour effectively. All this would suggest that conceptually, social capital still falls short of being a form of capital and that we are still in a primitive stage of thinking about social capital as a form of capital. On the other hand, there are social scientists who believe that social capital, while being constituted by social networks and relationships, is never disconnected from capital. For example, capital for Bourdieu (1986) is simultaneously economic and a set of power relations that constitute a variety of realms and social interactions normally thought of as non-economic. Two key components of his work suggest that the production and reproduction of capital is a process inherently about power and since his interest is in the social production of classes, he distinguishes between the social networks an individual is embedded in and out of which social capital and the outcomes of social relationships emerge (DeFilippis 2001).

There is little agreement on what constitutes social capital. Some view social capital as an individual asset that comes from access to networks and social connections, whereas others hold that it is a collective asset in the form of a homogeneous community with common interests and shared values. Some authors have focused on trust and tolerance, while others have focused on the degree of social engagements. Still others have highlighted issues of culture and social norms. Social capital stems from both subjective attributes and more profoundly from emergent and existing social infrastructures which facilitate individual and collective actions of many kinds.

Criticism has been applied as much to social capital in general as to Putnam's taxonomic innovation regarding bridging and bonding social capital. In this connection, Fischer (2001) rightly notes that Putnam's use of metaphors as 'bridging' and 'binding' social capital is somewhat unfitting as 'both terms are more suited to a metaphor around "ties" than around capital'.

Measures of social capital that are relevant for one set of cultures can be irrelevant for others. Roles, precedents, norms, values, attitudes, and beliefs are different among people who have different patterns of life. Moreover, social values are not static and change continuously. Social capital is an intrinsic and relational concept that cannot be adequately understood in instrumental, utilitarian terminology.

The most common measures of social capital look at participation in various forms of civic engagement, such as membership of voluntary associations, churches or political parties, or at levels of expressed trust in other people. More economistic interpretations put greater emphasis to the institutional capital and rules governing economic transactions at both micro and macro levels.

Despite some ambiguity, social capital is generally understood as a matter of relationships, as a property of groups rather than the property of individuals. Social capital focuses on networks: the relationships within and between them, and the norms that govern these relationships. Although this does not necessarily entail a specific value position on the part of those who use it as an analytic device, it has strong normative connotations, implying that trusting relationships are good for social cohesion and for economic success.

Needless to say that the social capital literature is also divided over how it is beneficial, that is, at the individual or societal level. Loury (1977), Bourdieu (1986), and Coleman (1988) all argued that social capital is not embodied in any particular person, but rather is embedded in people's social relationships. At the same time, however, they also stated that social capital was realized by individuals. The individualistic perspective of social capital differs from the aggregate/community perspective that has emerged as the dominant paradigm in the literature in the hands of Putnam. According to this aggregate perspective, social capital is a property of the group or the community or even the nation as a whole, although there is less than unanimity among authors what this property is. Some recent notable contributors to this aggregate perspective include Inglehart, Fukuyama, Bowles, Gintis, and Hayami. Inglehart (1997) equates social capital with culture, that is, 'a culture of trust and tolerance in which extensive network of voluntary associations form'. And to him, culture is 'a system of attitudes, values and knowledge that is widely shared within a society and is transmitted from generation to generation'. This preceding discussion suggests that the ingredients of what constitutes social capital have to be shared by a group but what is essentially individually lodged.

Much of the existing literature defines social capital in a way that tends to exaggerate its beneficial aspects. As Portes (1998) and Durlauf (1999) have noted, most definitions of social capital confuse its sources with consequences and its existence with functions. In other words, the evidence of the existence of social capital is often inferred from its positive outcomes and from the fact that without it collectives would not or could not exist. In a critique of Putnam's analysis, DeFilippis (2001) argues that 'social capital becomes divorced from capital (in the literal economic sense), stripped of power relations and imbued with the assumption that social networks are win-win relationships and that individual gains, interests and profits are synonymous with group gains, interests and profits'. Social capital for DeFilippis is about power relations, comprising a variety of realms and social interactions. He observes that it is groups who wield power and maintain control. For example, Rubio's (1997) study refers to what is called 'perverse' social capital—it derives from his study of Colombia where criminal activity is associated with strong networks. The impact therefore of social capital depends upon its social context (Fine 1999).

Social capital arises spontaneously as a product of iterated Prisoners' Dilemma (PD) games. The theory of repeated games has been used to interpret norms of behaviour, culture, and informal institutions—how they emerge and are sustained over time (Quibria 2003). A one-shot PD game does not lead to a cooperative outcome because defection constitutes a Nash equilibrium for both players: if the game is iterated, however, a simple strategy like tit-for-tat (playing cooperation for cooperation and defection for defection) leads both players to a cooperative outcome. In non-game theoretic terms, if individuals interact with each other repeatedly over time, they develop a stake in a reputation for honesty and reliability. Market interactions in a commercial society lead, as Adam Smith observed, to the development of bourgeois social virtues like honesty, industriousness, and prudence (Fukuyama 1999).

There is still no agreed upon definition for social capital, its measurement is problematic, and it is highly dependent on context, which causes particular difficulties when it comes to attempting to aggregate it across levels. In light of these conceptual and measurement problems, many economists are reluctant to label social capital as capital. Although there is a general consensus that social interactions influence economic outcomes, there is not much of a consensus whether these influences can be, or should be, meaningfully codified into such a metaphor as social capital.

Measurement and Conceptual Issues in Institutional Capital

The institutionalist analysis does not start by building mathematical models; it begins with stylized facts and theoretical inferences concerning causal mechanisms. Extensive use is made of historical and comparative empirical qualitative data related to socioeconomic institutions. In several of these respects, institutional economics is at variance with much of modern mainstream economic theory. Institutionalism is an 'evolutionary economics' and like all work in this vein, it is biased towards dynamic rather than equilibrium-oriented modes of theorizing (Hodgson 1998). Accordingly, it lacks a robust framework that provides guidelines for why and how institutional capital influences the large observed differences in per capita incomes across countries. Simon (1991) has charged the new institutional economics, and transaction cost economics in particular, with lacking sufficient empirical support. Until the relevant empirical studies have been done, he says, 'the new institutional economics and related approaches are acts of faith, or perhaps of piety'.

Empirical studies, which measure the importance of institutional capital for their growth and investment, are scarce due to a lack of data concerning the quality of institutional capital. It is impossible to find data that conforms to a most broad definition of governance or the quality of institutional capital, such as by Kaufmann et al. (1999) who define governance as 'the traditions and institutions by which authority in a country is exercised. This includes the process by which governments are selected, monitored, and replaced; the capacity of the government to effectively formulate and implement sound policies; and the respect of citizens and the state for the institutions that govern economic and social interactions among them'. Nevertheless, the past 10 years have provided an ever-increasing number of empirical studies on the influence of institutions. Some researchers based their empirical analyses of institutional capital on subjective indices of country-risk assessment collected by private sector companies. These data were first used by Knack and Keefer (1995) and subsequently by Hall and Jones (1999) and Acemoglu et al. (2001) to establish the influence of institutional capital on per capita income. Since then a hunt has begun to uncover ever better measures of institutions, as well as the mechanisms by which institutional capital influence growth.

Measures of institutional quality in empirical literature include a host of indicators such as property rights, bureaucratic structure, political rights, and civil liberties. Many indicators can shed light on various dimensions of governance. However, no single indicator or a combination of indicators can provide a completely reliable measure of any of these dimensions of governance because desirable institutional arrangements have a large element of context specificity. In any regression with change in per capita income (or its distribution) as the dependent variable, what is implicit is the change in production functions (or a change in ownership of the product thereof) and knowledge. It is institutions that make the change in production function possible, thus both the problems of endogeneity and embeddedness have failed the arguments of primacy and proximate cause.

The 'new' institutionalism attempts to explain the emergence of institutions, such as the firm or the state, by reference to a model of rational individual behaviour. An initial institution-free 'state of nature' is assumed. The explanatory movement is from individuals to institutions taking individuals as given. This approach is described as 'methodological individualism', But many authors, including the old institutionalists, suggest that in economic analysis, the individual should not be taken as given. Individuals interact to form institutions. At the same time, individual purposes or preferences are moulded by socio-economic conditions. The individual is both a producer and a product of his or her circumstances (Hodgson 1998). Such an analysis never reaches an end point as it is similar to the puzzle: which came first—the chicken or the egg?[1] Therefore, understanding and modelling the social context of economic decisions is distinct from the economic analysis of social decisions. Modelling the social context[2] requires non-standard or endogenous preferences.

Economic actors interact and organize themselves to generate growth and development through institutions. While organizations are material-bounded entities, institutions are systems of rules, decision-making procedures, and programmes that give rise to social practices, assign roles to participants in these practices, and guide their interactions. Institutions exhibit continuity and offer narrow and infrequent windows of opportunity for reform (Aghion and Howitt 1998; Rip et al. 1998). Institutions operate under settings characterized by material conditions such as the nature of available technologies and the distribution of wealth by cognitive conditions such as prevailing values, norms, and beliefs, and by transaction costs, costs of co-ordination, laws, etc. (Coase 1998; Young 1994). The market is a 'set of institutions, expectations, and patterns of behaviour that enable voluntary exchanges' based on the willingness of the parties to pay to the exchange (Haddad 2000).

One major concern of the new institutional economics is the boundary between the market on which transactions are negotiated and organizations, such as the firm (Simon 1991).

Notes

1. There are different points of view on how institutions emerge. Acemoglu et al. (2004) classifies these points of view on institutions into four categories. These are: (a) the efficient institutions view (the society will choose the institutions that maximize its total surplus), (b) the incidental institutions view (the institutions are a product of other social interactions), (c) the rent-seeking institutions view (the institutions emerge as a result of choices made by individuals, but they are not necessarily efficient), and (d) the costly institutions view (the institutions are created for solving economic problems and there is a tendency towards efficient institutions, but this view recognizes that it might be costly to design the right institutions).

2. According to Putnam (1993), social context is important as it conditions the effectiveness of institutions. Social context matters for several reasons: first, individuals may care about some characteristics, such as status, honour or popularity; second, preferences may be influenced by the environment and finally, even if individuals have exogenous preferences only over economic variables, the nature of interactions that facilitate economic activity can themselves be at least partially social in nature.

Appendix A.2

The following table provides a list of widespread definitions of social capital.

Author	Definitions of Social Capital
Coleman (1988)	'…obligations and expectations, information channels, and social norms'.
Coleman (1990)	'…social organization constitutes social capital, facilitating the achievement of goals that could not be achieved in its absence or could be achieved only at a higher cost'.
Putnam (1993)	'…features of social organization, such as trust, norms, and networks that can improve the efficiency of society'.
Fukuyama (1999)	'…the existence of a certain set of informal rules or norms shared among members of a group that permits cooperation among them. The sharing of values and norms does not in itself produce social capital, because the norms may be the wrong ones… The norms that produce social capital…must substantively include virtues like truth telling, the meeting of obligations and reciprocity'.
Knack and Keefer (1997)	'Trust, cooperative norms, and associations within groups'.
Narayan and Pritchett (1999)	'…the quantity and quality of associational life and the related social norms'.
Putnam (2000)	'…connections among individuals—social networks and norms of reciprocity and trustworthiness that arise from them'.

Ostrom (2000)	'...the shared knowledge, understandings, norms, rules and expectations about patterns of interactions that groups of individuals bring to a recurrent activity'.
Woolcock (2002)	'...the norms and networks that facilitate collective action...it is important that any definition of social capital focus on its sources rather than consequences... This approach eliminates an entity such as "trust" from the definition of social capital.'
Lin (2001)	'...resources embedded in social networks and accessed and used by actors for actions. Thus the concept has two important components: (1) it represents resources embedded in social relations rather than individuals, and (2) access and use of such resources reside with the actors.'
Bowles and Gintis (2002)	'...trust, concern for one's associates, a willingness to live by the norms of one's community and to punish those who do not'.
Keefer and Knack (2002)	'...government social capital to refer to institutions that influence people's ability to cooperate for mutual benefit. The most commonly analysed of these institutions... include the enforceability of contracts, the rule of law, and the extent of civil liberties permitted by the state'.
	'Civil social capital encompasses common values, norms, informal networks, and associational memberships that affect the ability of individuals to work together to achieve common goals.'
Sobel (2002)	'Social capital describes circumstances in which individuals can use membership in groups and networks to secure benefits.'
Durlauf and Fafchamps (2004)	'(1) social capital generates positive externalities for members of a group; (2) these externalities are achieved through shared trust, norms and values and their consequent effects on expectations and behaviour; (3) shared trust, norms and values arise from informal forms of organizations based on social networks and associations.'
World Bank (2005)	'[T]he norms and networks that enable collective action.'

Source: Knowles (2005).

Bibliography

Abramowitz, M., and P. David. 1996. 'Technological Change and the Rise of Intangible Investments: The US Economy's Growth Path in the Twentieth Century', in D. Foray and B.-Å. Lundvall (eds), *Employment and Growth in the Knowledge-based Economy*, pp. 11–32. Paris: OECD.

Acemoglu, D., S. Johnson, and J.A. Robinson. 2001. 'The Colonial Origins of Comparative Development: An Empirical Investigation', *American Economic Review*, 91(5): 1369–401.

———. 2004. 'Institutions as the Fundamental Cause of Long-term Growth', *NBER Working Paper*, No. 10481.

Addison, T., and M. Baliamoune-Lutz. 2004. 'The Role of Social Capital in Post-conflict Reconstruction', paper presented at the UNU-WIDER conference on 'Making Peace Work', UNU-WIDER, Helsinki, 4–5 June.

Adelman, Irma, and Cynthia T. Morris. 1967. *Society, Politics, and Economic Development: A Quantitative Approach*. Baltimore: John Hopkins Press.

Adler, P.S., and S-W Kwon. 2002. 'Social Capital: Prospects for a New Concept', *Academy of Management Review*, 27(1): 17–40.

Aghion, P., and P. Howitt. 1998. *Endogenous Growth Theory*. Cambridge, MA. MIT Press.

Alchian, Armen A., and Harold Demsetz. 1972. 'Production, Information Costs, and Economic Organization', *American Economic Review*, 62(5): 777–95.

Alexander, R.D. 1987. *The Biology of Moral Systems*. New York: Aldine de Gruyter.

Allen, F., J. Qian, and M. Qian. 2006. 'China's Financial System: Past, Present, and Future', in L. Brandt, and T. Rawski (eds), *China's Financial System: Past, Present, and Future*, Chapter 14, Cambridge: Cambridge University Press.

Allen, R.C. 2006. 'The British Industrial Revolution in Global Perspective: How Commerce Created the Industrial Revolution and Modern Economic Growth', *Unpublished paper Nuffield College*, Oxford University.

Amin, A., and P. Cohendet. 2004. *Architectures of knowledge: Firms, Communities, and Competencies*. Oxford: Oxford University Press.

Amit, Raphael, and Paul J. Schoemaker. 1993. 'Strategic Assets and Organisational Rent', *Strategic Management Journal*, 14(January): 33-46.

Amornthum, Somchai. 2002. 'Japan's Potential Growth: An HP Filter Approach', *Research Paper 614*, Department of Economics, University of Hawai'i at Manoa.

Andersen, E.S. 1994. *Evolutionary Economics: Post-Schumpeterian Contributions*. London and New York: Pinter.

Aoki, M. 1988. *Information, Incentives and Bargaining Structures in the Japanese Economy*. Cambridge and New York: Cambridge University Press.

———. 2001. *Toward a Comparative Institutional Analysis*. Cambridge, MA: MIT Press.

Araujo, Luis, Anna Dubois, and Lars-Erik Gadde. 2003. 'The Multiple Boundaries of the Firm', *Journal of Management Studies*, 40(5): 1255-77.

Argyres, N. 1996. 'Evidence on the Role of Firm Capabilities in Vertical Integration Decisions', *Strategic Management Journal*, 17(2): 129-50.

Arjona, Roman, Maxime Ladaique, and Mark Pearson. 2001. 'Growth, Inequality and Social Protection', *OECD Labor Market and Social Policy Occasional Paper No. 51*, OECD, Paris.

Arora, Ashish, and Surendrakumar Bagde. 2006. 'The Indian Software Industry: the Human Capital Story', *Working Paper*, Heinz School of Public Policy & Management, Carnegie Mellon University.

Arrow, K.J. 1962. 'The Economic Implications of Learning by Doing', *Review of Economic Studies*, 29(3): 155-73.

———. 1969. 'The Organization of Economic Activity: Issues Pertinent to the Choice of Market versus Nonmarket Allocation', in *The Analysis and Evaluation of Public Expenditure: The PPB System*, pp. 59-73. Washington, DC: US Government Printing Office.

———. 1972. 'Gifts and Exchanges', *Philosophy and Public Affairs*, 1(4): 343-62.

———. 1996. 'The Economics of Information: An Exposition', *Empirica*, 23(2): 119-28.

———. 1999. 'Observations on Social Capital', in Partha Dasgupta and Ismail Serageldin (eds), *Social Capital: A Multifaceted Perspective*, pp. 3-5. Washington, DC: The World Bank.

Astone, N., C. Nathanson, R. Schoen, and Y. Kim. 1999 'Investment in Social Capital', *Population and Development Review*, 25(1): 1-31.

Axelrod, R. 1984. *The Evolution of Cooperation*. New York: Basic Books.

———. 1997. *The Complexity of Cooperation*. New Jersey: Princeton University Press.

Bagde, Surendrakumar. 2008. 'Human Capital and Economic Development in India', Research Paper, Heinz College, Carnegie Mellon University.

Bagnasco, A. 1999. 'Trust and Social Capital', in K. Nash and A. Scott (eds), *Blackwell Companion to Political Sociology*, pp. 230-9. Oxford: Blackwell.

Baliamoune-Lutz, Mina. 2005. 'Institutions, Social Capital, and Economic Development in Africa: An Empirical Study', *ICER Working Papers*, No. 18-2005, International Centre for Economic Research.

Bardhan, P. 1989. 'The New Institutional Economics and Development Theory: A Brief Critical Assessment', *World Development*, 17(9): 1389-95.

———. 2001. 'Inequality and Collective Action', The Institute of Advanced Studies, University of Princeton (mimeo).

Barney, J.B. 1991. 'Firm Resources and Sustained Competitive Advantage', *Journal of Management*, 17(1): 99-120.

———. 1996. 'The Resource-based Theory of the Firm', *Organization Science*, 7(5): 469-96.

Barney, J.B., and W. Lee. 1998. 'Governance under Uncertainty: Transaction Costs, Real Options, Learning, and Property Rights', paper presented at the Annual Meeting of the Academy of Management, San Diego.

Barnow, B.S. and C. Smith. 2005. *Job training policy in the United States*. Kalmazoo, Michigan: W.E. Upjohn Institute for Employment Research.

Baron, James N., and Michael T. Hannan. 1994. 'The Impact of Economics on Contemporary Sociology', *Journal of Economic Literature*, 32(September): 1111-46.

Barro, R.J. 1996. 'Democracy and Growth', *Journal of Economic Growth*, 1(1): 1-27.

———. 1998. 'Human Capital and Growth in Cross-country Regressions', *Swedish Economic Policy Review*, 6(2): 237-77.

Barro, R.J. and X. Sala-i-Martin. 1995. *Economic Growth*. McGraw-Hill, Inc.

Barron J.M., M.C. Berger, and D.A. Black, 1997. *On-the-Job Training*. Kalamazoo: Upjohn Institute for Employment Research.

———. 1997. 'How Well do we Measure Training?', *Journal of Labor Economics*, 15(3): 507-28.

Barzel, Y. 1989. *Economic Analysis of Property Rights*. Cambridge: Cambridge University Press.

Becker, Gary S. 1962. 'Investment in Human Capital: A Theoretical Analysis', *Journal of Political Economy*, 70(5): 9-49.

———. 1964. *Human Capital: A Theoretical and Empirical Analysis with Special Reference to Education*, 1st ed. New York: Columbia University Press.

———. 1975. *Human Capital: A Theoretical and Empirical Analysis with Special Reference to Education*, 2nd ed. New York: Columbia University Press.

———. 1993. *Human Capital: A Theoretical and Empirical Analysis with Special Reference to Education*, 3rd ed. Chicago: The University of Chicago Press.

———. 1996. *Accounting for Tastes*. Cambridge: Harvard University.

Becker, Gary S., Elizabeth Landes, and Robert Michael. 1977. 'An Economic Analysis of Marital Instability', *Journal of Political Economy*, 85(6): 1141–88.

Behrman, J.R., and N. Stacey. 1997. *The Social Benefits of Education*. Ann Arbor: University of Michigan Press.

Benavot, Aaron. 1989. 'Education, Gender and Economic Development: A Cross-National Study', *Sociology of Education*, 62(1): 14–32.

Benhabib, Jess, and Mark M. Spiegel. 1994. 'The Role of Human Capital in Economic Development: Evidence from Aggregate Cross-country Data', *Journal of Monetary Economics*, 34(2): 143–73.

Benham, Lee, and Alexandra Benham. 1975. 'Regulating through the Professions: A Perspective on Information Control', *Journal of Law and Economics*, 18(2): 421–47.

Birke, D., and G.M.P. Swann. 2005. 'Social Networks and Choice of Mobile Phone Operator', *Industrial Economics Division Occasional Paper Series No. 2005-14*, Nottingham University Business School.

Bloom G, and X. Gu. 1997. 'Health Sector Reform: Lessons from China', *Social Science and Medicine*, 45(3): 351–60.

Bloom, D.E., and D. Canning. 2003. 'Health as Human Capital and its Impact on Economic Performance', *Geneva Papers on Risk and Insurance*, 28(2): 304–15.

Bloom, D.E., D. Canning, and J. Sevilla. 2004. 'The Effect of Health on Economic Growth: A Production Function Approach', *World Development*, 32(1): 1–13.

Blumenthal D., and W. Hsiao. 2005. 'Privatization and its Discontents—The Evolving Chinese Health Care System', *New England Journal of Medicine*, 353(11): 1165–70.

Blundell, R., L. Dearden, and B. Sianesi. 2001. 'Estimating the Returns to Education: Models, Methods and Results', University College London and Institute for Fiscal Studies.

Boisot, M. 1998. *Knowledge Assets: Securing Competitive Advantage in the Information Economy*. Oxford: Oxford University Press.

Bolton, Patrick, and Matthias Dewatripont. 2005. *Contract Theory*. Cambridge, MA: MIT Press

Bourdieu, Pierre. 1980. 'Le capital social', *Actes de la Recherche en Sciences Sociales*, 31(31): 2–3.

———. 1986. 'The Forms of Capital', in John G. Richardson (ed.), *Handbook of Theory and Research for the Sociology of Education*, 241–58. New York: Greenwood Press.

———. 1996. *The Rules of Art*. Cambridge, England: Polity.

Bourguignon, François, and Thierry Verdier. 2000. 'Oligarchy, Democracy, Inequality and Growth', *Journal of Development Economics*, 62(2): 285–313.

Bowles, S., and H. Gintis. 2002. 'Social Capital and Community Governance', *Economic Journal*, 112(Nov.): F419–36.
Brandenburg, U., and J. Zhu. 2007. 'Higher Education in China in the Light of Massification and Demographic Change: Lessons to be learned for Germany', *CHE Working paper No.97*, Germany.
Brehm, John, and Wendy Rahn. 1997. 'Individual-Level Evidence for the Causes and Consequences of Social Capital', *American Journal of Political Science*, 41(3): 999–1023.
Breschi, S., and F. Malerba. 2001. 'Geography of Innovation and Economic Clustering', *Industrial and Corporate Change*, 10(4): 817–33.
Brewer, John. 1982. 'Commercialization and Politics', in Neil McKendrick, John Brewer, and J.H. Plumb (eds), *The Birth of a Consumer Society: The Commercialization of Eighteenth century England*, pp. 197–262. Bloomington: Indiana University Press.
Burt, Ronald. 1992. *Structural Holes*. Cambridge MA: Harvard University Press.
Buttery, E. Alan, and Y.H. Wong. 1999. 'The Development of a Guanxi Framework', *Marketing Intelligence and Planning*, 17(3): 147–55.
Byrd, William, and Qingsong Lin. 1990. *China's Rural Industry: Structure, Development, and Reform*. Oxford: Oxford University Press.
Cain, Peter, and Anthony G. Hopkins. 1993. *British Imperialism: Innovation and Expansion*. Harlow, Essex: Longman.
Carroll, G.R., J. Goodstein, and A. Gyenes. 1988. 'Organizations and the State: Effects of the Institutional Environment on Agricultural Cooperatives in Hungary', *Administrative Science Quarterly*, 33(2): 33–256.
Casson, Mark C. 2005. 'Entrepreneurship and the Theory of the Firm', *Journal of Economic Behaviour and Organization*, 58(2): 327–48.
Castle, E.N. 1998. 'A Conceptual Framework for the Study of Rural Places', *American Journal of Agricultural Economics*, 80(3): 621–31.
Chadha, D. 2011. 'Is Blood Thicker than Water? An Analysis of Social Capital as a Risk-sharing Mechanism in Children's Development in India', *Young Lives Student Paper*, June.
Chandler, Alfred Dupont, Takashi Hikino, and Andrew von Nordenflycht. 2001. *Inventing the Electronic Century: The Epic Story of the Consumer Electronics and Computer Industries*. Ithaca, NY: Free Press.
Che, Jiahua, and Yingyi Qian. 1998. 'Insecure Property Rights and Government Ownership of Firms', *The Quarterly Journal of Economics*, 113(2): 467–96.
Chen, X., 2005. 'Magic or Myth? Social Capital and its Consequences in the Asian, Chinese, and Vietnamese Contexts', in Gerd Mutz, and Rainer Klump (eds), *Modernization and Social Transformation in Vietnam: Social Capital Formation and Institutional Building*, pp. 49–62. Hamburg, Germany: Institut für Asienkunde.

Chen, X., and C. Chen. 2004. 'On the Intricacies of the Chinese *Guanxi*: A Process Model of *Guanxi* Development', *Asia Pacific Journal of Management*, 21(3): 305-24.

Cheung, Steven N.S. 1983. 'The Contractual Nature of The Firm', *Journal of Law and Economics*, 26(3): 1-21.

Choi, Young B. 1993. *Paradigms and Conventions: Uncertainty, Decision-making and Entrepreneurship*. Ann Arbor: University of Michigan Press.

Chow, G.C. 2006. 'Rural Poverty in China: Problem and Policy'. Available at: www.princeton.edu/~gchow/ruralpovertyinchina.doc, last accessed in July 2008.

Chwe, Michael Suk-Young. 1999. 'Structure and Strategy in Collective Action', *American Journal Sociology*, 105(1): 128-56.

Cialdini, R.B. 2001. *Influence: Science and Practice*. Boston: Allyn and Bacon.

Clark, J.C.D. 1986. *Revolution and Rebellion: State and Society in England in the Seventeenth and Eighteenth Centuries*. Cambridge: Cambridge University Press

Clarke, Donald C. 1996. 'Power and Politics in the Chinese Court System: The Enforcement of Civil Judgment', *Columbia Journal of Asian Law*, 10(1): 1-91.

Coase, Ronald. 1937. 'The Nature of the Firm', *Economica*, 4(16): 386-405.

———. 1964. Discussion of 'Direct Regulation and Market performance in the American economy' by Richard E. Caves, and 'The Effectivenss of Economic Regulation: A legal view' by Roger C. Crampton, *American Economic Review*, 54: 194-7.

———. 1998. 'The New Institutional Economics', *American Economic Review*, 88(2): 72-4.

Cochrane, Thomas C. 1998. 'An Innovative Business System', in Gary Kornblith (eds), *The Industrial Revolution in America*, pp. 12-23. Boston and New York: Houghton Mifflin Company.

Cohendet, P. Llerena. 1999. 'La Conception de la Firme Comme Processeur de Connaissances', *Revue d'Economie Industrielle*, 88(2): 211-36.

Coleman, James. 1988. 'Social Capital in the Creation of Human Capital', *American Journal of Sociology*, Supplement, 94(suppl.): S95-S120.

———. 1984. 'Introducing Social Structure into Economic Analysis', *American Economic Review*, 74(2): 84-8.

———. 1990. *Foundations of Social Theory*. Cambridge, MA: Harvard University Press.

Colombatto, Enrico. 2004. 'Are Property Rights Relevant for Development Economics? On the Dangers of Western Constructivism' in *The Elgar Companion to the Economics of Property Rights*, pp. 363-7. Cheltenham (UK) and Northampton (MA): Edward Elgar.

Commons, John R. 1931. 'Institutional Economics', *American Economic Review*, 21(4): 648-57.

Conner, K.R. 1991. 'A Historical Comparison of Resource-based Theory and Five Schools of Thought Within Industrial Organization Economics', *Journal of Management*, 17(1): 121–56.

Conner, K.R., and C.K. Prahalad. 1996. 'A Resource Based of the Firm: Knowledge Versus Opportunism', *Organisation Science*, 7(5): 477–501.

Constant, A.F., B.N. Tien, and J. Meng. 2010. 'Can China Win the Tug-of-War for Talents', *DIWDC Synopsis*, No. 2, Washington, DC.

Cooter, Robert D. 1994. 'Structural Adjudication and the New Law Merchant: A Model of Decentralized Law', *International Review of Law and Economics*, 14: 215–31.

Coulombe, S., and J-F. Tremblay. 2004. 'Literacy, Human Capital, and Growth', *Ottawa University Working Papers*, n. 0407E.

Cunha, Flavio and James Heckman. 2010. 'Investing in Our Young People', *NBER Working Paper* 16201.

Cypher, J.M., and J.L. Dietz. 1997. *The Process of Economic Development*. London: Routledge.

Dagum, C., and D.J. Slottje. 2000. 'A New Method to Estimate the Level and Distribution of Household Human Capital with Application', *Structural Change and Economic Dynamics*, 11(1–2): 67–94.

Dam, Kenneth W. 2005. *The Law-Growth Nexus: The Rule of Law and Economic Development*. Washington: Brookings Institution Press.

Dasgupta, P. 1988. 'Trust as a Commodity', in D. Gambetta (ed.), *Trust: Making and Breaking Cooperative Relations*, pp. 49–72. Oxford: Blackwell.

———. 2001. *Human Well-Being and the Natural Environment*. Oxford: Oxford University Press.

Davenport, T.O. 1999. *Human Capital: What it is and Why People Invest it*. San Francisco: Jossey-Bass.

Davis, Lance E., and Douglass C. North. 1971. *Institutional Change and American Economic Growth*. Cambridge: The University Press.

de Tocqueville, Alexis. 1969. *Democracy in America*. Translated by J.P. Mayer. Garden City, New York: Anchor Books.

Dee, T.S. 2004. 'Are there Civic Returns to Education?' *Journal of Public Economics*, 88(9–10): 1697–720.

DeFilippis, James. 2001. 'The Myth of Social Capital in Community Development', *Housing Policy Debate*, 12(4): 781–806.

Denison, E.F. 1962. *The Sources of Economic Growth in the United States and the Alternatives before Us*. New York: Committee for Economic Development.

———. 1967. *Why Growth Rates Differ*. Washington DC: Brookings Institution.

Denzau, Arthur T., and Douglass C. North. 1994. 'Shared Mental Models: Ideologies and Institutions', *Kyklos*, 47(1): 3–31.

Dernberger, Robert F. 1980. *China's Development Experience in Comparative Perspective*. Harvard University Press.
Desai, Sonalde. 1994. *Gender Inequalities and Demographic Behavior in India*. New York: The Population Council.
Desai, Sonalde, and Katharine Sreedhar. 1999. 'India: Growth and Inequity', in Selig S. Harrison, Paul H. Kreisberg, and Dennis Kux (eds), *India and Pakistan: The First Fifty Years*. Cambridge: Cambridge University Press.
Dixit, Avinash. 2004. *Lawlessness and Economics*. Princeton, NJ and Woodstock, UK: Princeton University Press.
Djankov, Simeon, Rafael La Porta, Florencio Lopez-de-Silanes, and Andrei Shleifer. 2003. 'Courts', *Quarterly Journal of Economics*, 118(2): 453-517.
Dopfer, K., J. Foster, and J. Potts. 2004. 'Micro–Meso–Macro', *Journal of Evolutionary Economics*, 14(3): 263-79.
Dopfer, K., and J. Potts. 2004. 'Evolutionary Realism: A New Ontology for Economics', *Journal of Economic Methodology*, 11(2): 195-212.
Dore, Ronald. 1965. *Education in Tokugawa, Japan*. Berkeley: University of California Press.
Dossani, R. 2010. 'A Decade after the Y2K Problem: Has Indian IT Emerged?' in Dan Breznitz and John Zysman (eds), *Re-examining the Service Revolution*. New Haven, CT: Yale University Press.
Dossani, R., and Patibandla Murali. 2010. 'Technology and Educational Challenges in a Globalizing World—Case Study of India', *The Handbook of Technology Management*, 3 Volumes. Hoboken, NJ: John Wiley & Sons, Inc.
Drucker, P.F. 1993. *Post-capitalist Society*. Oxford: Butterworth-Heinemann.
Durlauf, S.N. 1999. 'The Case "Against" Social Capital', *Working Papers 29*, Wisconsin Madison—Social Systems.
Durlauf, Steven, and Marcel Fafchamps. 2004. 'Social Capital', *NBER Working Paper* No. 10485.
Dworkin, J.B., R. Larson, and D. Hansen. 2003. 'Adolescents' Accounts of Growth Experiences in Youth Activities', *Journal of Youth and Adolescence*, 32(1): 17-26.
Eades, James Seymour, Roger Goodman, and Yumiko Hada. 2005. *The 'Big Bang' in Japanese Higher Education: The 2004 Reforms and the Dynamics of Change*. Melbourne: Trans Pacific Press.
Eamon, William. 1990. 'From the Secrets of Nature to Public Knowledge', in David C. Lindberg, and Robert S. Westman (eds), *Reappraisals of the Scientific Revolution*, pp. 333-65. Cambridge: Cambridge University Press.
Easterly, W., and R. Levine. 1997. 'Africa's Growth Tragedy: Policies and Ethnic Divisions', *Quarterly Journal of Economics*, 112(4): 1203-50.
Eden, C. 1992. 'On the Nature of Cognitive Maps', *Journal of Management Studies*, 29(3): 261-5.

Edwards, Bob, and Michael Foley. 1998. 'Civil Society and Social Capital beyond Putnam', *American Behavioural Scientist*, 42(1): 124–39.

Eggleston, K., and W. Yip. 2004. 'Hospital Competition under Regulated Prices: Application to Urban Health Sector Reforms in China', *International Journal of Health Care Finance and Economics*, 4(4): 343–68.

Ehrenberg, R., and R. Smith. 1994. *Modern Labor Economics: Theory and Public Policy*, 5th ed. New York: HarperCollins.

Ellickson, R.C. 1991. *Order without Law: How Neighbors Settle Disputes*. Cambridge, MA: Harvard University Press.

Elster, Jon. 1989. 'Social Norms and Economic Theory', *Journal of Economic Perspectives*, 3(4): 99–117.

Engineer, Asghar A. 2001. *Muslim Middle Class and Its Role*. Mumbai, India: Center for Study of Society and Secularism.

Evans, Peter. 1992. 'The State as Problem and Solution: Predation, Embedded Autonomy, and Structural Change', in Stephan Haggard, and Robert Kaufman (eds), *The Politics of Economic Adjustment: International Constraints, Distributive Conflicts, and the State*, pp. 139–81. Princeton, NJ: Princeton University Press.

———. 1995. *Embedded Autonomy*. Princeton, NJ: Princeton University Press.

———. 1996. 'Government Action, Social Capital and Development: Reviewing the Evidence on Synergy'. *World Development*, 24(6): 1119–32.

Fafchamps, Marcel, and Susan Lund. 2003. 'Risk Sharing Networks in Rural Philippines', *Journal of Development Economics*, 71: 261–87.

Farrell, D., U.A. Gersch, and E. Stephenson. 2006. 'The Value of China's Emerging Middle Class', *The McKinsey Quarterly*, 2(1): 60–9.

Fine, Ben. 1999. 'The Developmental State Is Dead—Long Live Social Capital?' *Development and Change*, 30(1): 1.

———. 2003. *Social Capital versus Social Theory: Political Economy and Social Science at the Turn of the Millennium*. London: Routledge.

———. 2010. *Theories of Social Capital: Researchers Behaving Badly* (IIPPE series). London: Pluto Press.

Fine, Ben and Costas Lapavitsas. 2004. 'Social Capital and Capitalist Economies', *South Eastern Europe Journal of Economics*, 2(1): 17–34.

Fischer, C.S. 2001. 'Bowling Alone: What's the Score?' *paper presented at the American Sociological Association*, Anaheim, CA, 17–21 August.

Foss, K., and N.J. Foss. 2005. 'Resources and Transaction Costs: How Property Rights Economics Furthers the Resource-based View', *Strategic Management Journal*, 6(6): 541–53.

Foss, N.J. 1998. 'Firms and the Coordination of Knowledge: Some Austrian Insights', *DRUID Working Papers 98–19*, DRUID, Copenhagen Business School, Department of Industrial Economics and Strategy/Aalborg University, Department of Business Studies.

Foss, N.J. 2005. *Strategy and Economic Organization in the Knowledge Economy*. Oxford: Oxford University Press.

Foss, N.J. and C. Knudsen (eds). 1996. *Towards a Competence Theory of the Firm*. London: Routledge.

Foss, N.J., H. Lando, and S. Thomsen. 2000. 'The Theory of the Firm', in B. Bouckaert, and G. De Geest (eds), *Encyclopedia of Law and Economics*, Volume III—The Regulation of Contracts, pp. 631–58. Cheltenham: Edward Elgar.

Foss, N.J., and Mark Lorenzen. 2002. 'Analogy and the Emergence of Focal Points: Some Suggestions for Bringing Cognitive Coordination into the Theory of Economic Organization', in Klaus Nielsen (ed.) *Uncertainty in Economic Decision-Making: Ambiguity, Mental Models and Institutions*, Cheltenham: Edward Elgar.

Foster, John and J. Stanley Metcalfe. 2001. 'Modern Evolutionary Economic Perspectives: An Overview', in John Foster, and J. Stanley Metcalfe (eds) *Frontiers of Evolutionary Economics: Competition, Self-organization, and Innovation Policy*, pp. 1–19. Northampton, MA: Edward Elgar.

Fountain, J.E. 1998. 'Social Capital: A Key Enabler of Innovation', in L.M. Branscomb, and J.H. Keller (eds), *Investing in Innovation: Creating a Research and Innovation Policy that Works*, 85–111. Cambridge, MA: MIT Press.

Francois, P., and J. Zabojnik. 2005. 'Trust as Social Capital and the Process of Economic Development', *Journal of the European Economic Association*, 3(1): 51–94.

Fransman, M. 1994. 'Information, Knowledge, Vision and Theories of the Firm', *Industrial and Corporate Change*, 3(2): 1–45.

Friedman, T. 2005. *The World Is Flat: A Brief History of the Twenty-First Century*. New York: Farrar, Straus and Giroux.

Fukuyama, F. 1995. *Trust: The Social Virtues and the Creator of Prosperity*. London: Harnish Hamilton.

———. 1999. 'Social Capital and Civil Society', *paper presented at the International Monetary Fund Conference on Second Generation Reforms*, Washington, DC.

Gargiulo, M., and M. Benassi. 2000. 'Trapped in Your Own Net? Network Cohesion, Structural Holes, and the Adaptation of Social Capital', *Organization Science*, 11(2): 183–96.

Garrouste, Pierre, and Stephane Saussier. 2005. 'Looking for a Theory of the Firm: Future Challenges', *Journal of Economic Behavior & Organization*, 58(2): 178–99.

Gerlach, M.L. 1992. *Alliance Capitalism: The Social Organization of Japanese Business*. Berkeley: University of California Press.

Gerschenkron, A. 1962. *Economic Backwardness in Historical Perspective: A Book of Essays*. Cambridge: Harvard University Press.

Gibb, George. 1946. 'The Pre-Industrial Revolution in America: A Field for Local Research', *Business History Review*, 04: 103–16.
Gibbons, M., C. Limoges, H. Nowotny, S. Schwartzman, P. Scott, and M. Trow. 1994. *The New Production of Knowledge: The Dynamics of Science and Research in Contemporary Societies*. London: SAGE.
Glaeser, E.L, D. Laibson, and B. Sacerdote. 2000. 'The Economic Approach to Social Capital', *NBER Working Paper No. 7728*.
———. 2002. 'An Economic Approach to Social Capital', *Economic Journal*, 112(483): 437–58.
Glaeser, E.L., D. Laibson, J.A. Scheinkman, and C.L. Soutter. 1999. 'What Is Social Capital? The Determinants of Trust and Trustworthiness', *NBER Working Paper 7216*, July.
Godo, Y., and Y. Hayami. 2000. *Development Economics: From the Poverty to the Wealth of Nations*. Oxford: Oxford University Press.
Gordon, James, and Poonam Gupta. 2004. 'Understanding India's Services Revolution', *IMF Working Paper*, WP/04/171.
Gore, L. 1998. *Market Communism: The Institutional Foundation of China's post-Mao Hyper-growth*. Hong Kong and New York: Oxford University Press.
Gouldner, Alvin W. 1960. 'The Norm of Reciprocity: A Preliminary Statement', *American Sociological Review*, 25(2): 161–78.
Gradstein, M., and M. Justman. 2001. 'Education, Social Cohesion and Growth', *American Economic Review*,
Granovetter, M. 1985. 'Economic Action and Social Structure: The Problem of Embeddedness', *American Journal of Sociology*, 91(3): 481–510.
———. 1973. 'The Strength of Weak Ties', *American Journal of Sociology*, 78(6): 1360–80.
Granstrand, O., P. Patel, and K. Pavitt. 1997. 'Multi-technology Corporations: Why they have "Distributed" Rather than "Distinctive" Core Competencies', *California Management Review*, 39(4): 8–25.
Grant, R.M. 1991. 'The Resource-based Theory of Competitive Advantage: Implications for Strategy Formulation', *California Management Review*, 33(Spring): 114–35.
———. 1996. 'Toward a Knowledge-Based Theory of the Firm', *Strategic Management Journal*, 17(Winter Special Issue): 109–22.
Greene, Jack. 1999. 'Social and Cultural Capital in Colonial British America: A Case Study', *Journal of Interdisciplinary History*, 29(3): 491–509.
Greif, Avner. 1992. 'Institutions and International Trade: Lessons from the Commercial Revolution', *American Economic Review*, 82(2): 128–33.
Greif, Avner, Paul R. Milgrom, and Barry R. Weingast. 1994. 'Coordination, Commitment, and Enforcement: The Case of the Merchant Guild', *Journal of Political Economy*, 102(1): 745–76.

Grootaert, Christiaan, and Thierry van Bastelaer. 2002. *Understanding and Measuring Social Capital: A Multidisciplinary Tool for Practitioners*. Washington, DC: The World Bank.

Grossman, Sanford, and Oliver Hart. 1986. 'The Costs and Benefits of Ownership: A Theory of Vertical and Lateral Integration', *Journal of Political Economy*, 94(4): 691–719.

Guest, Avery M. 2005. 'Frontier and Urban-Industrial Explanations of US Occupational Mobility in the late 1800s', *Social Science Research*, 34(2): 140–64.

Guiso, Luigi, Paola Sapienza, and Luigi Zingales. 2003. 'People's Opium? Religion and Economic Attitudes', *Journal of Monetary Economics*, 50(1): 225–82.

Gupta, Dipankar. 2000. *Interrogating Caste; Continuous Hierarchies and Discrete Castes*. New Delhi: Penguin Books India.

Gupte, D.M., V. Ramachandran, and R.K. Mutatkar. 2001. 'Epidemiological Profile of India: Historical and Contemporary Perspectives', *Journal of Biosciences*, 26(4): 437–64.

Gyimah-Brempong, K., and M. Wilson. 2004. 'Health Human Capital and Economic Growth in Sub-Saharan Africa and OECD Countries', *Quarterly Review of Finance and Economics*, 44(2): 296–320.

Haddad, G. 2000. 'University and Society: Responsibilities, Contracts, Partnerships', in G. Neave (ed.), *The Universities' Responsibilities to Society*. International Perspectives Series. Oxford: Pergamon Press.

Hall, Peter A., and David Soskice. 2000. 'An Introduction to Varieties of Capitalism', in Peter A. Hall and David Soskice (eds), *Varieties of Capitalism: The Institutional Foundations of Comparative Advantage*, pp. 1–70. New York: Oxford University Press.

Hall, Robert E., and Charles I. Jones. 1999. 'Why Do Some Countries Produce so Much More Output per Worker than Others?' *Quarterly Journal of Economics*, 114(1): 83–116.

Halpern, D. 2005. *Social Capital*. Cambridge: Polity Press.

Hamilton, Walton H. 1932. 'The Problem of Anti-trust Reform', *Faculty Scholarship Series Paper No. 4665*, Yale Law School.

Hanifan, Lyda J. 1916. 'The Rural School Community Center', *Annals of the American Academy of Political and Social Science*, 67: 130–38.

Hardin, R. 1999. 'Social Capital', in J. Alt, and M. Levi (eds), *Competition and Cooperation: Conversations with Nobelists about Economics and Political Science*, pp. 170–89. New York: Russell Sage.

Harris, M. 1975. *Culture, People, Nature: An Introduction to General Anthropology*. New York: Thomas Y. Crowell.

Hart, Oliver. 1995. *Firms, Contracts, and Financial Structure*. Oxford: Clarendon Press.

Hart, Oliver, and John Moore. 1990. 'Property Rights and the Nature of the Firm', *Journal of Political Economy*, 98(6): 1119-58.
Hartog, J. 2002. 'On Human Capital and Individual Capabilities', *Review of Income and Wealth*, 47(4): 515-40.
Hartwell, R.M. 1971. *The Industrial Revolution and Economic Growth*. London: Methuen and Co. Ltd.
Harvie, C. 1999. 'Economic Transition: What can be Learned from China's Experience', *International Journal of Social Economics*, 26(7-9): 1091-119.
Haveman, Robert H., and Barbara Wolfe. 1984. 'Schooling and Economic Well-Being: The Role of Non-Market Effects', *Journal of Human Resources*, 19(3): 377-407.
Hayek, F.A. 1945. 'The Use of Knowledge in Society', *American Economic Review*, 35(4): 519-30.
Heckman, J. 2001. 'Heterogeneity, Microdata and Public Policy Evaluation', *Journal of Political Economy*, 109(4): 673-749.
Heeks, R. 1996. *India's Software Industry: State Policy, Liberalisation and Industrial Development*. New Delhi: Naurang Rai Concept Publishing Company.
Helmke, Gretchen, and Steven Levitsky. 2004. 'Informal Institutions and Comparative Politics: A Research Agenda', *Perspectives in Politics*, 2(4): 725-40.
Hessler, Peter. 2007. 'Boomtowns', *National Geographic*, June issue: 88-117.
Heyer, J., F. Stewart, and R. Thorpe (eds). 2002. *Group Behaviour and Development: Is the Market Destroying Cooperation?* Oxford: Oxford University Press.
Hideo, Totsuka. 1983. 'Japanese Trade Union Attitudes Towards Rationalization', in *East Asia: International Review of Economic, Political and Social Development* (Frankfurt Campus), 1: 29.
Hill, C.W.L. 1995. 'National Institutional Structures, Transaction Cost Economizing and Competitive Advantage: The Case of Japan', *Organization Science*, 6(1): 119-31.
Hiromi, A. 2006. 'Investing in Education in India: Inferences from an Analysis of the Rates of Return to Education across Indian States'. PhD Dissertation, Stanford University.
Hirschman, A.O. 1958. *The Strategy of Economic Development*. New Haven: Yale University Press.
———. 1970. *Exit, Voice, and Loyalty: Responses to Decline in Firms, Organizations, and States*. Cambridge, MA: Harvard University Press.
Hirschman, C., and L. Mogford. 2009. 'Immigration and the American Industrial Revolution from 1880 to 1920', *Social Science Research*, 38(4): 897-920.
Hodgkinson, V., and M. Weitzman. 1988. *Giving and Volunteering in the United States: Findings from a National Survey*. Washington, DC: Independent Sector.
Hodgson, Geoffrey. 1998. 'Evolutionary and Competence-based Theories of the Firm', *Journal of Economic Studies*, 25(1): 25-56.

Hoff, Karla and Joseph Stiglitz. 2001. 'Modern Economic Theory and Development', in G.M. Meier, and Joseph Stiglitz (eds), *Frontiers of Development Economics*, pp. 389-459. New York: Oxford University Press.

Hollis, Martin. 1998. *Trust within Reason*. Cambridge: Cambridge University Press.

Holmström, Bengt R. 1982. 'The Moral Hazard of Teams', *Bell Journal of Economics*, 13: 324-40.

——. 1999. 'The Firm as a Subeconomy', *Journal of Law, Economics, and Organization*, 15(1): 74-102.

Holmström, Bengt R., and J. Roberts. 1998. 'The Boundaries of the Firm Revisited', *Journal of Economic Perspectives*, 12(4): 73-95.

Holmström, Bengt R., and J. Tirole. 1989. 'The Theory of the Firm', in R. Schmalensee and R.D. Willig (eds), *Handbook of Industrial Organization*, vol. 1, ch. 3, pp. 61-133. Amsterdam: North Holland.

Holmström, Bengt R., and Paul Milgrom. 1994. 'The Firm as an Incentive System', *American Economic Review*, 84(4): 972-91.

Humphries, J. 2003. 'Child Labour in Industrial Revolution: The Evidence from Working Class Autobiographies', *Oxford University Economic and Social History Working Papers*.

——. 2007. *Through the Mill: Child Labour and the British Industrial Revolution*. Cambridge: Cambridge University Press.

Idson, T.L. 1995. 'Team Production Effects on Earnings', *Economics Letters*, 49(2): 197-203.

Inglehart, Ronald. 1997. *Modernization and Postmodernization: Cultural, Economic, and Political Change in 43 Societies*. Princeton: Princeton University Press.

Inkeles, Alex. 1978. 'National Differences in Individual Modernity', *Comparative Studies in Sociology*, 1(1): 47-72.

Inkeles, Alex, and David Smith 1974. *Becoming Modern: Individual Change in Six Developing Countries*. Cambridge, MA: Harvard University Press.

Inkster, I. 1980. 'Lunacy and the Industrial Revolution', *Bulletin of Society for Social History of Medicine*, 27: 42-47.

——. 1991. *Science and Technology in History: An Approach to Industrial Development*. Houndsmill: Macmillan.

Isham, J. 2002. 'Can Investment in Social Capital Improve Local Development and Environmental Outcomes? A Cost-Benefit Framework to Assess the Policy Options', in J. Isham, T. Kelly, and S. Ramaswamy (eds), *Social Capital and Economic Development: Well-being in Developing Countries*, pp. 159-75. Cheltenham: Edward Elgar Publishing.

Ito, T. 1992. 'Economic Growth', in *The Japanese Economy*. MIT Press.

Iyigun, Murat F., and Ann L. Owen. 1999. 'Entrepreneurs, Professionals, and Growth', *Journal of Economic Growth*, 4(2): 213-32.

Jacob, Margaret C. 1997. *Scientific Culture and the Making of the Industrial West*. Oxford: Oxford University Press.

Jacobides, M.G., and S. Billinger. 2006. 'Designing the Boundaries of the Firm: From "Make, Buy, or Ally" to the Dynamic Benefits of Vertical Architecture', *Organization Science*, 17(2): 249-61.

Jacobs, Jane. 1961. *The Death and Life of Great American Cities.* New York: Random House.

Jacoby, H., and E. Skoufias. 1997. 'Risk, Financial Markets, and Human Capital in a Developing Country', *Review of Economic Studies*, LXIV(311-35): 50-61.

Jensen, M.C., and W.H. Meckling. 1976. 'Theory of the Firm: Managerial Behavior, Agency Costs and Ownership Structure', *Journal of Financial Economics*, 3(4): 305-60.

Johnson, Chalmers. 1982. *MITI and the Japanese Miracle: The Growth of Industrial Policy: 1925-1975.* Stanford: Stanford University Press.

Johnson, Thomas. 1970. 'Returns from Investment in Human Capital', *American Economic Review*, 60(4): 546-60.

Joskow, P.L. 2005. 'Regulation of Natural Monopolies', *Working Paper 05-008*, Center for Energy and Environmental Policy Research, MIT.

Kapur, Devesh. 2001. 'Diasporas and Technology Transfer', *Journal of Human Development*, 2(2): 265-8.

Kapur, Devesh, and Pratap Bhanu Mehta. 2005. *Public Institutions in India: Performance and Design.* New Delhi: Oxford University Press.

Karlan, D. 2003. 'Social Capital and Group Banking', mimeo. Woodrow Wilson School, Princeton University.

Kaufmann, Daniel, Aart Kraay, and Pablo Zoido-Lobaton. 1999. 'Aggregating Governance Indicators', *Policy Research Working Paper Series 2195*, The World Bank.

Ke, W. 2006. 'Low Income, Poverty, and Aging—Rural Difficulties'. Available at: http://www.china.org.cn/english/2006/Aug/178393.htm, last accessed in July 2008.

Keesing, R.M. 1981. *Cultural Anthropology: A Contemporary Perspective.* New York: Holt, Rinehart, and Winston.

Kelly, G.A. 1963. *A Theory of Personality: The Psychology of Personal Constructs.* New York: W.W. Norton.

Kenney, M., and R. Florida. 1993. *Beyond Mass Production: The Japanese System and Its Transfer to the U.S.* New York: Oxford University Press.

——. 1994. 'Institutions and Economic Transformation: The Case of Post-war Japanese Capitalism', *Growth and Change*, 25(2): 247-62.

Khan, Zorina B., and Kenneth L. Sokoloff. 1993. 'Entrepreneurship and Technological Change in Historical Perspective: A Study of Great Inventors During Early American Industrialization', *Advances in the Study of Entrepreneurship, Innovation, and Economic Growth*, 6: 37-66.

Kiker, B.F. 1966. 'The Historical Roots of the Concept of Human Capital', *Journal of Political Economy*, 74(5): 481-99.

Kirzner, Israel. 1963. *Competition and Entrepreneurship*. Chicago: The University of Chicago Press.

Kitamura, I. 2001. 'The Role of Law in Contemporary Japanese Society', Lecture Presented at the Institut de Droit Comparé de Paris and Published as Chapter II of Droit GLOBAL Law 2001/1: Unifier le Droit: le Rêve impossible? Paris: Ed Pantheon-Assas.

Klein, Benjamin, Robert G. Crawford, and Armen A. Alchian. 1978. 'Vertical Integration, Appropriable Rents, and the Competitive Contracting Process', *Journal of Law and Economics*, 21(2): 297–326.

Klein, Peter. 1999. 'New Institutional Economics', Working Paper, Department of Economics, University of Georgia.

Knack, S., and P. Keefer. 1995. 'Institutions and Economic Performance: Cross-country Tests using Alternative Institutional Measures', *Economics and Politics*, 7(3): 207–27.

Kneller. 2000. 'Japan Inc. "University and Industry Cooperation"' July. Available at: http://www.japaninc.net/mag/comp/2000/07/jul00_uni.html, last accessed in August 2011.

Knight, J. 1992. *Institutions and Social Conflict*. Cambridge: Cambridge University Press.

Knight, John, and Song, Lina. 1999. *The Rural–Urban Divide. Economic Disparities and Interactions in China*. Oxford: Oxford University Press.

Knowles, S. 2005. 'Is Social Capital Part of the Institutions Continuum?', *Research Paper No. 05/11*, Centre for Research in Economic Development and International Trade, University of Nottingham.

Knudsden, D.C., F.R. Jacobs, D. Conway, and M.K. Blake. 1994. 'A Survey of Group Technology Adoption in the American Midwest', *Growth and Change*, 25(2): 183–205.

Kogut, B., and U. Zander. 1992. 'Knowledge of the Firm, Combinative Capabilities, and the Replication of Technology', *Organization Science*, 3(3): 383–97.

——. 1996. 'What Firms do? Coordination, Identity, and Learning', *Organization Science*, 7(5): 502–18.

Krishna, A. 2004. 'Escaping Poverty and Becoming Poor: Who Gains, Who Loses, and Why?' *World Development*, 32(1): 121–36.

Landry, R., Amara, N., and Lamari, M. 2002. 'Does Social Capital Determine Innovation? To What Extent?' *Technological Forecasting & Social Change*, 69(7): 681–701.

Langford, Paul. 2000. *Englishness Identified: Manners and Character, 1650–1850*. Oxford: Oxford University Press.

Langlois, R. 1992. 'Transaction Cost Economics in Real Time', *Industrial and Corporate Change*, 1(1): 99–127.

Langlois, R., and P. Robertson. 1995. *Firms, Markets and Economic Change*. London: Routledge.

Lareau, A., and E.B. Weininger. 2003. 'Cultural Capital in Educational Research: A Critical Assessment', *Theory and Society*, 32(5-6): 567-606.

Le, T., J. Gibson, and L. Oxley. 2003. 'Cost- and Income-based Measures of Human Capital', *Journal of Economic Surveys*, 117(3): 271-308.

Levi, Margaret. 1998. 'A State of Trust', in V. Braithwaite, and M. Levi (eds), *Trust & Governance*, pp. 77-101. New York: Russell Sage Foundation.

Levine, R., and D. Renelt. 1992. 'A Sensitivity Analysis of Cross-country Growth Regressions', *American Economic Review*, 82(4): 942-63.

Lewin, L. 1992. *Samhället och de organiserade intressena*. Stockholm: Norstedts.

Li, Meng, and J. Zhang. 2008. 'Why Do Entrepreneurs Enter Politics? Evidence from China', *Economic Inquiry*, 44(3): 559-78.

Li, Wensheng. undated. 'Financing of Higher Education in China', Peking University. Available at: http://iee.hedu.pku.edu.cn/jjlw/jjlw0020/jjlw0020. asp, last accessed in July 2008.

Lim, M.K., H. Yang, T. Zhang, W. Feng, and Z. Zhou. 2004. 'Public Perceptions of Private Health Care in Socialist China', *Health Affairs*, 23(6): 222-34.

Limerick, D. and B. Cunnington. 1993. *Managing in the New Organisation*. Sydney: Business & Professional Publishing.

Lin, J.Y. 1992. 'Rural Reforms and Agricultural Growth in China', *The American Economic Review*, 82(1): 34-51.

———. 2007. 'Developing Small and Medium Bank to Improve Financial Structure', *Working Paper*, China Center for Economic Research, Peking University.

Lin, J.Y., F. Cai, and Z. Li. 1996. *The China Miracle: Development Strategy and Economic Reform*. Hong Kong: Chinese University Press.

Lin, N. 2001. *Social Capital: A Theory of Social Structure and Action*. Cambridge: Cambridge University Press.

Lincoln, E.J. 2001. *Arthritic Japan: The Slow Pace of Economic Reform*. Washington DC: Brookings Institution Press.

Linton, R. 1936. *The Study of Man: An Introduction*. New York: D. Appleton-Century.

Liu, Y., and K. Rao. 2006. 'Providing Health Insurance in Rural China: From Research to Policy', *Journal of Health Politics, Policy and Law*, 31(1): 71-92.

Liu, Y., K. Rao, and W.C. Hsiao. 2003. 'Medical Expenditure and Rural Impoverishment in China', *Journal of Health, Population, and Nutrition*, 21(3): 216-22.

Loasby, Brian J. 1991. *Economics and Evolution*. Manchester: Manchester University Press.

———. 1999. *Knowledge, Institutions and Evolution*. London and New York: Routledge.

———. 2001a. 'Time, Knowledge and Evolutionary Dynamics: Why Connections Matter', *Journal of Evolutionary Economics*, 11(4): 393-412.

Loasby, Brian J. 2001b. 'Organisation as Interpretative Systems', *Revue d'economie Industrielle*, 97(1): 17–34.

Loury, G. 1977. 'A Dynamic Theory of Racial Income Differences', in P. Wallace, and A. LeMund (eds), *Women, Minorities and Employment Discrimination*, pp. 151–86. Lexington, MA: Lexington Books.

Lucas, R.E. 1988. 'On the Mechanics of Economic Development', *Journal of Monetary Economics*, 22(1): 3–42.

Lüdke, Michael. 1999. 'Die ländlichen Unternehmen im Spannungsfeld zwischen Zentrale und Peripherie: Lenkungsversuche der Zentrale und Ausweichmanöver an der Peripherie?', in Susanne Weigelin-Schwiedrzik, und Dagmar Hauff (eds) *Ländliche Unternehmen in der Volksrepublik China*, pp. 217–44, Berlin: Duncker und Humblot.

Luo, Y., J. Tan, and O. Shenkar. 1998. 'Strategic Responses to Competitive Pressure: The Case of Township and Village Enterprises in China', *Asia Pacific Journal of Management*, 15(1): 33–50.

Luzzati, T. 2000. 'Social Norms and Individual Sanctioning', *Economia Politica*, 17(1): 53–67.

Ma, Sai, and Neeraj Sood. 2008. 'A Comparison of the Health Systems in China and India', Rand Corporation Occasional Paper, Center for Asia Pacific Policy, Santa Monica, CA.

Maddison, Angus. 2002. 'Growth and Interaction in the World Economy: The West and the Rest, 1000–2000 AD', *paper Presented at Harvard University*.

Madhok, A. 2002. 'Reassessing the Fundamentals and Beyond: Ronald Coase, the Transaction Cost and Resource-based Theories of the Firm, and the Institutional Structure of Production', *Strategic Management Journal*, 23(6): 535–50.

Mankiw, N.G., D. Romer, and D.N. Weil. 1992. 'A Contribution to the Empirics of Economic Growth', *Quarterly Journal of Economics*, 102(2): 407–37.

Manor, James. 1996. 'Ethnicity and Politics in India', *International Affairs*, 72(3): 459–70.

Manski, C. 2000. 'Identification Problems and Decisions Under Ambiguity: Empirical Analysis of Treatment Response and Normative Analysis of Treatment Choice', *Journal of Econometrics*, 95(2): 415–42.

Marshall, Alfred. 1920. *Principles of Economics*, 8th Edition. London: Macmillan and Co.

Martin, Steve. 2002. 'Marital Dissolutions Involving Young Children: Trends by Education and Race since 1970'. Paper presented at the Institute for Research on Poverty Low Income Workshop, Madison, Wisconsin.

Maskell, P. 2001. 'Social Capital, Innovation, and Competitiveness', in S. Baron, J. Field and T. Schuller (eds), *Social Capital: Critical Perspectives*, pp. 111–23. Oxford: Oxford University Press.

Mason, R.M. 1982. *Participatory and Workplace Democracy: A Theoretical Development in Critique of Liberalism.* Carbondale, Illinois: Southern Illinois University Press.

Mathews, J.A. 2002. 'A Resource-based View of Schumpeterian Economic Dynamics', *Journal of Evolutionary Economics,* 12(1): 29-54.

McFadyen, M. Ann, and Albert A. Cannella, Jr. 2004. 'Social Capital and Knowledge Creation: Diminishing Returns of the Number and Strength of Exchange Relationships', *Academy of Management Journal,* 47(5): 735-46.

McMillan, John, John Whalley, and Lijin Zhu. 1989. 'The impact of China's Economic Reforms on Agricultural Productivity Growth', *Journal of Political Economy,* 97(4): 781-807.

McNally, Christopher, Hong Guo, and Guangwei Hu. 2007. 'Entrepreneurship and Political Guanxi Networks in China's Private Sector', *East–West Center Working Papers,* No. 19, Honolulu: East-West Center.

Meng, X., R. Gregory, and Y. Wang. 2005. 'Poverty, Inequality and Growth in Urban China, 1986-2000', *Journal of Comparative Economics,* 33(4): 710-29.

Michael, Robert. 1982. 'Measuring Non-monetary Benefits of Education: A Survey', in W. McMahon, and T. Geske (eds), *Financing Education: Overcoming Inefficiency and Inequity,* pp. 19-49. Urbana: University of Illinois Press.

Milgrom, Paul R., Douglass C. North, and Barry R. Weingast. 1990. 'The Role of Institutions in the Revival of Trade: The Law Merchant, Private Judges, and the Champagne Fairs', *Economics and Politics,* 2(1): 1-23.

Minami, Ryoshin. 1986. *The Economic Development of Japan: A Quantitative Study.* New York: St. Martin's Press.

Miyazawa, K. 2010. 'Measuring Human Capital in Japan', *RIETI Discussion Paper Series 11-E-037.*

Mokyr, Joel. 2003. 'Mercantilism, the Enlightenment, and the Industrial Revolution', *presented to the Conference in Honor of Eli F. Heckscher,* May, Stockholm.

——. 2005. 'Long-term Economic Growth and the History of Technology', in Philippe Aghion and Steven Durlauf (eds), *The Handbook of Economic Growth,* pp. 1225-73. Elsevier Science, North Holland.

——. 2006. 'The Great Synergy: The European Enlightenment as a Factor in Modern Economic Growth', in Wilfred Dolfsma and Luc Soete (eds), *Understanding the Dynamics of a Knowledge Economy,* pp. 3-41. Cheltenham: Edward Elgar.

——. 2007. 'The Institutional Origins of the Industrial Revolution', in Elhanan Helpman (ed.), *Institutions and Economic Performance.* Cambridge, MA: Harvard University Press.

——. 2008. 'The Institutional Origins of the Industrial Revolution', in Elhanan Helpman (ed.), *Institutions and Economic Performance,* pp. 64-119. Cambridge, Massachusetts: Harvard University Press.

Morck, Randall, and Masao Nakamura. 2005. 'A Frog in a Well knows nothing of the Ocean: A History of Corporate Ownership in Japan', in Randall Morck (ed.), *A History of Corporate Governance around the World: Family Business Groups to Professional Managers*, pp. 367–459. Chicago: University of Chicago Press.

Mukherjee, Anit, and Xiaobo Zhang. 2007. 'Rural Industrialization in China and India: Role of Policies and Institutions', *World Development*, 35(10): 1621–34.

Mullins, R. 2005. 'Test fever', *Follow Our China Today*. Available at: www.china-today.com.cn/English/e2005/e200506/p34.htm, last accessed in July 2008.

Nahapiet, J., and S. Ghoshal. 1998. 'Social Capital, Intellectual Capital, and the Organizational Advantage', *Academy of Management Review*, 23(2): 242–66.

Nakamura, J.I. 1981. 'Human Capital Accumulation in Premodern Rural Japan', *Journal of Economic History*, 41(2): 263–81.

Nakamura, Takafusa, and Konosuke Odaka (eds). 2003. *The Economic History of Japan: 1914–1955—a Dual Structure*. Oxford, UK: Oxford University Press.

Narayan, Deepa. 1999. 'Social Capital and the State: Complementarity and Substitution', *Working Paper* 2167, World Bank Policy Research.

——. 2002. 'Bonds and Bridges: Social Capital and Poverty', in Sunder Ramaswamy (ed.), *Social Capital and Economic Development: Well-being in Developing Countries*, pp. 58–83. Cheltenham, UK: Edward Elgar.

NASSCOM. 2006. 'e-Governance in India accelerating, but roadblocks exist', available at, http://www.nasscom.in/Nasscom/templates/NormalPage.aspx?id=2513, last accessed in April 2012.

Naudé, W.A. 1999. 'Technology, Growth and Creative Destruction: Institutional Prerequisites for Entrepreneurship', *Management Dynamics*, 8(1), Stellenbosch, South Africa.

Naughton, Barry. 2007. *The Chinese Economy: Transition and Growth*. Cambridge, MA: MIT Press.

Nee, Victor. 1992. 'Organizational Dynamics of Market Transition: Hybrid Forms, Property Rights, and Mixed Economy in China', *Administrative Science Quarterly*, 37(1): 1–27.

Neem, Johann. 2009. 'Creating Social Capital in the Early American Republic: The View from Connecticut', *Journal of Interdisciplinary History*, 39(4): 471–95.

Nelson, R. 00. 'Knowledge and Innovation Systems', in *Knowledge Management in the Learning Society*. Paris: OECD.

Nelson, R., and E. Phelps. 1966. 'Investments in Humans, Technological Diffusion, and Economic Growth', *American Economic Review*, 56(2): 69–75.

Nelson, R., and S. Winter. 1982. *An Evolutionary Theory of Economic Change*. Cambridge, MA: Belknap Press (Harvard University Press).

Ng, Yingchu, Li Sung-ko and Tsang Shu-ki. 1998. 'The Incidence of Surplus Labour and the Economic Performance of Villages in Rural China'. *BRC Papers on China* CP98008, School of Business, Hong Kong Baptist University.

Nishiguchi, T. 1994. *Strategic Industrial Sourcing: The Japanese Advantage*. Oxford: Oxford University Press.

Nishimoto, Mitoji. 1952. 'Educational Change in Japan After the War', *Journal of Educational Sociology*, 26(1): 16–26.

Nonaka, I. 1994. 'A Dynamic Theory of Organizational Knowledge Creation', *Organization Science*, 5(1): 14–37.

Nonaka, I., and H. Takeuchi. 1995. *The Knowledge-creating Company*. New York: Oxford University Press.

North, Douglass C. 1974. 'Beyond the New Economic History', *Journal of Economic History*, 34(1): 1–7.

———. 1981. *Structure and Change in Economic History*. New York: W.W. Norton & Co.

———. 1990. *Institutions, Institutional Change and Economic Performance*. Cambridge: Cambridge University Press.

North, Douglass C., and Barry R. Weingast. 1989. 'Constitutions and Commitment: The Evolution of Institutions Governing Public Choice in Seventeenth-Century England', *Journal of Economic History*, 49(4): 803–32.

North, Douglass C., and Robert Paul Thomas. 1973. *The Rise of the Western World: A New Economic History*. Cambridge: Cambridge University Press.

North, Douglass C., John Joseph Wallis, and Barry R. Weingast. 2006. 'A Conceptual Framework for Interpreting Recorded Human History', *NBER Working Papers 12795*, National Bureau of Economic Research.

OECD. 1996. *The Knowledge-based Economy*. Paris: OECD.

———. 2000. *Knowledge Management in the Learning Society*. Paris: OECD.

———. 2004. *Ageing and Employment Policies*: Japan. Paris: OECD.

———. 2010. *Economic Surveys of China*. Paris: OECD.

Okazaki, T. 2011. 'Evaluation and Formation of Human Capital in Pre-war Japan: The Case of White-Collar Workers in Mitsubishi Zaibatsu', *CIRJE-F-788 Discussion Paper*, University of Tokyo.

Okimoto, Daniel. 1989. *Between MITI and the Market: Japanese Industrial Policy for High Technology*. Stanford, CA: Stanford University Press.

Olson, Mancur. 1982. *The Rise and Decline of Nations: Economic Growth, Stagflation, and Social Rigidities*. New Haven: Yale University Press.

Ostrom, Elinor. 1999. 'Coping with Tragedies of the Commons', *Annual Review of Political Science*, 2(1): 493–535.

———. 2000. 'Collective Action and the Evolution of Social Norms', *Journal of Economic Perspectives*, 14(3): 137–58.

———. 2005. *Understanding Institutional Diversity*. Princeton: Princeton University Press.

Ouyang, K. 2004. 'Higher Education Reform in China Today', *Policy Futures in Education*, 2(1): 141–49.

Pandey A, A. Aggarwal, R. Devane, and Y. Kuznetsov. 2004. *India's Transformation to Knowledge-based Economy: Evolving Role of the Indian Diaspora*. Washington, DC: The World Bank.

Parker, William. 1996. 'Revolutions and Continuities in American Development', in Mikulas Teich, and Roy Porter (eds), *The Industrial Revolution in National Context*. Cambridge: Cambridge University Press.

Parnell, M.F. 2005. 'Chinese Business Guanxi: An Organization or Non-organization?' *Journal of Organisational Transformation & Social Change*, 2(1): 29–47.

Parsons, T. 1951. *The Social System*. Glencoe, IL: The Free Press.

Parthasarathy, B. 2004. 'Globalizing Information Technology: The Domestic Policy Context for India's Software Production and Exports', *Iterations: An Interdisciplinary Journal of Software History*, 3: 1–38.

Passin, Herbert. 1965. *Society and Education in Japan*. New York: Teachers College, Columbia University.

Pearson, Margaret M. 1997. *China's New Business Elite: The Political Consequences of Economic Reform*. Berkeley: University of California Press.

Pearson, R. 1991. 'Collective Diversification: Manchester Cotton Merchants and the Insurance Business in the Early Nineteenth Century', *Business History Review*, 65(2): 379–414.

Pearson, R., and D. Richardson. 2001. 'Business Networking in the Industrial Revolution', *Economic History Review*, 54(4): 657–79.

Penrose, E.T. 1959. *The Theory of the Growth of the Firm*. New York: John Wiley.

Peoples, J., and G. Bailey. 1997. *Humanity: An Introduction to Cultural Anthropology*. Belmont, CA: Cengage Higher Learning.

Perkins, Dwight. 2005. 'China's Economic Growth: Implications for the Defense Budget', in Ashley J. Tellis, and Michael Wills (eds), *Strategic Asia 2005–06: Military Modernization in an Era of Uncertainty*, pp. 363–85. Seattle: National Bureau of Asian Research.

Perugini, M., M. Gallucci, F. Presaghi, and A.P. Ercolani. 2003. 'The Personal Norm of Reciprocity', *European Journal of Personality*, 17(4): 251–83.

Peters, D.H., A. Wagsta, L. Pritchett, N.V. Ramana, and R.R. Sharma. 2002. *Better Health Systems for India's Poor: Findings, Analysis, and Options*. New Delhi: World Bank Publications.

Peters, D.H., K.S. Rao, and R. Fryatt. 2003. 'Lumping and Splitting: The Health Policy Agenda in India', *Health Policy and Planning*, 18(3): 249–60.

Ping Li, J.D. 2003. 'Rural Land Tenure Reforms in China: Issues, Regulations and Prospects for Additional Reform', *Land Reform, Land Settlement and Cooperatives (FAO)*, 3: 59–72.

Platteau, Jean-Philippe. 1994. 'Behind the Market Stage Where Real Societies Exist', [Parts I & II], *Journal of Development Studies*, 30(3–4): 533–77, 753–817.

Platteau, Jean-Philippe. 2000. *Institutions, Social Norms, and Economic Development, Fundamentals of Development Economics*, vol. 1. Reading, UK: Harwood Academic.

Podolny, J.M., and K.L. Page. 1998. 'Network Forms of Organization', *Annual Review of Sociology*, 24(1): 57-76.

Portes, Alejandro. 1998. 'Social Capital: Its Origins and Applications in Modern Sociology', *Annual Review of Sociology*, 24(1): 1-24.

Posner, Eric A. 2000. *Law and Social Norms*. Cambridge, MA: Harvard University Press.

Posner, R.A. 1997. 'Social Norms and the Law: An Economic Approach', *Papers and Proceedings from the 104th Meeting of the American Economic Association*, 87(2): 333-38.

Potts, J. 2001. 'Knowledge and Markets', *Journal of Evolutionary Economics*, 11(4): 413-31.

———. 2003. 'Toward an Evolutionary Theory of Homo Economicus: The Concept of Universal Nomadism', in J. Laurent (ed.), *Evolutionary Economics and Human Nature*, pp.195-216. Edward Elgar: Cheltenham.

Powell, W.W. 1990. 'Neither Market nor Hierarchy: Network Forms of Organizations', *Research in Organizational Behaviour*, 12: 295-313.

PricewaterhouseCoopers (PWC). 2005. 'Global Integration through Knowledge Process', PWC India.

Pritchett, Lant, and Lawrence H. Summers. 1996. 'Wealthier is Healthier', *Journal of Human Resources*, 30(4): 841-68.

Prude, Jonathan. 1998. 'Social Conflict in early Mills', in Gary Kornblith (ed.), *Industrial Revolution*, pp. 40-53. Boston and New York: Houghton Mifflin Company.

Putnam, Robert D. 1993. *Making Democracy Work: Civic Traditions in Modern Italy*. Princeton: Princeton University Press.

———. 1995. 'Bowling Alone: America's Declining Social Capital', *Journal of Democracy*, 6(1): 65-78.

———. 2000. *Bowling Alone: The Collapse and Revival of American Community*. New York: Simon and Schuster.

Qadeer, I. 2000. 'Health Care Systems in Transition III: India, Part I. The Indian Experience', *Journal of Public Health Medicine*, 22(1): 25-32.

Qiu, Ai-Jun. 2008. 'Policy Forming Mechanisms in Rural China', *Working Papers No. 08-11*, Center for Social Development.

Quibria, M.G. 2003. 'The Puzzle of Social Capital: A Critical Review', *Asian Development Review*, 20(2): 19-39.

Rajan, Raghuram G., and Luigi Zingales. 2006. 'Persistence of Underdevelopment: Institutions, Human Capital or Constituencies?' *NBER Paper No. 12093*, National Bureau of Economic Research.

Ramadorai, S. 2002. CEO of TCS: Personal Communication with Rafiq Dossani, 29 November 2012.

Rathe, K., and U. Witt. 2001. 'The "Nature" of the Firm—Static vs. Developmental Interpretations', *Journal of Management and Governance*, 5(3-4): 331-51.

Ravailion, Martin, and Shaohua Chen. 1997. 'What can New Survey Data Tell us about Recent Changes in Distribution and Poverty?' *World Bank Economic Review*, 11(2): 357-82.

Ray, D. 1998. *Development Economics*. Princeton: Princeton University Press.

Redding, R.E. 2001. 'Sociopolitical Diversity in Psychology: The Case for Pluralism', *American Psychologist*, 56(3): 205-15.

Reich, R.B. 1991. *The Work of Nations*. New York: Alfred A. Knopf.

Richard, Camille, Yan Zhaoli, and Du Guozhen. 2006. 'The Paradox of the Individual Household Responsibility System in the Grasslands of the Tibetan Plateau, China', in Donald J. Bedunah, E. Durant McArthur, and Maria Fernandez-Gimenez (eds), *Rangelands of Central Asia*, pp. 83-91. Fort Collins, Colorado: USDA Rocky Mountains Research Station Proceedings RMRS-P-39.

Rip, A., and R. Kemp. 1998. 'Human Choice and Climate Change', in S. Rayner, and E.L. Malone (eds), *Technological Change*, pp. 327-99. Battelle Press.

Rizzo, J., and Richard Zeckhauser. 1992. 'Advertising and the Price, Quantity, and Quality of Primary Care Physician Services', *Journal of Human Resources*, 27(3): 381-421.

Robison, Lindon, Allan Schmid, and Marcelo Siles. 2000. 'Is Social Capital Really Capital?' *Review of Social Economy*, 60(1): 1-21.

Robison, Lindon J. and Marcelo E. Siles (2002). 'Social Capital: Toward A Maturing Paradigm'. Agricultural Economics Staff Paper No. 00-45, Michigan State University.

Rodrik, Dani. 1994. 'King Kong Meets Godzilla: The World Bank and The East Asian Miracle', in A. Fishlow, C. Gwin, S. Haggard, and R. Wade (eds), *Miracle or Design? Lessons from the East Asia Experience* pp. 55-79. Washington, DC: Overseas Development Council.

———. 2003. 'What do we Learn from Country Narratives?' in Dani Rodrik (ed.), *In Search of Prosperity: Analytic Narratives on Economic Growth*, pp. 1-20. Princeton, NJ: Princeton University Press.

Rodrik, Dani, and Arvind Subramanian. 2004. 'From "Hindu Growth" to Productivity Surge: The Mystery of the Indian Growth Transition', paper presented at the IMF Jacques Polak Annual Research Conference, 4-5 November 2004, IMF, Washington, DC.

Romer, P.M. 1986. 'Increasing Returns and Long-Run Growth', *Journal of Political Economy*, 94(5): 1002-37.

———. 1987. 'Growth Based on Increasing Returns Due to Specialization', *American Economic Review*, 77(2): 56-62.

Romer, P.M. 1989. 'Human Capital and Growth: Theory and Evidence', *Journal of Political Economy*, 98(2): 71-102.

———. 1990. 'Endogenous Technological Change', *Journal of Political Economy*, 98(5): S71-S102.

Rosenzweig, Mark R. 1988. 'Human Capital, Population Growth, and Economic Development: Beyond Correlations', *Journal of Policy Modeling*, Elsevier, 10(1): 83-111.

Rothstein, Bo. 2005. *Social Traps and the Problem of Trust*. Cambridge: Cambridge University Press.

Rothstein, Bo, and Jan Teorell. 2008. 'What is Quality of Government? A Theory of Impartial Government Institutions', *Governance*, 21(2): 165-90.

Rowen, Henry, S., and A. Maria Toyoda. 2002. 'From Keiretsu to Startups: Japan's Push for High Tech Entrepreneurship', Working Paper, Asia/Pacific Research Center, Stanford, CA.

Rubin, B. 1985. 'Economic Liberalisation and the Indian State', *Third World Quarterly*, 7(4): 942-57.

Rubinstein, W.D. 1983. 'The End of "Old Corruption" in Britain 1780-1860', *Past and Present*, 101: 55-86.

Rubio, M. 1997. 'Perverse Social Capital: Some Evidence From Colombia', *Journal of Economic Issues*, 31(3): 805-6.

Russo, Fabio. 1999. 'Developing Indian Clusters: UNIDO's Experience', Interdisciplinary Research Institute for Asian Studies.

Rumelt, Richard P. 1984. 'Towards a Strategic Theory of the Firm', in Richard B. Lamb (ed.), *Competitive Strategic Management*, pp. 566-70. Engelwood Cliffs, NJ: Prentice-Hall.

Ryle, G. 1949. *The Concept of Mind*. London: Hutchinson.

Sako, M. 1992. *Prices, Quality, and Trust: Inter-firm Relations in Britain and Japan*. Cambridge: Cambridge University Press.

Salaff, Janet, Arent Greve, and Siu-Lun Wong. 2006. 'Business social Networks and Immigrant Entrepreneurs from China', in Eric Fong and Chiu Luk (eds), *Chinese Ethnic Business: Global and Local Perspectives*, pp. 99-119. London: Routledge.

Sala-i-Martin, X. 1997. 'I Just Ran Two Million Regressions', *American Economic Review*, 87(2): 178-83.

Samuels, R.J. 1987. *The Business of the Japanese State: Energy Markets in Comparative and Historical Perspective*. Ithaca, NY: Cornell University Press.

Sanchez, R. 1998. 'Uncertainty, Flexibility, and Economic Organization: Foundations for An Options Theory of the Firm', Paper presented at the DRUID Summer Conference, Copenhagen Business School.

Saxenian, A. 1999. 'Silicon Valley's New Immigrant Entrepreneurs', *Monograph submitted to the Public Policy Institute of California*, February 1999.

Schaede, Ulrike. 2000. *Cooperative Capitalism: Self-Regulation, Trade Associations, and the Anti-Monopoly Law in Japan*. Oxford: Oxford University Press.

Schmid, Allan. 2003. 'Discussion: Social Capital as an Important Lever in Economic Development Policy and Private Strategy', *American Journal of Agricultural Economics*, 85(3): 716.

——. 2004. *Conflict and Cooperation. Institutional and Behavioural Economics*. Oxford: Blackwell Publishing.

Schotter, Andrew. 1981. 'Why Take a Game Theoretical Approach to Economics? Institutions, Economics and Game Theory', Working Papers 81-08, C.V. Starr Center for Applied Economics, New York University.

Schultz, T. Paul. 1994. 'Human Capital Investment in Women and Men: Micro and Macro Evidence of Economic Returns', Occasional Papers Number 44, International Center for Economic Growth, San Francisco.

——. 1999. 'Health and Schooling Investments in Africa', *Journal of Economic Perspectives*, 13(3): 67–88.

Schultz, T.W. 1961. 'Investment in Human Capital', *The American Economic Review*, 1(2): 1–17.

——. 1975. 'The Value of the Ability to Deal with Disequilibria', *Journal Economic Literature*, 13(3): 827–46.

Scott Morton, F., F. Zettelmeyer, and J. Silva-Risso. 2001. 'Internet Car Retailing', *Journal of Industrial Economics*, 49(4): 501–20.

Seeley, J.R., A.R. Sim, and E.W. Loosley. 1956. *Crestwood Heights: A Study of the Culture of Suburban Life*. New York: Basic Books.

Seligman, A.B. 1997. *The Problem of Trust*. Princeton: Princeton University Press.

Sen, Amartya. 1989. 'Development as Capabilities Expansion', *Journal of Development Planning*, 19(1): 41–58.

——. 1999. *Development as Freedom*. Oxford: Oxford University Press.

Sherer, P.D. 1995. 'Leveraging Human Assets in Law Firms: Human Capital Structures and Organizational Capabilities', *Industrial and Labour Relations Review*, 48(4): 671–91.

Sheshinski, E. 1967. 'Tests of the Learning by Doing Hypothesis', *Review of Economics and Statistics*, 49(4): 568–78.

Shinohara, M. 1976. 'MITI's Industrial Policy and Japanese Industrial Organisation—A Retrospective Evaluation', *The Developing Economies*, 14(4): 366–80.

Shirai, T. 1983. 'Japanese Labour Unions and Politics', in T. Shirai (ed.), *Contemporary Industrial Relations in Japan*. Madison, WI: University of Wisconsin Press.

Sianesi B., and J. van Reenen. 2003. 'The Returns to Education: Macroeconomics', *Journal of Economic Surveys*, 17(2): 157–200.

Simon, Herbert A. 1959. 'Theories of Decision-making in Economics and Behavioral Science', *American Economic Review*, 49(1): 253–83.

Simon, Herbert A. 1976. *Administrative Behavior: A study of Decision-making Processes in Administrative Organization*, 3rd edition. New York: The Free Press.
———. 1991. 'Organizations and Markets', *Journal of Economic Perspectives*, 5(2): 25–44.
Singh, Nirvikar. 2003. 'Some Economic Consequences of India's Institutions of Governance: A Conceptual Framework', paper for the International Law and Economics Conference, New Delhi.
———. 2008. 'Holding India Together: The Role of Institutions of Federalism', MPRA Paper No. 12432, Munich: University of Munich.
Sinha, Aseema. 2005. *The Regional Roots of Development Politics in India: A Divided Leviathan*. Bloomington: Indian University Press.
Smart, A. 1993. 'Gifts, Bribes and Guanxi: A Reconsideration of Bourdieu's Social Capital', *Cultural Anthropology*, 8(3): 388–408.
Smart, J., and A. Smart. 1991. 'Personal Relations and Divergent Economies: A Case Study of Hong Kong Investment in China', *International Journal of Urban and Regional Research*, 15(2): 216–33.
Smith, Adam. 1976. *An Inquiry into the Nature and Causes of the Wealth of Nations*. Edited by Edwin Cannan. Chicago: University of Chicago Press.
Sobel, Joel. 2002. 'Can we trust social capital?', *Journal of Economic Literature*, XL: 139–54.
Solow, Robert. 1956. 'A Contribution to the Theory of Economic Growth', *Quarterly Journal of Economics*, 70(1): 65–94.
———. 1995. 'Trust: The Social Virtues and the Creation of Prosperity (Book Review)', *The New Republic*, 213(September): 36–40.
———. 2000 [1999]. 'Notes on Social Capital and Economic Performance', in P. Dasgupta and I. Serageldin (eds), *Social Capital: A Multifaceted Perspective*, pp. 3–5. Washington, DC: The World Bank.
Spender, J.C. 1996. 'Making Knowledge the Basis of a Dynamic Theory of the Firm', *Strategic Management Journal*, 17(Winter): 45–62.
Squire, L. 1993. 'Fighting Poverty', *AEA Papers and Proceedings*, 83(2): 377–82.
Sridharan, E. 1996. *The Political Economy of Industrial Promotion: Indian, Brazilian and Korean Electronics in Comparative Perspective, 1969–94*. Praeger: Westport, CT.
Srinivas, M.N., and Andre Beteille. 1964. 'Networks in Indian Social Structure', *Man*, 64: 165–8.
Srinivasan, T. 2005. 'China, India and the World Economy', Stanford Center for International Development, Stanford University (Mimeo).
Standifird, S., and R. Marshall. 2000. 'The Transaction Cost Advantage of Guanxi-based Business Practices', *Journal of World Business*, 35(1): 21–42.
Stewart, C.L. 2004. 'Chile Mental Health Country Profile', *International Review of Psychiatry*, 16(1–2): 73–82.

Stigler, George. 1971. 'The Theory of Economic Regulation', *Bell Journal of Economics and Management Science*, 2: 3–21.

Stiglitz, Joseph. 1998. 'Towards a New Paradigm for Development: Strategies, Policies, and Processes', Presented as the 1998 Prebisch Lecture at UNCTAD, Geneva.

——. 1999. 'Whither Reform?' *Annual Bank Conference on Development Economics*, April, Washington, DC.

——. 2000. 'Formal and Informal Institutions', in P. Dasgupta, and I. Serageldin (eds), *Social Capital: A Multifaceted Perspective*, 59–68. Washington, DC: The World Bank.

Stiles, P., and S. Kulvisaechana. 2003. *Human Capital and Performance: A Literature Review*. Judge Institute of Management. Cambridge: University of Cambridge.

Stokey, Nancy. 1991. 'Human Capital, Product Quality and Growth', *Quarterly Journal of Economics*, 106(2): 587–616.

Strauss, J., and D. Thomas. 1998. 'Health, Nutrition and Economic Development', *Journal of Economic Literature*, 36(2): 766–817.

Stuart, T. E., H. Hoang, and R.C. Hybels. 1999. 'Interorganizational Endorsements and the Performance of Entrepreneurial Ventures', *Administrative Science Quarterly*, 44(2): 315–49.

Subramanian, C.R. 1992. *India and the Computer: A Study of Planned Development*. New Delhi: Oxford University Press.

Suzuki, Hiroto. 1999. *Foreign Press Center/Japan*. 'Venture Business in Japan'. November. Available at: http://www.fpcj.jp/e/shiryo/bim/vbj.html, last accessed in July 2011.

Swart, I. 2005. 'Mobilising Faith-based Organisations for Social Development through a Participatory Action Research (PAR) Process', *Maatskaplike Werk/Social Work*, 41(4): 323–36.

Szreter, S., and M. Woolcock. 2004. 'Health by Asociation? Social Capital, Social Theory, and the Political Economy of Public Health', *International Journal of Epidemiology*, 33(4): 650–67.

Sztompka, Piotr. 1998. 'Trust, Distrust and Two Paradoxes of Democracy', *European Journal of Social Theory*, 1(1): 19–32.

Szulanski, G., and R. Jensen. 2004. 'Overcoming Stickiness: An Empirical Investigation of the Role of the Template in the Replication of Organizational Routines', *Managerial and Decision Economics*, 25(6–7): 347–64.

Tarrow, Sidney. 1996. '"Making Social Science Work Across Space and Time: A Critical Reflection" on Robert Putnam's *Making Democracy Work*', *American Political Science Review*, 90(2): 389–97.

Taylor, M. 1982. *Community, Anarchy and Liberty*. Cambridge, UK: Cambridge University Press.

Teece, D.J., and G. Pisano. 1994. 'The Dynamic Capabilites of Firms: An Introduction', *Industrial and Corporate Change*, 3(3): 537-56.

Thorat, Sukhadeo. 2006. 'Higher Education in India: Emerging Issues Related to Access, Inclusiveness and Quality', Nehru Memorial Lecture, University of Mumbai, November, Mumbai.

Tomasevski, K. 2002. 'Economic, Social, and Cultural Rights, The Right to Education', Report of the Special Rapporteur, Item 10, *Fifty-ninth Session*, submitted Pursuant to Commission on Human Rights Resolution 2002/23.

Toshio, Y. 2003. 'Trust and Social Intelligence in Japan', in Frank J. Schwartz, and Susan Pharr (eds), *The State of Civil Society in Japan*. New York: Cambridge University Press.

Townsend, Robert. 1994. 'Risk and Insurance in Village India', *Econometrica*, 62(3): 539-91.

Tsai, Kellee S. 2002. *Back-Alley Banking: Private Entrepreneurs in China*. Ithaca: Cornell University Press.

Tung, Rosalie L., and Verner Worm. 2001. 'Network Capitalism: The Role of Human Resources in Penetrating the China Market', *International Journal of Human Resource Management*, 12(4): 517-34.

Tyler, T.R. 2001. 'Public Trust and Confidence in Legal Authorities: What do Majority and Minority Group Members want from the Law and Legal Authorities?' *Behavioural Science and Law*, 19(2): 215- 35.

Tylor, E.B. 1871. *Primitive Culture*. London: J. Murray.

Uekusa, Masu. 1987. 'Industrial Organisation: The 1970s to the Present', in Kozo Yamamura and Yasukichi Yasuba (eds) *The Political Economy of Japan, Vol 1: The Domestic Transformation*, pp. 469-515. Stanford: Stanford University Press.

Unger, Jonathan. 1996. 'Bridges: Private Business, the Chinese Government and the Rise of New Associations', *China Quarterly*, 147: 795-819.

Uzzi, B. 1996. 'Embeddedness and Economic Performance: The Network Effect', *American Sociological Review*, 61(4): 674-98.

———. 1997. 'Social Structure and Competition in Inter-firm Networks: The Paradox of Embeddedness', *Administrative Science Quarterly*, 42(1): 35-67.

Vaessen, J., and J. Bastiaensen. 1999. 'Social Capital and Institutions: In Search of a Conceptual Framework for the Analysis of Local Rural Development', *Research Paper No. 99-036*, Department of Development Studies, Faculty of Applied Economics, Antwerp.

van Wolferen, K. 1989. *The Enigma of Japanese Power*. London: Macmillan.

Varatharajan, D., R. Thankappan, and J. Sabeena. 2004. 'Assessing the Performance of Primary Health Centres Under Decentralized Government in Kerala, India', *Health Policy and Planning*, 9(1): 41-51.

Veblen, Thorstein B. 1919. *The Place of Science in Modern Civilization and Other Essays*. New York: Huebsch.

Velthuis, O. 1999. 'The Changing Relationship between Economic Sociology and Institutional Economics: From Talcott Parsons to Mark Granovetter', *American Journal of Economics and Sociology*, 58(4): 629–49.

Walder, A. 1996. 'Markets and Inequality in Transitional Economies: Toward Testable Theories', *American Journal of Sociology*, 101(4): 1060–73.

Wallace, Anthony. 1998. 'The Fraternity of Mechanicians', in Gary Kornblith (eds), *The Industrial Revolution in America*, pp. 23–9. Boston and New York: Houghton Mifflin Company.

Wallis, John Joseph, and Douglass C. North. 1986. 'Measuring the Transaction Sector in the American Economy, 1870–1970', with a Comment by Lance Davis, in Stanley L. Engerman, and Robert E. Gallman (eds), *Long-Term Factors in American Economic Growth*, pp. 95–162. Chicago: University of Chicago Press.

Wang, H., L. Zhang, and W.C. Hsiao. 2006. 'Ill Health and Its Potential Influence on Household Consumptions in Rural China', *Health Policy*, 78: 167–77.

Wang, Y. and Y. Yao. 2003. 'Sources of China's Economic Growth 1952–1999: Incorporating Human Capital Accumulation', *China Economic Review*, 14: 32–52.

Wank, David. 1998. 'Embedding Greater China: Kin, Friends, and Ancestors in Overseas Chinese Investment Networks', Paper presented at the International Conference on 'City, State and Region in a Global Order: Toward the 21st Century', Hiroshima University, Hiroshima, Japan, December 19–20.

Weber, Max. 1925. *The Theory of Social and Economic Organization*. New York: Free Press.

Weitzman, M., and C. Xu. 1994. 'Chinese Township Village Enterprises as Vaguely Defined Cooperatives', *Journal of Comparative Economics*, 18(2): 121–45.

Wernerfelt, B. 1984. 'A Resource-based View of the Firm', *Strategic Management Journal*, 5(2): 171–80.

Williamson, Oliver. 1975. *Markets and Hierarchies: Analysis and Antitrust Implications*. New York: Free Press.

——. 1985. *The Economic Institutions of Capitalism*. New York: Free Press.

——. 1996. 'Revisiting Legal Realism: The Law, Economics, and Organization Perspective', *Industrial and Corporate Change*, 5(2): 383–420.

——. 2000. 'Contract and Economic Organization', *Revue d'Économie Industrielle, Programme National Persée*, 92(1): 55–66.

——. 2002. 'The Theory of the Firm as Governance Structure: From Choice to Contract', *Journal of Economic Perspectives*, 16(3): 171–95.

Winter, S. 1995. 'Four R's of profitability: Rents, Resources, Routines, and Replication', in C.A. Montgomery (ed.), *Resources in an Evolutionary Perspective:*

A Synthesis of Evolutionary and Resource-based Approaches to Strategy. Norwell, MA and Dordrecht: Kluwer Academic.
Winters, L.A., and S. Yusuf. 2007. 'Introduction: Dancing with Giants', in L.A. Winters, and S. Yusuf (eds), *Dancing with Giants: China, India, and the Global Economy*, pp. 1-34. World Bank and Institute of Policy Studies.
Witt, M.A. 2006. *Changing Japanese Capitalism: Societal Coordination and Institutional Adjustment*. Cambridge, UK: Cambridge University Press.
Witt, Ulrich. 1999. 'Do Entrepreneurs Need Firms? A Contribution to a Missing Chapter in Austrian Economics', *Review of Austrian Economics*, 11(1): 99-109.
Wolfe, B., and R. Haveman. 2001. 'Accounting for the Social and Non-Market Benefits of Education', in J. Helliwell (ed.), *The Contribution of Human and Social Capital to Sustained Economic Growth and Well-Being*, pp. 221-50. Vancouver: University of British Columbia Press.
Wong, Y.H. 1998. 'The Dynamics of Guanxi in China', *Singapore Management Review*, 20(2): 25-42.
Woolcock, M. 1998. 'Social Capital and Economic Development: Toward a Theoretical Synthesis and Policy Framework', *Theory and Society*, 27(2): 151-208.
———. 1999. 'Learning from Failures in Microfinance: What Unsuccessful Cases tell us about How Group-Based Programs Work', *American Journal of Economics and Sociology*, 58(1): 17-42.
———. 2002. 'Social Capital in Theory and Practice—Where do we Stand?' in J. Isham, T. Kelly, and S. Ramaswamy (eds), *Social Capital and Economic Development: Well-being in Developing Countries*, pp. 18-39. Aldershot: Edward Elgar.
Woolcock, Michael, and Deepa Narayan. 2000. 'Social Capital: Implications for Development Theory, Research, and Policy', *World Bank Research Observer*, 15(2): 225-50.
World Bank. 1993. *The East Asian Miracle: Economic Growth and Public Policy*. Oxford: Oxford University Press.
———. 2005. *Community Driven Development and Social Capital: Designing a Baseline Survey in the Philippines*. Social Development Department. Washington, DC: World Bank.
Wrong, D. 1961. 'The Oversocialized Conception of Man in Modern Sociology', *American Sociological Review*, 26(2): 183-93.
———. 1994. *The Problem of Order*. Cambridge, Massachusetts: Harvard University Press.
Wu, Xiaogang. 2002. 'Embracing the Market: Entry into Self-employment in Transitional China, 1978-1996', *Working Paper No. 512*, William Davidson Institute.

Xiao Zhou, Kate. 1996. *How the Farmers Changed China: Power of the People*. Boulder, CO: Westview Press.

Xu, Chenggang. 2008. 'The Institutional Foundations of China's Reforms and Development', *Working Paper*, University of Hong Kong.

Xu, Chenggang, and Xiaobo Zhang. 2009. 'The Evolution of Chinese Entrepreneurial Firms Township-Village Enterprises Revisited', *IFPRI Discussion Paper 00854*, International Food Policy Research Institute.

Yamagishi, T. 1988. 'The Provisioning of a Sanctioning system in the US and Japan', *Social Psychology Quarterly*, 51(3): 265–71.

Yang, J.Y., and J.T. Li. 2008. 'The Development of Entrepreneurship in China', *Asia Pacific Journal of Management*, 25(2): 355–9.

Yang, Mayfair M.H. 1994. *Gifts Favors & Banquets: The Art of Social Relationships in China*. Ithaca, NY: Cornell University Press.

Young, H.P. 1994. *Equity in Theory and Practice*. Princeton, NJ: Princeton University Press.

Zhang, H. 2007. 'The Relationship between Higher Education Internationalization and National Identity, and its Impact on Curriculum', in S. Liu, and Y. Zhang (eds), *Higher Education Reform: Ideas and Reforms*. Shanghai: Jiao Tong University Press.

Zhang, Jian, Linxiu Zhang, Scott Rozelle, and Steve Boucher. 2006. 'Self-Employment with Chinese Characteristics: The Forgotten Engine of Rural China's Growth', *Contemporary Economic Policy*, 24(3): 446–58.

Zhou, L., W. Wu, and X. Luo. 2007. 'Internationalization and the Performance of Born-global SMEs: The Mediating Role of Social Networks', *Journal of International Business Studies*, 38(4): 673–90.

Zhou, Yongming. 2000. 'Social Capital and Power: Entrepreneurial Elite and the State in Contemporary China', *Policy Sciences*, 33(3–4): 323–40.

Zhu, Kangdui. 2007. 'Local Government Freedom of Choice in Privatization and Market-oriented Reform: Private and Government Interaction Perspectives on the History of Wenzhou Model'. Mimeo, Wenzhou Public Administration Institute.

Zott, C., and R. Amit. 2006. 'Exploring the Fit between Business Strategy and Business Model: Implications for Firm Performance', *Working paper*, INSEAD, Fontainebleau, France.

Index

abilities, 13
absorptive capacity, *See under* knowledge
agreements, xxiv
　institutional, 43*n*6
America, industrial revolution (IR) in, 79–80, 85
　adoption of machine methods and factory organization, 112
　all-purpose artisans, 111
　American colonies, role of, 103
　Anglo-American culture, role of, 108
　development of new settlements, 112
　diverse artisan knowledge, significance of, 104
　division of labour, 106
　export of machines and emigration of mechanics, 105
　heterogeneity of workers, 104
　human capital, role of, 104–6
　human, social, and institutional capital, interaction between, 103, 110–13
　institutional capital, role of, 108–10
　integrated enclaves, establishment of, 109–10
　manufacturers, role of, 111
　mass membership and voluntary associations, role of, 106–7
　migrants, role of, 108, 111
　missionary societies, role of, 106
　Patent Act of 1790, 108
　significant changes, 102–3
　social capital, role of, 106–7
　state and local governments, support of, 108–9
　technological improvements, 106
American Patent system, 91, 108–9
Austrian economics, xxvi, xxxiv*n*10

bargaining economics, 74, 76*n*3
bargaining transaction, 66*n*1
behavioural skills, 14, 20*n*6
bonding, 30–31, 43*n*6, 73, 75, 168, 227
bridging, 30–31, 43*n*6, 75, 98
Britain, industrial revolution (IR) in, 79–80, 83–100
　apprenticeship system, 87, 97–8
　artisans, role of, 87
　barriers to entry and exclusionary arrangements, 92–3
　Bill of Rights of 1689, 90
　civil legal system, 99

entrepreneurship and technical skills, 88
formal institutions, role of, 91
form of exclusive coalitions or thugs, 90
gentlemanly ideals, 94–95
Glorious Revolution of 1688, 90
human capital and, 85–9
Industrial Enlightenment and, 85–6
innovations, 86–8
institutional capital and, 89–93
institutional setups, 88–9
inventors, 88
knowledge-induced economic growth, 83–4
link between human, social, and institutional capital, 96–100
norms of cooperation and decency, 93–5
Parliamentary support, 90, 98–9
practical knowledge, economic application of, 86–7
scientific culture, development of, 86
social capital and, 93–6
technological innovation and institutional change, 98
theories, 84
trust relations, 93, 95–6
working class, role of, 89
British Patent system, 91

capabilities and skills, 13–15
capital, forms of, xxviii–xxxi; *see also* human capital, institutional capital, social capital
causality, 8
Chinese economy
  aggregate GDP growth, 131
  allocation for education and, 134–6
  behaviours and practices, acceptable, 140
  Company Law (1993, amended in 1999), 142
  comparison with India, 131–3
  financial and banking system, 143
  formal institutions, importance of, 142
  ganqing (emotions or effect), 138
  growth phases, 144
  household responsibility system (HRS), 144–51
  human capital, role of, 134–7
  Individual-owned Enterprise Law (1999), 142
  institutional capital, role of, 141–3
  manufacturing sector, 133
  mianzi (face preserving), 138
  Partnership Enterprise Law (1997), 142
  political environments and, 131
  population growth and, 134
  private entrepreneurship, 156–60
  property rights, 143
  regional disparities as source of inequality, 135
  renqing (reciprocal favour), 138
  social capital (*guanxi*), role of, 137–41
  Special Economic Zones (SEZs), development of, 141–2
  state-owned enterprises (SOEs), autonomy of, 141–2
  township-village enterprises, 151–6
  as a transitional economy, 139
  vocational training, setting up of, 136–7
codified knowledge, 44n9
cognitive capabilities, 14, 20n7

Index

collective action, 48
collective norms and values, xx, 43n1
combine-and-exchange process, 37
competition, 65
consumer efficiency, 17
cooperation, 61
cooperative action, 34
cooperative relationship, 30
culture, 60–61

decay (maintenance), xxix
dependability, xxx
development theories, evolution of, xxvi–xxviii
division of labour, 3–4
durability, xxix

economic agents, 45
economic expansion of East Asia, xix
economic problem of society, xxiv
economics; *see also* evolutionary economics
   conventional notions of capital, xxii
   explanatory power of, xxii
   institutional, xxii
   study of, xxi
economic theory, xxvi, xxxivn10,
   tools of, 46
education system
   in China, 134–36
   human capital, contribution of, 9, 12, 17
   in India, 165–66
   in Japan, 118–20
entrepreneurship, 76n1
evolutionary economics, 3–4, 7n2, 23
   competencies and capabilities, 4
   economic system as a rule-based system, 7n1
   effects of complementarity and substitution, 69
   link between human capital, social capital, and institutional capital, 4, 6, 68–75
   micro–meso–macro framework, 5–7
   nature of, 3

firm, theories of
   analysis of economic organization in terms of, 192
   boundaries of firm, 206–10
   categories of, 194
   contracts, transaction costs, and entrepreneurship, 191–3
   evolutionary approach to firm, 202–3
   firm as a communication-hierarchy, 199–200
   firm as a governance mechanism, 195–7
   firm as an employment relation, 194–5
   firm as an incentive system, 201
   firm as a solution to moral hazard in teams, 200
   firm as a source of leverage from composite resources, 203–6
   implicit contracts, 199
   incomplete contracting theories, 194–200
   models of, *See* theories of the firm, models of
   nexus of contracts, 200
   principal–agent theories, 200–201
   property rights theories, 197–9
   resource-based view, 201–2
   seminal contributions, 193
flexibility, 14, xxix
formal and informal institutions, xx
formal institutions, 59–63

270 Index

governance structures, 50
group-level social capital, 26
groups with economic functions, 77n5

habit, 49
heterogeneous labour, 20n4
human capital, xx, xxii, xxiii, xxix, 4, 217, 219
  abilities, 13
  apprenticeship systems, 12
  assumptions, 69–70
  capabilities and skills, 13–15
  contribution of education, 9, 12, 17
  contribution to rational thought and reason, trust and social norms, 74
  and economic growth, 9
  entrepreneurial, 21n9
  expenditures on, 11
  framework, 12–15
  intra- and inter-community exchanges, 72
  meaning and definition, 10–12
  measurement issues, 222–6
  micro and macro implications, 15–18
  modern theory of, 9–10
  modern values and attitudes, 15–17
  in money terms, 20n3
  occupation-specific, 21n10
  OECD's definition, 11
  in pre-modern period, 12
  productive capacity, 11, 18
  relationship between social capital, institutional capital and, 68–75
  role of, 8

India
  comparison with Chinese economy, 131–3
  education regulatory bodies, 166
  education system, 165–8
  foreign direct investment (FDI), 173
  growth experience, 174
  heterogeneous society, 168
  human capital in, 165–8
  Institutional capital in, 172–5
  Insurance Development Regulation Act (IDRA), 172
  political structure in, 169
  reforms in markets, 175
  Right to Information (RTI) Act, 172
  Securities and Exchange Board of India (SEBI), 172
  social capital in, 168–71
  social identities in, 169–71
  Telecommunications Regulatory Authority of India (TRAI), 172
Indian IT industry, 163–4, 175–86
  Dot.com companies, 184
  entrepreneurship and innovation, 176
  government's policies and, 180–1
  Minicomputer Policy of 1978, 179
  non-profit associations, formation of, 185
  regulatory or institutional scenario, 177
  1970s, 175–80
  1980s, 180–3
  1990s and beyond, 183–6
  software exports, 178
  transnational corporations and domestic firms, 181–2
  Y2K problem, case of, 185–6

Index 271

informal institutions, 59–63
information sharing, 36
institutional capital, xx, 4, 220
  in an interdependent society, 58
  assumptions, 70–1
  basic roles, 45
  categorization of theories, 48
  contributions, 64–5
  framework, 52–9
  functioning of institutional environment and arrangements, 50–2
  meaning and definitions, 47–52
  measurement and conceptual issues in, 229–32
  micro and macro implications of, 63–5
  'old' institutionalism *vs* 'new institutional economics' (NIE), 46–7
  relationship between human capital, social capital and, 68–75
  role in economic development, 47
  role in providing people support and confidence, 64
  rules, 61
  as 'sets of opportunities', 52
institutional change, 77n7
institutions, types of, 53–56
  formal and informal, 59–63
intangible capital, xxiii, xxix, xxx, xxxiiin5
intellectual development, 17
intensity, xxx
investment (disinvestment), xxx

Japanese economy
  amakudari and *genkyoku* principle, 125
  complementarity between human, social, and institutional capital, 126–9
  cooperative interaction between government and business, 120–1
  driving forces of, 116
  education system, development of, 118–20
  first phase of development, 115
  giri norm, 124
  human capital in, 118–20
  industrial policy, 123
  industry associations, 126
  institutional capital in, 120–4
  institutional change in, 123–4
  Japanese management, 123
  manufacturing industry, growth of, 116
  Meiji Restoration, 118–19
  Ministry of International Trade and Industry (MITI), *See* Ministry of International Trade and Industry (MITI) of Japan
  National School Ordinance Enforcement Regulations, 119
  network-centric nature of, 126–7
  networks and business groups, 124–5
  organizational and industrial arrangements, 115
  post-War period, 117
  Primary School Order of 1886, 118
  real economic growth in, 117
  relationships between manufacturers and suppliers, 122
  relationships of commitment and cooperation, 124
  role of government, 117

272 Index

School System Rule, 118
social capital in, 124-6

*keiretsu*ization, 122
keiretsu networks, 122, 124-5, 128-30
know-how capabilities, 14
knowledge, 19n1, 20n7
  absorptive capacity, xx
  access to, 171
  codified, 44n9
  creation of, 5, 19, 37, 69-70, 219
  development of, 14, 192
  diffusion of, xxiv, 37, 45, 69-70, 85, 219
  distinction between 'knowing that' and 'knowing how,' 13-14
  growth of, 1, 5
  and knowledge-based economy, xxxiin3, xxxiiin4, 23-4, 219
  mobilization of, 127
  as power, 219
  practical application of, 171
  as source of value, 127
  strengthening of, 147, 185, 219
  tacit, 44n8
  transfer of, 68, 202-3, 209
  utilization of, 68

labour, xix
laissez-faire capitalism, xxvii
linking, 30-31, 43n6
longevity, xxx

Mechanics Institutes, 89
micro-meso-macro framework; *see also under* evolutionary economics
  human capital, 15-18
  institutional capital, 63-5
  social capital, 36-41
Ministry of International Trade and Industry (MITI) of Japan, 121-3, 125, 127-8

networks, 35-6, 41, 73-4, 76n2
  amakudari, 125-9; *see also under* Japanese economy
  creation and strengthening of, 111, 149, 184
  genkyoku, 125-9; *see also under* Japanese economy
  guanxi, see under chinese economy
  human capital's potential for, 148
  keiretsu, see keiretsu
  social network, *see* social networks

orthodoxy, xix

physical capital, xix, xxix, 11, 57, 226
  properties of, xxix
political economy, xxi
primary social groups, 41
procedural capabilities, 14

rational individuals, xxvi, 43n3
reciprocity, 30, 33-6, 42, 59, 137-8
  direct, 34
  indirect, 34
  renqing (reciprocal favour), *see under* Chinese economy
  transactions, 25
reliability, xxx
rent seeking, prevention of, 73, 98-101, 128-30, 220
Royal Institution, 89

sanctions, xxiv, 25, 29-31, 34-6, 74, 128
scientific knowledge, accumulation of, 148
self-organizing governance systems, xxv
Smith, Adam, 4-5, 8, 46, 64, 75, 229
social capabilities, 14
social capital, xix, xx, xxiv, xxx, 4, 217-18, 220

allocation of power and assets, 31
application of, 24
assumptions, 70
basic traditions in, 26
bounded solidarity, 25
categorization of theories, 26-8
cognitive dimension, 29
contributions, 38, xxvii-xxviii
cooperative relationship, 30
in economic thinking, xxii
form of bonding, bridging, and linking, 30-1, 43n6
framework, 30-2
group-level, 26
guanxi, see under chinese economy
meaning and definitions, 25-30
measurement and conceptual issues in, 226-9
micro, meso, and macro perspectives, 36-41
neoclassical framework, 24
networks, 35-6
networks' view, 39
origins and effects of, 25
outcomes from, 41
personal relationships, 27
reciprocity, *See* reciprocity
relational dimension, 29
relationship between human capital, institutional capital and, 68-75
reputation, 27
role in economic evolution, 39
sanctions, 34-5
social cohesion, 28
solidarity behaviour, 28
structural dimension, 29
as a tool for for knowledge and information, 38
trustworthiness, 27, 32-3
social dimension, xxvii

social embeddedness, xxxii$n$2
social integration, 31
social interactions, 23
social knowledge, 4
social networks, 4, 27
   and knowledge, 159, 161,
social structures, 36-7
Society of Arts, 88
Solow growth model, xxvi-xxvii, xxxiv$n$11
state-society relations, xxiii
superego, 25
system integration, 31

tacit knowledge, 44n8
tangible capital, xxix
technical skills, 14
theories of the firm, models of
   incomplete contracting model, 194
   principal-agent model, 194
   knowledge-based model, 194
transformation capacity, xxix
trust, xvi, 43n5, 71, 138-40, 159, 169
   in Britain, 93, 95-7
   and behaviour, 61
   human capital and, 74
   social capital and, 27, 32-3, 35-7

unpredictability, xxx

voting behaviour, 17
vocational education, 10
   in China, 136-7
   in Japan, 119

Western values, xxvi

X-Club, 88

zaibatsu, 125

About the Author

Lalita Som has worked for the Organisation for Economic Co-operation and Development (OECD), Paris and the Commonwealth Secretariat, London. She holds a PhD from the University of London and was a Post-doctoral Research Fellow at ESSEC Business School, France and Singapore. She has previously authored *Stock Market Capitalization and Corporate Governance* (Oxford University Press 2006).